D0205769

CRITICAL INSIGHTS

The Fantastic

GRACE LIBRARY CARLOW UNIVERSITY
PITTSBURGH PA 15213

CRITICAL INSIGHTS

The Fantastic

Editor
Claire Whitehead
University of St. Andrews

PN
56
F34
F355
2013

SALEM PRESS
A Division of EBSCO Publishing
Ipswich, Massachusetts

CATALOGUED

Cover Photo: Midsummer Eve by Edward Robert Hughes
© Christie's Images/CORBIS

Editor's text © 2013 by Claire Whitehead

Copyright © 2013, by Salem Press, A Division of EBSCO Publishing, Inc. All rights reserved. No part of this work may be used or reproduced in any manner whatsoever or transmitted in any form or by any means, electronic or mechanical, including photocopy, recording, or any information storage and retrieval system, without written permission from the copyright owner. For permissions requests, contact proprietarypublishing@ebscohost.com.

∞ The paper used in these volumes conforms to the American National Standard for Permanence of Paper for Printed Library Materials, Z39.48-1992 (R1997).

Library of Congress Cataloging-in-Publication Data
The fantastic / editor, Claire Whitehead.
    p. cm. -- (Critical insights)
 Includes bibliographical references and index.
 ISBN 978-1-4298-3735-4 (hardcover)
 1. Fantasy literature--History and criticism. 2. Fantastic, The, in literature. I. Whitehead, Claire.
 PN56.F34F355 2012
 809'.915--dc23

2012014118

PRINTED IN THE UNITED STATES OF AMERICA

Contents

About This Volume

Claire Whitehead

The impulse toward fantasy (the unreal, the irrational, the supernatural) is as old as humankind itself. We have likely always used our imaginations to conjure up stories and pictures of that which lies beyond our familiar everyday reality and which challenges many of our deeply held beliefs. As a narrower and more historically specific instance of this general impulse, the genre (or mode, as some critics prefer) of the fantastic has nevertheless also been with us for more than two hundred years. Beginning in the late eighteenth or early nineteenth century, the fantastic has captivated writers and readers across the world ever since. Of course, in a volume of essays such as this, it is impossible to do full justice to the amazing variety of writing that constitutes the genre. We must content ourselves with offering a snapshot of the type of imaginative writing we label "fantastic" and the sort of critical thinking it inspires. One major aim informing this volume is the desire to represent examples of the fantastic from across the full span of its historical reach as well as its popularity in many different national traditions. To this end, it includes essays dedicated to some of the earliest practitioners of fantastic writing, such as E. T. A. Hoffmann and Washington Irving, as well as contemporary authors including Sarah Waters and Marie NDiaye. The volume also features reflections on the work of writers from the United States, Great Britain, Ireland, France, Germany, Austria, the Czech Republic, Italy, Russia, and Argentina. And while the majority of the contributions here are dedicated to an analysis of the literary fantastic, there are also essays acknowledging the place of the fantastic in both television and film.

The volume opens with four Critical Context essays designed to give the reader a broadly based introduction to the fantastic. David Sandner's essay on the emergence and evolution of the fantastic outlines historical trends and contexts in the critical history of the genre from the eighteenth to the twentieth century. He identifies as significant a cultural shift in the eighteenth century represented by the discourse around aesthetics and the sublime and an emerging theory of the creative imagination. During the nineteenth century, the critical history of the fantastic began to place an emphasis on the issue of childhood, viewing children as more imaginative than adults. In the twentieth century, Sandner considers the ongoing discussion of the fantastic to have been heavily influenced by Austrian psychologist Sigmund Freud's ideas of the relationship between fear and the fantastic. For Sandner, it is the fantastic's ability to inspire fear, perplexity, and wonder in readers that ensures its lasting appeal.

Dimitra Fimi's chapter on J. R. R. Tolkien confronts head-on the often thorny issue of the relationship between fantasy and the fantastic. She suggests a simple distinction: whereas the fantastic seeks to confuse its readers about whether the events depicted are real or not, fantasy does not. Fimi regards Tolkien as both a highly influential critical thinker about fantasy as well as the author of the work of fantasy against which all others are judged: *The Lord of the Rings*. Tolkien's essay "On Fairy Stories" (1939) identifies fantasy as a genre in which the human mind is able to create an imagined world out of language and in which language is all-important. His literary work helps to highlight the relationship between fantasy and myth that, Fimi argues, provides an effective way "of thinking about the world and fundamental questions of human existence."

In her Critical Lens chapter, Amaryll Chanady develops Fimi's claim about the importance of geographical setting to fantasy, arguing that spatial theory can help to provide a broader perspective on the social and cultural dimension of various modes of the fantastic, fantasy, the marvelous, and magical realism. Using Washington Irving's 1819 tale "Rip Van Winkle," Chanady demonstrates how adopting a spatial approach to the literary treatment of nonrealistic material can illustrate different ways of conceptualizing cultural difference as well as humankind's relationship to knowledge. She uses her reading to challenge previous definitions of Irving's story as fantastic. Rather, she shows how the natural surroundings of the village are constructed differently according to different belief systems. And this brings it into the realm of magical realism, a mode that the story hints at but does not develop.

Complementing Amaryll Chanady's spatial approach, Bernice Murphy's chapter compares and contrasts the motif of the haunted house in works by three American authors: Shirley Jackson, Richard Matheson, and Stephen King. The haunted house is the perfect expression of a past that refuses to remain buried and of the fact that often the most terrifying threats are those that come from within. The chosen works by these three authors all illustrate a particular subsection of the haunted house genre: where the characters have set out actively somehow to be haunted and where the houses know how to exploit their psychological vulnerabilities. Murphy's analysis successfully demonstrates how all three novels illustrate literary critic Renée Bergland's claim that "all houses built on American soil are in some way haunted."

Lucie Armitt's essay, "Women Writers in the Haunted House of Fiction," forms an effective bridge between these four introductory essays and the nine more in-depth considerations of the fantastic that follow. Contrasting with Murphy's focus on the horror genre, Armitt's interest lies in the gothic mode and, most especially, in works authored by women. In their hands, she argues, the popular maxim "a woman's place is in the home" renders the gothic or haunted house a particularly conflicted space. The chapter considers as examples of this phenomenon Emily Brontë's *Wuthering Heights* (1847), Elizabeth Gaskell's "The Old Nurse's Story" (1852), Mary Elizabeth Braddon's *Lady Audley's Secret* (1862), Daphne du Maurier's *My Cousin Rachel* (1951), and Sarah Waters's *The Little Stranger* (2009).

The volume then moves on to consider the works of individual authors of the fantastic in greater depth. Birgit Röder's essay considers the nineteenth-century German author E. T. A. Hoffmann, in whose work almost all of the defining features of the fantastic appear. Hoffmann is also extremely important for the profound influence he exerted upon many of his successors in the genre. His interest in the fantastic, Röder argues, is the consequence both of a turbulent personal biography and the social context of radical upheaval in the wake of the French Revolution in 1789. The failure of this revolution, for Hoffmann, proved that man was not merely a rational creature, and his œuvre consequently engages with the idea that human behavior involves a range of inexplicable and irrational forces. Hoffmann's work constantly reminds the reader of the productive tension that exists between the real and the fantastic, between reason and imagination.

Staying with nineteenth-century European practice in the fantastic, Peter Cogman's chapter considers the treatment of the fantastic in the work of the French writer Prosper Mérimée. Mérimée used this literary genre to communicate to his readership a number of his underlying preoccupations: the fragility of civilization and of the control of reason, and a fascination with the primitive and its associations with violence and sexuality. Cogman analyzes three stories by Mérimée and sees each one as mapping effectively onto a different category in Tzvetan Todorov's influential tripartite division of the fantastic, as outlined in his *Introduction à la littérature fantastique* (1970). "The Vision of Charles XI" exemplifies the "marvellous" in which the supernatural is accepted. "Il Viccolo di Madama Lucrezia" represents the "uncanny," in which the apparently supernatural is given a rational explanation. "Lokis," however, showcases the "pure fantastic" in which the reader's interpretive ambiguity is never resolved.

Slobodan Sucur argues that a fruitful comparison can be made between the work of Edgar Allan Poe and the little-known, but fascinating, Russian writer Vladimir Odoevsky. Sucur takes issue with Todorov's view that the fantastic is not present in the work of Poe. Rather, he believes that both Poe's *Narrative of Arthur Gordon Pym* and Odoevsky's *The Salamander* have something new to tell us about the nature of the fantastic and the "marvellous." Specifically, Sucur contends that in each author the promise of the pleasure to be found in learning or discovering something new, perhaps in the realm of the occult, is fundamental to how interpretations of the fantastic unfold. Sucur calls this combination the "pedagogical fantastic" and shows how Poe and Odoevsky use it to exploit a subtly metaphysical fantastic that seeks to dissolve conventional boundaries and contradictions.

Moving into the twentieth century, Donald Shaw considers the relationship of the work of the Argentine writer Jorge Luis Borges to the fantastic. For Shaw, Borges's stories are representative of the way in which much so-called "high" (or canonical) literature has moved from incorporating reassuring metaphors of the intelligibility of the universe and human behavior to disturbing metaphors that radically interrogate some of our assumptions about our surroundings and selves. Moreover, Borges's legacy can be seen to teach us three things: the reality surrounding us, which we often take for granted, is in fact mysterious and we may not be programmed to understand it; our inner, psychological reality is just as difficult to comprehend; and that even if these two postulates did not apply, language is inadequate and utterly incapable of conveying anything meaningful about reality.

Tomáš Kubíček, like Sucur, adopts a comparative approach by choosing to consider the practice of the fantastic in two novels by Hermann Broch and Milan Kundera. He argues that in Broch's *The Sleepwalkers* (1932) and Kundera's *The Farewell Party* (1976), the reader confronts the presence of fictional polyphony, or multivoicedness, which establishes an equality between different voices so that no single one dominates. Although the polyphony in these cases derives from the use of features associated with the genre of the fantastic (the unreliability of the fictional world and the narrative voice; a disconnect between logic and action; the tension between rationality and irrationality), the works do not themselves necessarily become truly fantastic. However, both Broch and Kundera often provoke the hesitation essential to the fantastic, and they also succeed in authoring what the latter labeled "ethical" novels in which the disintegration of society's values leaves the reader feeling disconcerted and bewildered.

Eugenio Bolongaro takes as his subject the work of the American novelist Thomas Pynchon. Using *Gravity's Rainbow* (1973) as his point of reference, Bolongaro argues that Pynchon's fantastic emerges as an interrogation of the accepted distinctions between the real and the imaginary. He believes that Pynchon is driven by the desire to overcome an insufficient understanding of both the real and the conventions of literary realism. As such, Pynchon's use of the fantastic seeks to puncture the real ironically with the sudden irruption of the sort of chaos that undermines our assumptions about what constitutes reality and realistic representation in aesthetic forms. In *Gravity's Rainbow*, according to Bolongaro, these irruptions cajole the reader into contemplating the unthinkable: a world where human technology embodies monstrous fantasies and in which reason is driven by the insane desire for orgasmic death.

Daniela De Pau considers the rather more genteel presence of the fantastic in the work of the Italian writer Italo Calvino. She contends that throughout his career and in both his fiction and nonfiction Calvino explored his interest in the fantastic with recourse to the fairy tale. He believed categorically that the fantastic was distinct from fantasy, being rooted firmly in rationality. And it represented for Calvino an intellectual tool with which he could attempt to understand the complex relationship between perception and reality or, rather, the different levels through which reality presented itself. De Pau uses two of Calvino's *Stories for Children* to illustrate precisely how he exploits the specific combination of the fantastic and the fairy tale to identify a specific perspective from which to construct a narrative and as a means of modulating his writing according to specific categories, such as "quickness" and "exactitude."

Moving to the late twentieth and early twenty-first centuries, Daisy Connon offers a reading of several works by the contemporary French novelist Marie NDiaye. She argues that NDiaye's writing exhibits a constant tension between the familiar and the strange and is characterized by her tendency to exploit the "uncanny." NDiaye borrows from a repertoire of fantastic imagery and techniques in a unique fashion and thereby revives and estranges the reader's perception of what she might have taken to be everyday reality. Linking back to the essays of Murphy and Armitt, Connon identifies the haunted house as one of NDiaye's favorite motifs. The reader also confronts images related to metamorphosis, which is often intended to have metaphorical meaning, and the figure of the double. Alongside these motifs, and particularly in NDiaye's more recent novels, the experience of the "uncanny" derives less from specific events and is rather inscribed into the language of the narrative itself.

The final essay in this volume returns to a more general treatment of a crucial element of much fantastic art (literature, film, and television): monsters. Joseph Andriano highlights the fact that, whatever medium they might appear in, monsters continue to proliferate in the human imagination. For Andriano, monsters demonstrate that the boundaries between animal and human are elusive and illusory; and they frequently refuse to remain safely in the category of the "other." Andriano's essay initially distinguishes between the impossible monsters of the supernatural and fantasy and the rather more possible (and therefore far more disturbing) monsters depicted in science fiction. As examples of the former category, Andriano takes various incarnations of the mythical sea dragon Leviathan as encountered in Melville's *Moby-Dick* (1851), a Japanese anime series, and an episode of the British TV series *Doctor Who*. The possible monsters are represented by the extraterrestrials or aliens found in H. G. Wells's *War of the Worlds* (1898) and Catherine Moore's "Shambleau" (1933). Andriano concludes that the more we think about monsters, the more we are forced to conclude that, semiotically at least, there is no significant difference between possible and impossible monsters.

What all of these fourteen essays have in common is a recognition that the fantastic (and fantasy) interrogates the type of boundaries that humankind has always used to safeguard itself. Boundaries between the real and the unreal, between order and chaos, between reason and imagination, between civilization and nature, between knowledge and ignorance, and between self and other. While recognizing that the undermining or dissolution of such comforting binaries might induce fear in both fictional protagonists and readers alike, there is also an insistence upon the productive sense of wonder and discovery that can be generated by the fantastic's examination of these categories. And, finally, what all of these essays demonstrate is the crucial role played by language in the genre of the fantastic and our need to recognize both its potential and its limitations.

On the Fantastic

Claire Whitehead

Certain phenomena in our contemporary world make it seem as if "reality" were among the most highly prized cultural commodities. The apparently inexorable rise of reality television, for instance, suggests that we attach greater value to that which is deemed "real" than to that which is apparently "unreal" or "fictitious." The rise of social networking sites or blogs, where people derive entertainment by detailing their day-to-day activities, speak to a similar obsession. Reality television, in its various incarnations, is touted as being somehow more "true" than the invented dramas that previously dominated: carefully crafted scripts are substituted with everyday scenarios; actors are replaced by "ordinary," "real" people like you and me.

However, how real or true is it actually to isolate a dozen or so people on a desert island, in a jungle, or in a purpose-built house, to surround them with numerous cameras and to record their every word and movement around the clock? Even if the people are "real" at the outset, such situations certainly border on the contrived and "unreal" and frequently end up making "real" people seem somehow "unreal." A fundamental problem that arises both in this narrow context, and much more broadly, is that before trying to attach any values to "reality," you need to know what it is. But are you absolutely certain you know what is real and what is unreal? Do you and I perceive exactly the same things as real in precisely the same way? Who decides what is real? Which factors modify our perception of what is real? Is our perception of what is "real" or "the truth" fixed, or does it change over time? Such questions lie at the very heart of the literary fantastic.

Although the particular twist that our current preoccupation with "reality" puts on such questions may be historically unique, the simple phenomenon of valuing the "real" above its opposites (variously seen as the unreal, the imaginary, or the supernatural) is nothing new. Indeed, the difference between the real and the unreal, between the this-worldly and the otherworldly, is one of humankind's most fundamentally held beliefs. However, in the specific context of the genre of the fantastic, which is the subject of this volume, it is what we might label "the rise of the real" in the Age of Enlightenment that is the most significant.

In Europe in the second half of the eighteenth century, various philosophers, scientists, and other intellectuals challenged the prevailing view that wisdom and knowledge were derived from revelation and mysticism (i.e., granted to the lucky few thanks to communion with a divine figure). Instead, they advocated reason as the desired means of establishing an authoritative system of aesthetics, ethics, logic, and government. This rationally based system, they argued, would allow humankind to arrive at an understanding of the objective truth(s) about the reality of the universe. These three interrelated notions of reason, truth, and reality represent a powerful trinity whose influence is still being felt today.

The Enlightenment approach, along with the results it was considered capable of yielding, is well illustrated by the work and discoveries of Sir Isaac Newton (1643–1727). Newton's famous scientific discoveries with regard to universal gravitation and the three laws of motion led to a revolution in the sphere of physics. They also emboldened many others who believed that the type of systematic thinking that had permitted Newton's discoveries could be beneficially applied to the entire range of human activities. What all such Enlightenment figures had in common, regardless of their specific field of expertise, was a desire to understand the reality of the world surrounding them and to identify certain truths related to that reality by means of investigations based on the application of reason above all else. Although the Enlightenment period did not provoke a single or uniform response in the fields of art and literature, its principles found their most obvious expression in the mode of neoclassicism. Neoclassical art emphasized ideals of order, logic, reason, and common sense and looked back to Greek and Roman originals for inspiration.

However, just as the advent of the Enlightenment period and the ideas that it promoted should be understood as a response to previously dominant worldviews (based on faith), this period in turn engendered its own reaction, which included the birth of the fantastic. There were many thinkers and artists who considered the post-Enlightenment insistence upon an understanding of the world predicated entirely upon the real and the rational to be just as unsatisfactory as one rooted in mysticism. Such figures believed that the Enlightenment view told only a partial story and that, in spite of its insistence upon reason and reality as the keys to an understanding of certain fundamental truths, the universe continued to harbor many irrational and apparently unreal phenomena. In the field of literature, such beliefs began to find expression primarily with the rise of the gothic novel, an essential precursor to the fantastic.

The British writer Horace Walpole's *Castle of Otranto*, published in 1764, is widely recognized as being the first such novel. The excesses of its plot are clearly intended as a rebuttal of the idea of a rational and natural order governing the world: one character is killed by an enormous military helmet of unknown provenance; other characters subsequently confront a similarly oversized and seemingly evil arm and leg; facial features on the portrait of family ancestors apparently move; and, eventually, a skeleton appears to warn the protagonist, Manfred, off his incestuous designs toward his deceased son's fiancée. And reflecting the growing interest in the functioning of the human mind during this period, these excesses equally speak of subconscious or unconscious impulses that appear to control the characters' actions just as much, if not more so, than reasoned consideration. In Walpole's novel, like many other examples of gothic literature, in fact, it is conventional laws in general, whether they be rational, scientific, moral, or religious, that are challenged. This explains the prevalence of plots in such novels that feature apparently spectral or otherwise unreal beings, impossible-seeming disappearances and reappearances frequently explained by hidden tunnels or doorways, sexual deviance, and numerous characters with diabolical intent.[1]

In a related development, in 1799, the Spanish artist Francisco Goya released a series of eighty aquatint prints, entitled *Los Caprichos* (*The Caprices*), by means of which he intended to criticize the foolishness he perceived in contemporary Spanish society. Plate 43 in the collection is known, after the inscription that features on it, as "The Sleep of Reason Produces Monsters." The original legend on the print reads: "Fantasy abandoned by reason produces impossible monsters; united with reason, fantasy is the mother of the arts and the source of their wonders" (my translation). This notion that there exists an interdependence between reason and fantasy, that you cannot have one without the other, and that a combination of the two can be harnessed for artistic purposes is evident in the gothic novel, but, as we shall see below, it is an even more important cornerstone of the fantastic.

Although the fantastic enjoyed its first flowering in the nineteenth century, it is a genre that, as this volume will demonstrate, has maintained its relevance for generations of readers and writers right up to the present day. Back in the early nineteenth century, one of the most important figures in popularizing the genre across Europe was the German writer E. T. A. Hoffmann (1776–1822). Works such as *The Golden Pot* (1814), *The Sandman* (1815), and *The Devil's Elixirs* (1817), combined with the wider burgeoning interest in the nonrational, inexplicable sides of life, captured the public imagination. The subtitle to *The Golden Pot*, which reads "A Modern Fairy Story," clearly corresponds to Goya's idea of uniting fantasy (the fairy tale) and reason (as implied by the adjective "modern" and its overtones of scientific rationality).

Hoffmann's *Sandman*, which, perhaps because of the influence of Austrian neurologist Sigmund Freud, remains a well-known and widely read work to this day, provides an excellent example of how the fantastic can serve as an expression of deep psychological fears and buried memories. (Freud places a reading of Hoffmann's story at the heart of his 1919 article "The Uncanny," which is a key text in the development of his theories of psychoanalysis.) These works and others inspired writers in many different countries to produce imitations of Hoffmann in their own language and, perhaps more importantly, to translate them so that readers who did not understand German might appreciate them.

Beginning in the mid-1820s, this nascent genre also began to attract serious critical attention: the Scottish writer Sir Walter Scott sketched its basic features with reference to the gothic novel in two articles from 1826 and 1829; and in 1830, the French writer Charles Nodier first employed the term "fantastique" to categorize the nature of works by Hoffmann and his German contemporaries, Johann Wolfgang von Goethe and Johann Ludwig Tieck. According to Nodier, the fantastic is a genre that enjoys popularity at precisely those times when "the empire of real or convenient truths comes to an end," and without it, he says, he "does not know what would remain of humanity's moral and intellectual instinct in times of extreme historical pressure" (10; my translation). Furthermore, in one of his more florid pronouncements, Nodier characterizes the fantastic as "the font of eternal youth for the imagination" (28; my translation).

While the articles by Scott and Nodier make clear that the fantastic garnered a certain amount of critical attention from the time of its earliest appearance, it is largely in the post–Second World War period that study of the genre seriously developed. Beginning with French critics such as Pierre-Georges Castex, Louis Vax, and Marcel Schneider, the field of critical investigation of the fantastic blossomed and branched out in a variety of quite different, though ultimately complementary, directions. These three French critics adopted a broadly thematic and biographical approach to examining the history of the genre.

Others, such as Kathryn Hume, Tobin Siebers, and Amaryll Chanady, consider the fantastic in terms of its relationship to neighboring genres, such as realism, romanticism, or magical realism. José Monleón approaches the fantastic in sociohistorical terms and emphasizes, in particular, factors such as the French Revolution and the rise of the bourgeoisie as essential contributors to the popularity of the fantastic. Rosemary Jackson, meanwhile, allies such sociohistorical considerations with an interest in the psychoanalytical significance of the genre. Jackson argues that fantasy is ultimately "a literature of desire" that traces the unseen and the unsaid of culture in order both to express and expel them.

Meanwhile, a number of critics have chosen to examine the genre in terms of its popular motifs: Deborah Harter focuses on "bodies in pieces" and the fragment more generally, while Irving Massey and Darko Suvin are more interested in the role played by images of metamorphosis. And, since 1970, many writers have examined the genre from a structural or narratological angle and have endeavored to uncover the particular rhetorical, narrative, or stylistic features that characterize the fantastic. Examples of such an approach would include the work undertaken by Christine Brooke-Rose, Nancy Traill, Fanfan Chen, and myself.

The year 1970 deserves to be highlighted as a watershed moment in the history of criticism of the fantastic because it saw the publication, originally in French, of arguably the most influential study of the genre: Tzvetan Todorov's *Introduction à la littérature fantastique* (published in English as *The Fantastic: A Structural Approach to a Literary Genre*). Among a sizeable group of critics to have analyzed the genre, Todorov is the one that any good student of the fantastic cannot afford to ignore. So why is Todorov's work deserving of such a reputation? For three reasons mainly: he offered a clear and workable definition of the genre; in so doing he distinguished the fantastic from other closely related genres; and he directed critical attention away from history and thematics and almost exclusively toward the narrative structures operating within the confines of the fictional text. Todorov belonged to a group of critics working in the 1960s and 1970s, mostly in France, who became known as structuralists. This designation clearly reveals their interest, first and foremost, in analyzing the narrative and linguistic structures of aesthetic artifacts such as literature. Structuralists also advocated a quasi-scientific approach to the study of literature in which a greater degree of critical rigor would be applied than in earlier, more descriptive approaches. At the root of Todorov's interest in the fantastic is the desire to identify rules that operate in various works across the genre, not just the individual or unique features in a single work, which might not be shared by another reader. In total, Todorov identifies nine different "rules" for the genre, subdivided into three different categories: rules, properties, and semantic features.

Arching over all of these is Todorov's proposal of a definition of the fantastic that, thanks to both its clarity and its accuracy, still holds sway today among the majority of contemporary critics. Todorov arrives at his definition by considering a passage from Jacques Cazotte's novel *The Devil in Love* (1772) that he considers to be of central importance. In Cazotte's novel, the protagonist, Alvaro, is pursued by a demonic figure, and, at a certain point, he reflects upon his experiences and asks himself:

> But what was there that was conceivable in my adventure? All of this seems like a dream, I said to myself; but is human life anything else? I dream more extraordinarily than another, and that's all there is to it. . . . Where is the possible? Where is the impossible? (Cazotte 245)

For Todorov, the uncertainty that Alvaro expresses here about the nature of his experiences (reality or dream; possible or impossible) is essential to the fantastic. Accordingly, he places it at the very heart of his definition of the genre, stating:

> In a world which is indeed our world, the one we know, a world without devils, sylphides, or vampires, there occurs an event which cannot be explained by the laws of this same familiar world. The person who witnesses the event must opt for one of two possible solutions: either he is the victim of an illusion of the senses, of a product of the imagination—and laws of the world then remain as they are; or the event has indeed taken place, it is an integral part of reality—but then this reality is controlled by laws unknown to us. . . . The fantastic occupies the duration of this uncertainty.

Once we choose one answer or the other, we leave the fantastic for a neighboring genre, the uncanny or the marvellous. The fantastic is that hesitation experienced by a person who knows only the laws of nature, confronting an apparently supernatural event. (Todorov 25)

This definition has several key angles that are worth highlighting. The first is that, in order to be fantastic, a text must provoke hesitation in the mind of the reader. But this hesitation needs to be linked specifically to the question of whether the events or characters being portrayed are natural or supernatural; more general hesitation on its own is not enough. Secondly, this definition helps us to situate the fantastic vis-à-vis other genres. If the reader's hesitation is never resolved, we are in the realm of the "pure fantastic"; if uncertainty is dispelled through the provision of a rational answer, a work becomes *étrange* ("uncanny," although this translation is not entirely satisfactory); but if the interpretation to be given to events is shown to be definitively otherworldly, or supernatural, then a work belongs to the category of the *merveilleux* ("the marvellous"). Finally, the fantastic literary text must create the impression of depicting "our world"; that is, it must convince the reader of its seeming realness or realism before disrupting it by introducing the unreal. Add to this definition the three rules, three properties, and three features that Todorov also identifies in his study, and we are left with a hugely insightful and inspiring introduction to the fantastic.

One area, however, that Todorov does not investigate as fully as necessary concerns the question of precisely how a fantastic text provokes hesitation in the mind of the reader. If the fantastic has this hesitation as its very lifeblood, then an understanding of exactly how a literary text first induces trust and belief in the reader, only then to undermine it, would seem to be absolutely key. In trying to identify and understand the techniques used by an author or narrator to induce uncertainty in the reader's mind, it is essential to acknowledge that any and all "events" presented in literary fictional narratives are, first and foremost, "discourse" events. That is, because we are dealing with fiction, they do not exist outside the text (they are not actually real) and so their primary mode of existence is in language and through the linguistic and narrative techniques used in the literary fictional text to create them. When we read about a young man seeing the outline of a female ghost in a mirror (Théophile Gautier's *Spirit*) or about a civil servant who wakes up one morning to find that his nose has disappeared (Nikolai Gogol's short story "The Nose"), for example, we do not experience these events directly; we are not eyewitnesses. We are only able to read about them as another voice tells us the story of their apparent occurrence. Therefore, what is especially interesting when considering the genre of the fantastic is to think about the various ways in which language and narration control and modulate how we as readers assess the status of an event or situation in the text as "real" or "natural" or not. In so doing, it becomes clear that, although the fantastic has always been a literary genre practiced in different countries using a variety of languages, many of the basic linguistic devices and narrative techniques remain broadly the same.

The best starting point for an analysis of the techniques employed to make a reader hesitate is, in actual fact, an examination of what first makes her believe. It is particularly in this regard that the intimate relationship between the fantastic and mimesis (imitation or representation of the physical world) or realism becomes obvious. For authors of the fantastic, it is crucially important to persuade the reader, at least initially, that the world being described within the text is subject to the same logical, rational rules that govern reality outside the text. The fantastic is, therefore, a genre that makes extensive use of techniques more commonly associated with the practice of realism. This explains, for instance, why many works of the fantastic (particularly during the nineteenth century) are set in named and recognizable "real" locations: Dresden in Hoffmann's *Golden Pot*, St. Petersburg in Pushkin's "Queen of Spades" (1834), or Eton School in England in Edgar Allan Poe's "William Wilson" (1839). Furthermore, these physical settings are then described in considerable detail so as to make them more convincing.

In Dostoyevsky's novella *The Double* (1846), for example, the narrator carefully sketches out the appearance of the protagonist's room and the furniture found in it. Similarly, the location of the action in many of Stephen King's novels is clearly contemporary North America, where nothing, initially, appears untoward.

However, by far the most important device in persuading a reader of the "realness" of the fictional world is the presence of a trustworthy and informative narrative voice. Although, in the case of third-person narrators (those not involved in the action of the fictional world as a character), the reader's natural instinct is to trust the voice telling the story, there are still techniques that can further promote this sense of reliability. For example, the temporal stance (the relationship between the time of the action and the time of the recounting of that action) of the narrator with relation to the story's action can be influential. It is conventional for most narrators not to begin telling their story until all of the action it involves has been concluded. Such a temporal stance (referred to as "posterior") implies that the narrator already knows the outcome of the story before he starts to relate it. Consequently, a sense of trust is created because the reader expects this voice to have all the information necessary to tell it well. Such third-person narrators can use this temporal perspective, as well as other techniques, to provide background information on characters or situations that will also persuade the reader that they are reliable reporters.

For first-person narrators, the job is a little harder. Precisely because of their relative unreliability, Todorov claims that first-person narrators are preferred by the genre of the fantastic. In fact, the fantastic contains numerous examples of stories told by such narrator-protagonists who also manage to persuade the reader of their reliability. For these voices, proof of their status as intelligent, rational, and skeptical characters is crucial; without it the reader might be able to dismiss their supernatural interpretation of events as merely the result of their suggestible personality. So, in Prosper Mérimée's short story "The Venus of Ille" (1837), the narrator is an archaeologist-historian on a field trip who initially rejects the idea that a statue of Venus unearthed close to his host's estate could in any way be alive. Similarly, in Mary Shelley's *Frankenstein*, the initial narrator, Robert Walton, is presented as an educated man, well versed in medicine and the physical sciences.

One of the most important ways in which such apparently trustworthy narrators then create hesitation about whether an event should be interpreted as natural or supernatural is through syntax—that is, the structure of sentences. The fantastic employs numerous methods of manipulating sentences and language to provoke uncertainty, but it is worth highlighting just a few here. The first is what Todorov himself identified as "modalization phrases," which are used to express the speaker's lack of conviction in what he describes. The most common type of such phrases are modal verbs such as "to seem" or "to appear." So, for example, in Ivan Turgenev's *Phantoms* (1864), when the phantom female figure makes her first appearance, the narrator states that "it seemed to me I fell asleep" (125). However, the crucial first phrase in this clause introduces unavoidable ambiguity: does he perceive the ghostly figure in reality or only in his dreams? On the basis of this type of phrasing, the reader cannot be sure of the answer. Equally, in Oscar Wilde's novel *The Picture of Dorian Gray* (1891), when the eponymous hero examines his apparently animated portrait, "the face seemed to him to be a little changed," "the expression seemed different," and "one would have said that there was a touch of cruelty in the mouth" (148). But again, the reader cannot fully trust the reliability of any of these statements, because the protagonist himself does not believe them.

Alongside such modalization phrases we find myriad other syntactic devices intended to ensure that the reader cannot be certain of their interpretation. For instance, the fantastic makes ample use of indefinite pronouns (someone, something, whoever, whatever) that mean that the identity of certain actors or objects remains obscure. For example, in Pushkin's short story "The Queen of Spades," before the protagonist is supposedly visited by the ghost of a deceased countess, the reader is told that "someone" looks in at his window from the street. Is this the countess or somebody else, and would this information help us to solve the mystery of who exactly visits the hero? Similarly, in Chekhov's short story "The Black Monk" (1894), the main character apparently begins to be visited by the figure from the title after hearing a legend that is "somehow strange," featuring "some sort of monk" who wanders "somewhere in Syria or Arabia" (233). The terms of this legend are so vague that they raise serious doubts about the reality of the "visits" that subsequently occur. A device closely related to these indefinite pronouns is supervention. This is a rather technical term simply used to indicate instances where, instead of stating that "this particular person opened the window," the human actor is masked and the result is a more ambiguous sentence, such as "the window opened [itself]."

So, for example, in Maupassant's short story "The Horla" (1887), in which the narrator fears he is haunted by an invisible being, roses "cut themselves off" a bush in his garden and the pages of his diary "turn themselves" in his study. Obviously such actions should not be able to complete themselves, but the lack of a clearly identified human performer confuses both protagonist and reader. Finally, in this brief survey of syntactic devices, comes the use the fantastic makes of multiple or indefinite adjectives (e.g., whitish, darkish, bluish) to describe phenomena experienced in the story world.

So, too, in Vladimir Odoevsky's short story "The Sylph" (1837), when the protagonist, having read a book of ancient magic, places his signet ring in a glass of water in the sunlight in order to try to conjure up a sylph, the water is shot with "greenish" and "opal-like" rays. And the beautiful creature who does, apparently, appear is said to be "amazing, indescribable, unbelievable" (50). In Théophile Gautier's *Spirit* (1865), the reader is told that the form that appears in the mirror, "whilst similar, did not resemble in any way that which passes, in this life, for the head of a beautiful woman. It had, granted, the same traits, but purified, transfigured, idealized, and made perceptible by a substance which was somehow immaterial" (236; my translation). By means of this technique, the fantastic repeatedly suggests the presence of the otherworldly by implying that human language is somehow insufficient as a tool to describe such events; if the events were natural, there would be no such difficulty.

Sometimes, although not necessarily, such syntactic devices are associated with another key technique employed by the fantastic to provoke hesitation: a restriction or shift in the point of view from which the narration of events is provided. This is a particularly effective method because it allows uncertainty to be injected into the account of events without the trustworthiness of the narrator being undermined. In Sarah Waters's novel *The Little Stranger* (2009), for example, the reader can never definitively determine the true nature of the strange and violent events occurring in the Ayres's household because we never experience them directly. The increasingly threatening scratches, noises, instances of fire-starting and, eventually, deaths are reported by the doctor-narrator who is never in the room to observe them directly, but only hears them through doors or through walls or has them reported to him. This means that the mystery surrounding where responsibility for the actions lies, either with a member of the household or with an unidentified supernatural being, is never fully uncovered.

The fantastic is also adept at switching the narrative point of view at crucial moments away from relatively reliable observers to far less reliable ones. This is the case, for instance, in Dostoevsky's *The Double,* when, as the protagonist walks along a street in St. Petersburg directly toward a figure who may or may not be his doppelgänger, the point of view moves from the more reliable third-person narrator to the highly untrustworthy protagonist, Goliadkin. Consequently, the crucial moment when this "double" is at closest proximity and could potentially be unambiguously identified is passed over because the protagonist does not look at him properly. The reader is thus left in the dark as to whether this other figure really is the protagonist's double or not. Such switches in point of view are employed adroitly by the fantastic so as to introduce uncertainty without upsetting the "decorum" (the reliability and honesty) of the text. If a narrator who has previously been considered trustworthy began inexplicably to fail to fulfill his storytelling duties by not reporting events fully, the reader would soon lose patience with him and potentially stop reading. Shifts in point of view allow hesitation to be provoked while preserving the "rules of the game" that were established at the outset of the narrative and remain important to the reader.

While shifts in point of view create hesitation because of a lack of information, the fantastic also makes ample use of a device that confuses by means of a surfeit of details: multiple voices. Authors of fantastic narratives are highly skilled at generating ambiguity by leaving the reader unable to distinguish between various interpretations of events suggested by a range of different voices. Some of these may consider an event to be entirely real or natural; others, however, may insist that they have witnessed an instance of the supernatural. The key issue, though, is that the reader is unable to choose between the different accounts. In Mérimée's story "The Venus of Ille," for instance, the allegation made by one voice that a character has been embraced to death by a supernaturally animated statue of Venus is not allowed to stand unchallenged. Other voices, including those of the archaeologist-narrator and the king's procurator, challenge such a seemingly far-fetched account with their view that the murder is the work of disgruntled locals.

In Henry James's novella *The Turn of the Screw* (1898), the reader has even more competing voices to contend with. The frame narrative introduces the voices of one first-person narrator, of the character Douglas who possesses the manuscript that contains the narrative that forms the main part of the novella, and of the various other characters gathered in the country house. Then, in the body of the novella, the reader has to deal with the voices of the governess; the housekeeper, Mrs. Grose; and the children Miles and Flora. And this multiplicity of voices in a narrative laden with ambiguous syntax ensures that the reader is never able to decide whether the children are actually visited by ghosts or whether the governess is mentally unstable.

Although what has been highlighted above is merely a selection of the syntactic and narrative techniques encountered in the fantastic, it hopefully succeeds in illustrating how this genre recognizes and exploits the endless capacity and power of language. In an important sense, one of the most significant qualities of the fantastic is that it makes absolutely central to its existence an issue that is actually the key to all literature: the role played in the manipulation of readers' responses by the structuring of language. The enduring popularity of the genre of the fantastic over the past two hundred years is thus explained, at least in part, by humankind's fascination with the status of language and its relationship to reality. In this era of postmodernity, arguably, humankind experiences a considerable degree of anxiety about its ability to read and interpret statements correctly and about the stability of language and representation. And so works of the fantastic speak to readers as reflections of this broader cultural phenomenon.

It is important to emphasize, however, that, in the context of the fantastic, hesitation and uncertainty should not be viewed as negative or unpleasant experiences. On the contrary, as a genre that resists closure and the creation of a single, stable meaning, the fantastic instead argues in favor of open-endedness, of multiple possible endings in which the reader is invited to play an active role. As Nicholas Royle argues in *The Uncanny* (2003): "Intellectual uncertainty . . . is just as well an experience of something open, generative, exhilarating (the trembling of what remains undecidable)" (52). The fantastic undoubtedly sets out to challenge the conventional wisdoms held by its readership. It expressly seeks to call into question notions such as the hegemony of post-Enlightenment rational-scientific discourses, the dominance of monolithic constructions of truth and reality, and the reliability and transparency of language. However, its aim in so doing is to empower readers to construct alternative discourses, to question the existence of a single truth, and to recognize language as the arch manipulator. In short, to make better, more sensitive readers.

Notes

1. Other early gothic novels include Ann Radcliffe's *The Mysteries of Udolpho* (1794) and *The Italian; Or, The Confessional of the Black Penitents* (1797); Matthew Lewis's *The Monk* (1796); Mary Shelley's *Frankenstein; Or, The Modern Prometheus* (1818); John Polidori's *The Vampyre* (1819); and Charles Maturin's *Melmoth the Wanderer* (1820).

Works Cited

Brooke-Rose, Christine. *A Rhetoric of the Unreal: Studies in Narrative and Structure, Especially of the Fantastic.* Cambridge, Eng.: Cambridge UP, 1981.

Castex, Pierre-Georges. *Le Conte fantastique en France de Nodier à Maupassant.* Paris: Corti, 1951.

Cazotte, Jacques. *The Devil in Love.* Sawtry, Eng.: Dedalus, 2011.

Chanady, Amaryll. *Magical Realism and the Fantastic: Resolved versus Unresolved Antinomy.* New York: Garland, 1985.

Chekhov, Anton. "The Black Monk." *Polnoe sobranie sochinenii.* Vol. 8. Moscow: Nauka, 1977.

Chen, Fanfan. *Fantasticism: Poetics of Fantastic Literature.* Oxford, Eng.: Lang, 2007.

Gautier, Théophile. *Spirit. L'œuvre fantastique: Romans.* Paris: Bordas, 1992.

Harter, Deborah. *Bodies in Pieces: Fantastic Narrative and the Poetics of the Fragment.* Stanford: Stanford UP, 1996.

Hume, Kathryn. *Fantasy and Mimesis: Representations of Reality in Western Literature.* New York: Methuen, 1984.

Jackson, Rosemary. *Fantasy: The Literature of Subversion.* New York: Methuen, 1981.

James, Henry. *The Turn of the Screw.* Boston: St. Martin's, 1995.

Massey, Irving. *The Gaping Pig: Literature and Metamorphosis.* Berkeley: U of California P, 1976.

Monleón, José. *A Specter Is Haunting Europe: A Sociohistorical Approach to the Fantastic.* Princeton: Princeton UP, 1990.

Nodier, Charles. "Du fantastique en littérature." *La Revue de Paris* (1830): 1–30.

Odoevsky, Vladimir. «The Sylph.» The Salamander *and other Gothic Tales.* Bristol: Bristol Classical, 1992.

Royle, Nicholas. *The Uncanny.* Manchester, Eng.: Manchester UP, 2003.

Schneider, Marcel. *Histoire de la littérature fantastique.* Paris: P.U.F., 1960.

Siebers, Tobin. *The Romantic Fantastic.* Ithaca: Cornell UP, 1984.

Suvin, Darko. *Metamorphoses of Science Fiction.* New Haven: Yale UP, 1979.

Todorov, Tzvetan. *The Fantastic. A Structural Approach to a Literary Genre.* Trans. Richard Howard. Ithaca: Cornell UP, 1975.

Traill, Nancy. *Possible Worlds of the Fantastic.* Toronto: Toronto UP, 1996.

Turgenev, Ivan. "Phantoms." *Dream Tales and Prose Poems*. Ed. Constance Garnett. New York: Macmillan, 1920.

Vax, Louis. *Histoire de la littérature fantastique en France*. Paris: Fayard, 1985.

Whitehead, Claire. *The Fantastic in France and Russia in the Nineteenth Century: In Pursuit of Hesitation*. Oxford, Eng.: Legenda, 2006.

Wilde, Oscar. *The Picture of Dorian Gray*. Cambridge, MA: Belknap, 2011.

CRITICAL
CONTEXTS

The Emergence and Evolution of the Fantastic _____

David Sandner

The fantastic is defined by what it is not—*un*real. We know when we read the story of a man waking from uneasy dreams to discover he is a monstrous bug, or of a girl following a rabbit with a pocket watch down a hole into Wonderland, that the story is fantastic because these things cannot happen. But how do we know what is impossible? Did the author of the Old English epic *Beowulf* believe in Grendel, the story's monster, roaming somewhere beyond the firelight? Is the story only "fantastic" now when we no longer know it as truth, when we no longer believe in monsters? All stories are fiction—by definition, lies—so why do we worry if one kind is more false than another? On what scale do we measure truth? Is there a different scale for measuring truth in fiction? Do we really not believe in ghosts? Why does the fantastic matter? Why name it and know it by a certain name—fantasy, fairy tale, wonder tale, and so many more—if, as Shakespeare writes, a rose by any other name would smell as sweet? Because the name matters a great deal, apparently. We know the fantastic, finally, only by its name, by what we call it, by what we believe it to be, and not by what it is . . . because it is not anything at all.

This essay outlines historical trends and contexts in the critical history—the ongoing discussion—of the fantastic. Because of space restrictions, only a selection of representative works in the critical tradition can be highlighted. This must necessarily remain a provisional sketch of the most influential ideas, meant to give an idea of the shape of the discourse. Another commentator would undoubtedly tell a different story of the cultural conversation on the field. For example, I am going to use the terms "fantasy" and "the fantastic" interchangeably. Others argue for specific uses for these terms: perhaps fantasy is the earlier and so more inclusive term; so the fantastic describes a kind of fantasy emerging from literary movements like postmodernism or magical realism; or, differently, the fantastic describes a mode, the use of the unreal in all stories; therefore, fantasy describes the commercial genre. For specific arguments, these or related differentiations have value; however, for a general overview of fantastic material, such distinctions only obscure work that, no matter how it is classified or when it was written, attempts to explore the presence of the impossible in literature and in our experience of life itself.

The first question is: where to begin? Any history of the fantastic must encounter the genre's claims for an "ancient" timelessness. Has not fantasy always been with us in ancient fables and epics and romances and fairy tales? Perhaps, but, as noted above, the matter of belief is thorny. Not until the eighteenth century does a modern sense of skepticism toward the supernatural arise, along with, not coincidentally, claims for the value of a new, realistic literature, allowing the fantastic to be defined as the modern literature of the unreal. Many works that might be considered criticism of the fantastic therefore precede fantasy literature as a discernible genre, though they influence its eventual form and function. In the classical era, for example, Aristotle discusses the unreal in his *Poetics,* generally disapproving of it but allowing what he calls the "marvelous" as a traditional part of the epic, and so allowing a precursor form of the fantastic into poetics generally. The early modern era witnesses more forceful defenses of the "marvelous." Giraldi Cinthio in "On the Composition of Romances" (1549) and Sir Phillip Sidney in "An Apology for Poetry" (1595) argue that "poet" means "maker," and as such the poet should be inventive and wildly imaginative. Sidney writes that the poet grows into "another nature, in making things either better than Nature bringeth forth, or quite anew, forms such as never were in Nature" (Sidney 85). Torquato Tasso in "Discourses on the Heroic Poem" (1594) claims that poetry should be true to life, but insists that something may be "marvelous and true." None of these critics, however, advance claims for the existence of a distinct genre.

A decisive shift in defining (and so discovering, or even inventing) the fantastic proved to be the eighteenth-century discourse on aesthetics (what we like in art and why), especially around the term "the sublime." The sublime describes that which inspires awe, reimaging the relationship between modern individuality and the transcendent (conceived of as divine or supernatural) in a skeptical age. The fantastic, through the presentation of difference, through strange or impossible images, compels the characteristically "sublime" movement beyond the proscribed limits of the imagination, occasioning an overwhelming moment that produces an intense breakdown of the imagination that motivates new insights and the experience of "surprise" and "wonder." In "The Pleasures of the Imagination" (1712)— an early discussion of the aesthetics of the sublime—Joseph Addison specifically links what he calls "the fairy way of writing" to the "great" or sublime, marking his essay as the first important critical essay on the fantastic. Addison offers the eighteenth century a working definition of fantastic literature:

> There is a kind of writing wherein the poet quite loses sight of nature and entertains his reader's imagination with the characters and actions of such persons as have many of them no existence but what he bestows on them. Such are fairies, witches, magicians, demons, and departed spirits. (No. 419)

Addison's definition contains a basic tension. On the one hand, the fantastic is presented as purely imaginary, as having "no existence." On the other hand, the fantastic is associated with a tradition of exploded supernatural beliefs from fairies to demons; that is, it exploits figures and characters we used to believe in but no longer do. But is something invented that has "no existence" but what the writer "bestows" the same thing as using the traditional elements of superstitious folklore? The first, something invented, "entertains his reader's imagination" with something new, never seen before; the second, folklore, the repository of past belief, deploys familiar ideas, if only for new effects.

Addison simply assumes the two sides of his definition fit together: for, of course, modern rationality no longer allows belief in fairies or any of the other claptrap of superstition. Fairies and the rest must have "no existence." Addison explains that the poet "has no pattern to follow and must work altogether out of his own invention," but insists he must also have "a particular cast of fancy and imagination" not only "naturally fruitful" but also "superstitious." Again, the power of the fantastic resides in the poet's creation of something new and original out of nothing, but also in its raising of the specter of a superstitious past supposedly laid to rest by the refinement of modern understanding. The fantastic is activated for Addison by a mixture of "memory" and story, built on the return of "childhood" fears that had seemed left behind by the reasoning adult (and modern culture) and on "secret terrors" that Addison indicates "naturally" underlie the mind. The fantastic at once defines modernity by its own backwardness (as a repository of exploded beliefs) and supposed childishness, its seeming unimportance; and yet the fantastic also haunts modernity with its presentation of inassimilable and wholly "different laws and economies," its "secret terrors" and pleasures that also "naturally" underlie, and so define, the modern mind. This contradiction lies at the heart of the fantastic as a form.

Fantastic literature initially emerges in the production of new, "modern" literary ballads, fairy tales, oriental tales, and the like, written in the style of those "ancient" works found in numerous popular eighteenth-century collections, such as Thomas Percy's *Reliques of Ancient English Poetry* (1765) and James MacPherson's dubious reconstruction of the "lost" epics of an ancient bard in *Fragments of Ancient Poetry* (1760) and *The Works of Ossian* (1765), among many others. The continued popular consumption of new works that look backward to the exploded supernatural for their style and subject matter raised critical questions about the purpose of literature in a "reasonable" age. (For isn't the rational purpose of literature to show us who we are? To reflect the world as it is? To be a mirror of society? If so, why is fantasy, which distorts and obscures reality, so popular?) Increasingly throughout the eighteenth century, the novel and romance (a category including gothic literature and other stories from the period set in remote locations or distant times) are marked off from one another as, respectively, realistic or fantastic. Fantastic literature and its criticism develops in inverse relationship to what has been characterized as the "rise" of the realistic novel in the eighteenth century (following an assertion of the form in midcentury prefaces to novels by Henry Fielding and Samuel Richardson, and criticism by Samuel Johnson, among many others), each mode seemingly requiring the other for self-definition.

The fantastic romance material fails to be superseded by the realistic novel in part because of a new focus on the interior faculties of the mind, especially the cultivation of the creative possibilities of the imagination that propels popular interest in supernatural fictions as fictions, even after belief in the supernatural wanes. For example, gothic literature, the first popular fiction genre, embraces the use of the imaginary, beginning in Horace Walpole's dynamic claim in the "Preface to the Second Edition" of the very first gothic novel, *The Castle of Otranto* (1765), "to blend the two kinds of romance, the ancient" (where "all was imagination and improbability") and "the modern" (123), or realistic. Ann Radcliffe in "On the Supernatural in Poetry" (1826) and Sir Walter Scott in "On the Supernatural in Fictitious Composition" (1827) develop theories of the supernatural fantastic based on the sublime of terror presented in Edmund Burke's *A Philosophical Enquiry of Our Ideas of the Sublime and Beautiful* (1757), the most famous British treatise on the subject. The sublime describes the imagination overworked and overwhelmed, an event that writers noted the fantastic could accomplish well. Scott argues for the need of sublime "obscurity" to the working of the fantastic. Radcliffe attempts to bridge the growing divide between realistic and gothic fiction by making an important distinction between "horror"—outright supernatural fictions— and "terror"—which uses the possibility (but not actuality) of the supernatural to underwrite narrative tension through sublime uncertainty.

In the romantic era, Samuel Taylor Coleridge defines a modern approach to the fantastic when he writes in his *Biographia Literaria*

(1817) of "the willing suspension of disbelief" necessary for the enjoyment of imaginative literature by skeptical readers. Coleridge counters the importance of "accurate observation" to literature with the claim that the literature of the imagination arises vitally and creatively from within, from the "depths" of the mind. His influential theories of the creative imagination license romantic experiments with supernatural ballads and ghost stories (the label Mary Shelley gives to her *Frankenstein* in 1818). But the romantic era's increasing interest in the imagination also witnesses an intensification of anxieties surrounding the fantastic. For example, Coleridge's critical writings claim the fantastic as a way to enter the divine world of the spirit, but his tragic gothic fantasies, such as *The Rime of the Ancient Mariner* (1798) or *Kubla Khan* (1816), express a profound failure and fragmentation of the imagination.

Beyond an emerging theory of the creative imagination, the early nineteenth century presides over a crucial new emphasis on childhood that refigures children as more imaginative than adults; this reconfiguration allows a new focus on fantasy produced for children in particular, as well as on the nostalgic adult looking back on childhood lost. William Wordsworth, Coleridge's collaborator in the collection *Lyrical Ballads* (1798), famously writes poems that turn to personal memory, "recollection in tranquility," and in so doing valorizes childhood as a site of adult feeling and reflection. Wordsworth's work popularizes a common but now contested view of fantastic literature that insists on the importance of imaginative fairy tales and other fantastic works for children in order to grow the imagination, while firmly dismissing (however sadly) outright fantastic literature for adults. The romantic viewpoint presides over a profound increase in the production and importance of fantasy literature for children in the late nineteenth century, repositioning the fantastic literature from a primarily gothic or superstitious literature haunting modernity to a vigorous children's literature confined by the Victorian era to the personal past of adult memory, as when Lewis Carroll insists on an Alice who can lead us into Wonderland. The adult becomes, finally, haunted not by history but by childhood innocence lost, as represented in fantastic literature.

Victorian fantasy is dominated by the "fairy tale." The nineteenth century, especially after the work of the Brothers Grimm (*Children's and Household Tales*, first volume published in 1812), witnesses a transformation of oral fairy tales originally meant for general readers into increasingly "enchanted" works suitable for children. Victorian essays on the fantastic produce numerous defenses of the morality of fantasy literature for children (though also offering covert explanations for its continued interest for adults), promoting an expansion of the material collected as "fairy tales" and the creation of new "fairy tale"–like works such as the nonsense poetry of Lewis Carroll and Edward Lear. For example, Charles Dickens, in "Frauds on the Fairies" (1853), makes a plea for the moral force and innocence of the fantastic. John Ruskin, in "Fairy Stories" (1868), argues that fairy tales should remain unbowdlerized—that is, unchanged—because of the importance of the imagination, unencumbered by adult concerns, to childhood. In the Edwardian essay "Fairy Tales" (1908), G. K. Chesterton goes further, asserting the moral innocence of the fantastic by finding, in the hard justice of fairy tales, the root of all morality in the capacity of the imagination to move us to an abstract world of "wonder" that underwrites moral law.

George MacDonald's piece "The Fantastic Imagination" (1890) is a defining work of fantastic criticism in the nineteenth century. MacDonald defends the delight of "calling up new forms" when coupled with respect for the "laws" of creation, stressing the inner consistency of a fantasy world, once invented. He argues that good fantasy expresses a moral truth found in the free play of the imagination: "It [the fairy tale] cannot help but have meaning; if it has proportion and harmony it has vitality, and vitality is truth" (MacDonald 66). He argues that true art will have many meanings and locates the vitality of fantasy in its ability to "wake a meaning," leading the reader to wonder. MacDonald prefigures the project explicitly proposed by J. R. R. Tolkien and C. S. Lewis to use fantasy literature to engender a feeling analogous to the feeling of the divine, using "wonder" to allow the reader to glimpse beyond words, beyond the world.

In the late nineteenth century and early decades of the twentieth century, a proliferation of popular genres, many related to the fantastic, influences the definition of what is increasingly called "fantasy" literature. Horror and science fiction, in particular, are genres closely related to fantasy, and their separate formal definition marks off important borders with fantasy. Moving off into their own separate critical discourses, they allow fantasy literature to further develop a genre identity of its own. For example, horror literature and "fantasy literature seem to be defined against one another, two sides of one coin: "fear" and "wonder" marking opposed key emotional responses to the unknown or mystery central to (and connecting) both.

H. P. Lovecraft's foundational "Supernatural Horror in Literature" (1927) defines fantastic works of what he calls "cosmic fear." His essay begins: "The oldest and strongest emotion of mankind is fear, and the oldest and strongest kind of fear is fear of the unknown," locating a fear in the obscurity and uncertainty embodied in fantastic literature. Sigmund Freud's essay "The Uncanny" (1919) brings his psychoanalytic insights to bear upon aesthetics, and the working of fantastic horror in particular. His notion of the uncanny is related to the sublime we have discussed earlier. However, Freud writes of an exclusively negative effect, emphasizing the possibility in the sublime (and fantastic) of fragmentation and a frightening breakdown of identity in the bewildering play of fantastic images. His ideas function as a critique of the positive views of the fantastic as expressed in Victorian opinions of children's fairy tales. Freud reads the fantastic image, "other" by definition, as expressive of the superstitious return of the repressed both in the individual and in culture.

Proto-science fiction writer H. G. Wells in his "Preface to *Seven Famous Novels*" (1934) discusses what he calls his "scientific romances" as "fantasies; they do not aim to project a serious possibility; they aim indeed only at the same amount of conviction as one gets in a good gripping dream. They have to hold the reader to the end by art and illusion and not by proof and argument, and the moment he closes the cover and reflects he wakes up to their impossibility" (253). Clearly, his speculations indicate another transformation in how the game of the impossible can be played. As Wordsworth shifted the locus of fantasy's power from the impossible past to childhood lost, so science fiction brilliantly moves the fantasy element from the past to the future, where it perhaps awaits us just out of reach, moving its fantasy into step with our progress-obsessed contemporary culture. Damon Knight's foundational essay "Critics" (1956) introduces the concept of "the sense of wonder" into science fiction criticism, revealing the early connection between science fiction's extrapolation from the possible and the fantastic's embrace of the impossible. Knight's claim remains an influential (if long contested) idea in science fiction and marks the crossroads where fantasy and science fiction move off from one another.

For early science fiction and other genres, the early twentieth-century American pulp magazines become the vehicle for identifying (and refining) "niches" for certain generic material from what had been more generalized "adventure" material in the Victorian era. For the fantastic, a brief mention of some notable pulps must include *Weird Tales*, the great horror magazine of the 1930s, where Lovecraft published; *Amazing Stories*, edited by Hugh Gernsback, starting in 1926, and *Astounding*, after editor John Campbell took over in 1937, both of which organized and defined a readership for science fiction; and, for fantasy, *Unknown* in 1939, which had only a short run but influenced other magazines through today. In this period, science fiction took precedence over fantasy in popularity, though the two became linked—because of their shared pulp past and overlapping readership—on bookstore shelves. A significant number of science fiction novels, from authors growing out of the pulps, appear in the 1950s, and some fantasy novels not marketed as children's literature would join them. However, modern fantasy literature trails science fiction and horror and does not really cohere as a genre until Tolkien's success in the 1960s. Much important criticism in this period on the fantastic, like the essays named above, is, in fact, not on the fantastic *per se* but on the neighboring genres of horror and science fiction.

An important exception is Tolkien's essay "On Fairy-stories" (1938), the most influential essay of fantasy criticism in the twentieth century. Tolkien defines fairy stories not by the presence of fairies (or any fantastic element alone) but faerie, "the Perilous Realm itself, and the air that blows in that country" (114). Tolkien's definition places the fantastic not in the text but in the reader's apprehension of something other, perceived beyond the text. He argues that fantasy is not the special province of children but belongs to a certain type of reader, whether young or old. He describes fantasy as subcreation, an art demanding inner consistency in the making of secondary worlds. He outlines a three-part structure of the fantastic: Recovery, Escape, and Consolation. Recovery describes fantasy's ability to make the familiar unfamiliar and to allow one to see it anew. Tolkien's structure of Escape answers the charge of escapism by asserting that fantasy is an escape but not a running away; rather, fantasy challenges the reader to break free from possessiveness, from a narrow greed of material objects. Consolation describes a joy glimpsed in the "*eucatastrophe*," the happy ending of fantasy literature, though it is a complex emotion: "It does not deny the existence of *dyscatastrophe*, of sorrow and failure: the possibility of these is necessary to the joy of deliverance; it denies (in the face of much evidence, if you will) universal final defeat and in so far is *evangelium*, giving a fleeting glimpse of Joy, Joy beyond the walls of the world, poignant as grief" (153). *Catastrophe* is a word used to describe an unhappy event; Tolkien separates "dyscatastrophe," the bad event, from "eucatastrophe," the happy accident. Undeserved on a strictly realistic level, the "sudden turn" of the "happy ending" becomes for Tolkien akin to religious grace.

Lewis, who belonged to the same writing group as Tolkien, The Inklings, also produced important essays on the fantastic. His "On Stories" (1947), for example, describes fantasy as motivated not by character (as in the realistic novel) but by story. He makes a further distinction between the lesser surprise of "mere story" or plot (as in action-adventures) and a quality of "surprisingness" in the fantastic that is not lessened by rereadings and motivates our encounter with mystery. In fantasy, the impossible leads one to imagine, to reach for something not quite embodied in the text itself; this reaching out is, for Lewis, like a yearning for the divine.

Before the 1970s, work on fantasy by academic critics in the twentieth century does not constitute a sustained inquiry into the genre. However, important work is produced in, for example, myth criticism, an important early- and midcentury critical "school" that seeks to explain the structure of literature by reference to anthropology and psychology. "The Mythos of Summer: Romance" from Northrop Frye's *Anatomy of Criticism* (1957), for instance, describes the importance of fantasy to the literary archetype of descent into and return from the underworld. Frye compellingly delineates fantasy's quest structure, granting fantasy a vital and organic place in his four "seasons" or literary modes. His work importantly brings ideas out of Jungian psychology to fantasy literature. Carl Jung's study of mythology developed the idea of archetypes—powerful symbolic characters, themes, and forms in myth and story. His work has been widely influential on fantasy criticism because it provides a vocabulary for the creations of the imagination and describes the psychological impact on readers of symbolic figures or motifs that appear repeatedly in fantasy, such as dragons or wizards. Archetypes, Jung argues, access a permanent and foundational level of the mind, rising up out of what he calls the "collective unconscious." Jung's ideas also underlie Joseph Campbell's use of archetypes to describe the quest structure of his Monomyth in his influential *Hero with a Thousand Faces* (1949).

The fantastic emerges in the twentieth century in international adult works by Franz Kafka, Russian experimenters, French and other European surrealists and existentialists such as Albert Camus or Eugène Ionesco, and in Latin American magical realists such as Gabriel Garcia

Márquez, all of which undermine the idea that the fantastic—fantasy—is not "serious" enough for mature adult readers. A representative commentary comes from Jean-Paul Sartre, in a review, "Aminadab; Or, The Fantastic Considered as a Language" (1947), which claims that in "order to achieve the fantastic, it is neither necessary nor sufficient to portray extraordinary things." (57). The fantastic is an all-or-nothing proposition: everything must be turned upside down. The purpose of the wholly "other" language of fantasy is to allow us to "see *from the outside*." Sartre's claim argues for the importance of fantasy to allow us to think in new ways about the world, marking its usefulness to Sartre's own existential philosophy.

Also of interest in international criticism of the fantastic, Russian critic Mikhail Bakhtin's dialogic criticism describes literature as a site for the interaction or dialogue of multiple voices (or modes of discourse). In, for example, "Characteristics of Genre and Plot Composition in Dostoevsky's Work" (1973), Bakhtin, in his inimitable style, describes the use of the fantastic in Dostoevsky by comparing it to the Menippean satire, an ancient comic form of abundant energy and imagination. The fantastic and its strangeness is importantly identified as a site for the "carnivalesque," a key term for dialogic criticism that locates the intense interaction of multiple discourses in a place (or text) outside of proscribed rules of form and decorum.

Closer to the present day, the persistence of the fantastic internationally drives an interest in the fantastic in postmodern literature, in authors as different as Donald Barthelme, Angela Carter, or Salman Rushdie. Representative academic work on the postmodern that accounts for the newfound critical value of the fantastic can be seen in Fredric Jameson's "Magical Narratives: On the Dialectical Use of Genre Criticism" from *The Political Unconscious* (1981). Jameson's Marxist work argues against the universalism of arguments like Frye's or Jung's and sets out to historicize the fantastic. The fantastic for Jameson, in other words, is written at certain historical moments for particular ideological reasons, whether those reasons are to bring forward what is otherwise unsayable or to avoid saying what must remain hidden.

The emergence of a coherent critical dialogue on the fantastic, however, coincides, not incidentally, with the increased production of fantasy literature itself as a genre. Tolkien's *Lord of the Rings* (1954–55), published as an adult sequel to his successful children's fantasy *The Hobbit* (1937), is embraced by the American counterculture of the 1960s, greatly expanding the readership of the genre and becoming, like J. K. Rowling's Harry Potter series at the end of the century, a commercial phenomenon. Attempts by eager publishers to repeat this success leads in the 1970s to the establishment of new publishing lines for fantasy; the resultant production of more fantasy books than ever pours forth vast quantities of formulaic hackwork but also makes room for good, new work that might have been unmarketable before.

One of those "new, good works" is Ursula Le Guin's *A Wizard of Earthsea* (1968), not only a classic fantasy novel, but an early young adult (YA) work, a new marketing area exclusively for the older teenager introduced during the 1970s. Just as fantasy has long dominated children's literature, it strongly influences YA literature and, in the 1990s, crossover novels, a new category for works marketed successfully to teens and adults, such as Francesca Lia Bloch's modern fairy tale *Weetzie Bat* (1989), often considered the first "crossover" novel. Rowling's *Harry Potter* series begins as children's literature but takes on darker themes (and grows in sheer wordage) in later novels, until it seems to move over into YA territory and end as a crossover series, exemplifying the contemporary trend and fantasy's importance in it.

Le Guin has been a vital critical voice for fantasy in this period thanks to collected essays from *The Language of the Night* (1979) through *Cheek by Jowl* (2009). Her piece "From Elfland to Poughkeepsie" (1973), for example, is perhaps the premier essay on the role of style in fantasy. Le Guin uses close readings of master stylists to show that heightened language is necessary to the working of affect in fantasy, and calls on writers of fantasy during the early post-Tolkien boom to take their work seriously. "Why Are Americans Afraid of Dragons?" (1974) argues for the importance of the imagination both to childhood and to a healthy adulthood. Later, "The Carrier Bag Theory of Fiction" (1986) sharply argues that fantasy does not need to be structured as a quest, but also holds out the possibility for a new kind of story, perhaps one which is less hierarchal and more essentially integrative in terms of gender and the environment, precisely because of fantasy's ability to imagine new places and ways of being.

Among many other writers who make important contributions, representative work includes Jane Yolen's "Fabling to the Near Night" (2000) and China Miéville's "Introduction" to a special issue he guest-edited on fantasy for the academic journal *Historical Materialism* (2002). Yolen's work defends fantasy in children's literature but also, moving beyond earlier critical defenses, details how its seemingly innocent symbolic forms can cloak racism, among other dark impulses. Miéville's discussion of Marxism and fantasy notes the conservative nature of Tolkienesque fantasy and its retrograde nostalgia, arguing for the liberating and transformational possibilities of fantasy as a form. Fiction writers hungry to understand their own work have always been an important source of critical insight on the field.

A coherent field of academic criticism on the fantastic appears, paradoxically, in response to one of the first full-length studies of the genre, Tzvetan Todorov's *The Fantastic: A Structural Approach to a Literary Genre* (1973). Todorov defines the fantastic as a "hesitation" between the marvelous (outright fantasy) and the uncanny (the strange but true). Later critics argue with Todorov's contention that, when the moment of uncertainty is resolved in a narrative, the fantastic disappears, but Todorov's structuralist study sets the immediate terms of the academic debate. Eric S. Rabkin, for example, describes the fantastic in structural terms in *The Fantastic in Literature* (1975): "One of the key distinguishing marks of the fantastic is that the perspectives enforced by the ground rules of the narrative world must be diametrically contradicted" (qtd. in Sandner 170). Rabkin sets out to expand Todorov's approach in order to include more forms of fantasy literature. W. R. Irwin does similar work with the narrative "rules" of fantasy in *The Game of the Impossible* (1976). In *Fantasy: The Literature of Subversion* (1981), Rosemary Jackson describes the structure of the fantastic on a linguistic level: "The fantastic . . . pushes towards an area of non-signification" (41). The fantastic does not simply exist in the moment of "hesitation" between the real and the supernatural, but rather expresses a desire for the unreal that subverts the "real" of the dominant culture by allowing for the presence of the otherwise silenced imaginary other. Another kind of characteristic definition appears in C. N. Manlove's *Modern Fantasy: Five Studies* (1975), which defines the fantastic by the presence of "wonder" and the "supernatural," connecting his work to the earliest definitions of the form in the eighteenth century and the romantic era.

As the critical discourse approaches the present day, the amount of work produced expands exponentially, and it becomes difficult to say with any certainty how best to characterize current interests. Therefore, what follows should perhaps best be considered to be one reader's "take" on a now lively field of inquiry. An important touchstone work has been Brian Attebery's *Strategies of Fantasy* (1992), which helpfully makes a distinction between fantasy as a mode, describing any use of the literary unreal, even in "mainstream" literature, and as a formula, describing the most limited fantasy tropes and themes of the popular literature as in derivative fantasy quest novels, and proposes the "fuzzy set" middle ground of genre. Attebery's "genre" moves away from fractious debates over what is and is not fantasy toward frames of reference that allow different sorts of discussion on fantasy to take place, as it must, in such a large field as the fantastic.

The history of the fantastic has been clarified by several critics. Karl Kroeber's *Romantic Fantasy and Science Fiction* (1988) makes clear fantasy's debt to romantic poetics. Kathryn Hume's *Fantasy and Mimesis* (1984) outlines the history of fantasy criticism in relation to the classic Greek term "mimesis," arguing that fantasy and mimesis are impulses equally expressed in literature. Stephen Prickett's *Victorian Fantasy* (1979) usefully identifies the Victorian era as a defining moment in the evolution of the word "fantasy" and the genre together. And David Sandner's *Critical Discourses of the Fantastic: 1712–1831* (2011) defines the emergence of the fantastic from the eighteenth-century aesthetic discourse of the sublime.

As the modern genre continues to evolve and change, new criticism attempts to provide useful frameworks for conversation. Among the many arguments about the form or shape of the fantastic, perhaps the most important attempt to produce a systematic response to the strangeness of the genre has been John Clute's sometimes idiosyncratic but fascinating and insightful criticism, which taken together details a complex structure (what he calls a "grammar") of the genre's affect. Of special interest for the fantastic has been his work in the *Encyclopedia of Fantasy* (1997) and *A Darkening Garden: A Lexicon of Horror* (2006), which offer definitions of terms that are often more meditations on the ability of the fantastic to tell the "story" of our world—that is, to aid our understanding of it through literary art. Another very recent work of interest because it deals with fantasy's dismantling of itself as a genre—its movement into the "mainstream" or into new, ephemeral genre designations such as "slipstream" or "interstitial fiction"—is Gary Wolfe's collection of essays, *Evaporating Genres* (2011), which considers how much new fantasy challenges and undermines (perhaps necessarily) the idea of genre boundaries around the fantastic, expanding the fantastic beyond genre confines but also perhaps losing the focus of being a genre, with an identifiable readership and shared interests.

Wolfe's work brings us back full circle to the question with which we began this essay: what's in a name? The answer is still: everything and nothing. The contradictory power of the fantastic imagination—its uselessness (as Oscar Wilde would say) and yet, because of that, its ability to draw us in to desire its strangeness, to experience stories that matter because they are manifestly not true, are only a story, only a representation of us and our thoughts—all this drives our continued interest in fantasy, from excavations of its history, to its present convoluted evolutions, and on into its impossible future. Fantasy induces us all to be critics, to look again, more closely—to be perplexed and wonder why? That wondering is part of its importance, part of its reason for being—or for not being, as the case may be, depending, fundamentally, on how you look at it.

Works Cited

Addison, Joseph. "The Pleasures of the Imagination." *Spectator* Nos. 411–21. 1712. *Essays in Criticism and Literary Theory*. Ed. John Loftis. Northbrook, IL: AHM, 1975. 138–82.

Aristotle. *The Poetics*. 335–322 BCE. *Criticism: Major Statements*. Ed. Charles Kaplan and William Anderson. New York: St. Martin's, 1991. 21–53.

Attebery, Brian. *Strategies of Fantasy*. Bloomington: Indiana UP, 1992.

Bakhtin, Mikhail. *Problems of Dostoevsky's Poetics*. Ann Arbor, MI: Ardis, 1973.

Burke, Edmund. *A Philosophical Enquiry into Our Ideas of the Sublime and the Beautiful*. 1757. Ed. James T. Boulton. 1968. Notre Dame: U of Notre Dame P, 1986.

Chesterton, G. K. «Fairy Tales.» 1908. *Fantastic Literature: A Critical Reader*. Ed. David Sandner. Westport, CT: Praeger, 2004. 70–73.

Cinthio, Giraldi. "On the Composition of Romances." 1549. *Literary Criticism: Plato to Dryden*. Ed. Allan H. Gilbert. New York: American, 1940. 262–73.

Clute, John. *The Darkening Garden: A Short Lexicon of Horror*. Cauheegan, WI: Payseur, 2006.

_____. *The Encyclopedia of Fantasy*. New York: St. Martin's, 1997.

Coleridge, Samuel Taylor. *Biographia Literaria*. 1847. Ed. James Engell and W. Jackson Bate. Princeton: Princeton UP, 1983. 2 vols.

Dickens, Charles. "Frauds on the Fairies." 1853. *Fantastic Literature: A Critical Reader*. Ed. David Sandner. Westport, CT: Praeger, 2004. 56–58.

Freud, Sigmund. "The Uncanny." 1919. *Standard Edition of the Complete Psychological Works*. Vol. 17. Trans. James Strachey. London: Hogarth, 1955. 218–56.

Frye, Northrop. *Anatomy of Criticism: Four Essays*. Princeton: Princeton UP, 1957.

Hume, Kathryn. *Fantasy and Mimesis: Responses to Reality in Western Literature*. New York: Methuen, 1984.

Irwin, W. R. *The Game of the Impossible*. Urbana: U of Illinois P, 1976.

Jackson, Rosemary. *Fantasy: The Literature of Subversion*. New York: Methuen, 1981.

Jameson, Fredric. *The Political Unconscious: Narrative as a Socially Symbolic Act*. Ithaca, NY: Cornell UP, 1981.

Johnson, Samuel. *Rambler* no. 4. 1750. Rptd. in *Novels and Romance 1700–1800: A Documentary Record*. Ed. by Ioan Williams. New York: Barnes, 1970. 142–46.

Jung, Carl. *Man and His Symbols*. Garden City, NY: Doubleday, 1971.

_____. *Memories, Dreams, Reflections*. New York: Vintage, 1989.

Knight, Damon. *In Search of Wonder*. Chicago: Advent, 1956.

Kroeber, Karl. *Romantic Fantasy and Science Fiction*. New Haven, CT: Yale UP, 1988.

Le Guin, Ursula. "The Carrier Bag Theory of Literature." 1986. *Dancing at the Edge of the World: Thoughts on Words, Women, Places*. New York: Grove, 1989.

_____. "From Elfland to Poughkeepsie." 1973. *The Language of the Night*. New York: Putnam, 1979. 83–96.

_____. "Why Are Americans Afraid of Dragons?" 1974. *The Language of the Night*. New York: Putnam, 1979. 39–48.

Lewis, C. S. *On Stories and Other Essays on Literature*. Ed. Walter Hooper. 1966. San Diego: Harcourt, 1982.

Lovecraft, H. P. "Supernatural Horror in Literature." 1927. New York: Dover, 1973.

MacDonald, George. "The Fantastic Imagination." 1890. *Fantastic Literature: A Critical Reader*. Ed. David Sandner, Westport, CT: Praeger, 2004. 64–69.

Manlove, C. N. *Fantasy Literature: Five Studies*. New York: Cambridge UP, 1975.

Mieville, China. "Marxism and Fantasy: Editorial Introduction." *Historical Materialism* 10.4 (2002): 39–49.

Prickett, Stephen. *Victorian Fantasy*. Bloomington: Indiana UP, 1979.

Rabkin, Eric. *The Fantastic in Literature*. Princeton: Princeton UP, 1976.

Radcliffe, Ann. "On the Supernatural in Poetry," *New Monthly Magazine* 16 (1826): 142–52.

Ruskin, John. "Fairy Stories." 1868. *Fantastic Literature: A Critical Reader*. Ed. David Sandner. Westport, CT: Praeger, 2004. 59–63.

Sandner, David, ed. *Fantastic Literature: A Critical Reader*. Westport, CT: Praeger, 2004.

Sartre, Jean Paul. "Aminadab, or the Fantastic Considered as a Language." Rptd. in *Literary Essays*. Trans. Annette Michelson. New York: Philosophical Library, 1958. 56–72.

Scott, Walter. "On the Supernatural in Fictitious Composition." 1827. *Sir Walter Scott on Novelists and Fiction*. Ed. Ioan Williams. London: Routledge, 1968. 312–53.

Sidney, Philip. "An Apology for Poetry." 1595. *Criticism: The Major Texts*. Ed. Walter Jackson Bate. New York: Harcourt, 1952. 82–106.

Tasso, Torquato. "Discourses on the Heroic Poem." 1594. *Literary Criticism: Plato to Dryden*. Ed. Allan H. Gilbert. New York: American, 1940. 467–503.

Todorov, Tzvetan. *The Fantastic: A Structural Approach to a Literary Genre*. Trans. Richard Howard. Cleveland, OH: P of Case Western Reserve U, 1970.

Tolkien, J. R. R. "On Fairy-Stories." 1938. *The Monsters and the Critics and Other Essays*. Ed. Christopher Tolkien. Boston: Houghton, 1984. 109–61.

Walpole, Horace. "Preface." *The Castle of Otranto*. 1764. Rptd. in *Novels and Romance 1700–1800: A Documentary Record*. Ed. Ioan Williams. New York: Barnes, 1970. 263–65.

_____. "Preface [to the Second Edition]" 1765. *The Castle of Otranto.* 1764. Rptd. in *Novels and Romance 1700–1800: A Documentary Record.* Ed. by Ioan Williams. New York: Barnes, 1970. 265–69.

Wells, H. G. "Preface." *Seven Famous Novels.* 1934. Rptd. in *The Time Machine.* Ed. Nicholas Ruddick. Peterborough, ONT: Broadview, 2001. 252–55.

Wolfe, Gary. *Evaporating Genres.* Middletown, CT: Wesleyan UP, 2011.

Yolen, Jane. "Fabling to the Near Night." 2000. *Touch Magic: Fantasy, Faerie, and Folklore in the Literature of Childhood.* Rev. ed. New York: August, 2007.

Žižek, Slavoj. *The Sublime Object of Ideology.* New York: Verso, 1989.

Tolkien and the Fantasy Tradition _____

Dimitra Fimi

I. Defining Fantasy Literature: "Fantasy" vs. "the Fantastic"

If literature of the fantastic is a broad term to refer to literature that deviates from realism and allows the exploration of "impossible," non-realistic occurrences within its narratives, then fantasy literature is a distinct category that not only allows fantastical elements to exist but takes them seriously as part of the narrative's "reality" and arranges them into a coherent system with its own internal rules.[1]

Consider the plotline of Henry James's novella *The Turn of the Screw* (1898), in which a young governess in charge of two orphaned children has visions of two ghosts that lived in the house and were involved in a guilty liaison while alive. The ghosts have now returned to corrupt the children and draw them to evil and sin. The novella presents incidents and beings that are "impossible" and nonrealistic. However, for decades readers and scholars have debated whether the ghosts the young governess sees are real or figments of her disturbed imagination (see James). The text never gives us a definite answer, and its ambiguity is intentional. This is a classic example of literature of the fantastic, described as "a mode of fiction in which the possible and the impossible (or most frequently 'reality' and the paranormal, or the supernatural) are confounded, so as to leave the reader (and usually the narrator and/or protagonist) with no satisfying explanation for the strange events which have occurred within a fictional world" (Cornwell).

Tzvetan Todorov, whose work laid the foundations for the study of literature of the fantastic, insisted on the importance of a lack of explanation for "impossible" events: "The fantastic occupies the duration of this *uncertainty*. . . . The fantastic is that *hesitation* experienced by a person who knows only the laws of nature, confronting an apparently supernatural event" (25, my italics). Fantasy, on the contrary, has its own internal rules, and all of the magical, supernatural, impossible, and unrealistic elements are taken seriously as true and occur within a clearly defined framework. As a general rule, a fantasy text will not attempt to confuse the reader about what is real in the world in which it is set: everything "impossible" that happens is possible in that world and has been thought through. Following this distinction, literature of the fantastic includes a great number of genres, from gothic novels to ghost stories and supernatural or "weird" tales, all the way to postmodernist genres like magical realism. But fantasy is a distinct category with its own rules, tradition, and structural and formal expectations, although many critics use the term "fantasy" to refer to both fantasy literature and "the fantastic," which often confuses students of the genre (e.g., Jackson, Armitt).

Devising a comprehensive definition of fantasy literature can be a difficult task, but let us take as a working model the relevant entry from *The Encyclopedia of Fantasy*, which sums up some of the ideas discussed above:

> A fantasy text is a self-coherent narrative. When set in this world, it tells a story which is impossible in the world as we perceive it; when set in an otherworld, that otherworld will be impossible, though stories set there may be possible in its terms. (Clute and Grant 338)

Unlike the disruptive dreamlike sequences, surreal elements, unexplained supernatural occurrences, or open endings often found in texts of "the fantastic," fantasy favors traditional forms of storytelling. It presents narratives with a coherent beginning, middle, and end, and in which one plot element leads consequentially to the next. This central quality sets fantasy apart from modernist or postmodernist texts that play with unreliable narrators, or draw attention to the artificiality of the narrative voice.

Clute and Grant's definition also focuses on the setting of fantasy literature. Fantasy can be set both in "the world as we perceive it," our world, or an otherworld, an entire invented cosmos. Many scholars use these two possible settings to distinguish between two different subgenres of fantasy: "low" fantasy and "high" fantasy, respectively (see Sullivan, Gamble and Yates, Clute and Grant). Low fantasy contains supernatural intrusions into our world, like the sand fairy in E. Nesbit's *Five Children and It* (1902), or the tiny people that live under our floorboards in Mary Norton's *The Borrowers* (1952). Some fantasy critics call this category "intrusion fantasy" (e.g., Mendlesohn). High fantasy is set in an otherworld, an entirely invented universe such as J. R. R. Tolkien's Middle-earth, C. S. Lewis's Narnia, or Ursula K. Le Guin's Earthsea.

In low or intrusion fantasy, the fantastic enters our own world, but in high fantasy there are different ways in which the otherworld is accessible. Given the way the characters enter the fantasy world, high fantasy can be further subdivided into three categories. In the first, "the primary world does not exist" (Gamble and Yates 121). Like with Tolkien's Middle-earth or Le Guin's Earthsea, the plot of this type of fantasy takes place directly in a secondary world, without any reference to our world. It is also called "immersive fantasy" (Mendlesohn), as we are "immersed" into the fantasy world without any introduction. In the second, "the alternative world is entered through a portal in the primary world" (Gamble and Yates 122). The classic example here is Lewis's *The Lion, the Witch and the Wardrobe* (1950), in which Lucy, Peter, Susan, and Edmund enter the magical land of Narnia through a wardrobe. In other books of the series, children enter Narnia via other such "portals," such as a painting (*The Voyage of the Dawn Treader*, 1952) or magic rings (*The Magician's Nephew*, 1955). In the third subcategory of high fantasy, "the alternative world is a world-within-a-world, marked off by physical boundaries" (Gamble and Yates 122). A good example here is the magical world of the Harry Potter series. As Gamble and Yates observe:

Although there is an invisible barrier that Harry has to pass through in order to board the Hogwarts Express [i.e., platform 9 ¾], the school is still in our world. Muggles and wizards inhabit the same space, although there are some areas that Muggles cannot access because they do not have the necessary powers. (122)

The last concern of the definition by Clute and Grant is to establish what is "possible" or "impossible" in fantasy. In high fantasy, a lot of what takes place in the fantasy world is impossible in our world, but within the fantasy world, it is possible and consistent. The fantasy otherworld has its own, internally coherent rules. In low fantasy, the fantastical intrusions to our world are impossible and nonrealistic, but we take them in good faith as "really" happening.

II. Theorizing Fantasy Literature: J. R. R. Tolkien's "On Fairy-Stories"

Students of fantasy who are familiar with Tolkien's work and terminology will have already discerned resonances between the introductory discussion above and Tolkien's exploration of fantasy in his seminal essay "On Fairy-Stories" (*Tree and Leaf* 3–73). A number of other fantasy writers have attempted to theorize their own work and defend, discuss, and analyze the genre they write in (e.g., George MacDonald, Le Guin), but Tolkien's essay is one of the most influential theoretical explorations of fantasy literature. Verlyn Flieger and Douglas A. Anderson have recently claimed that:

"On Fairy-stories" is . . . [Tolkien's] most explicit analysis of his own art. . . . It is the template on which he shaped his idea of sub-creation, and the manifesto in which he declared his particular concept of what fantasy is and how it ought to work. (9)

Tolkien's essay was originally a lecture delivered at the University of St. Andrews in 1939. The essay is beautifully written, but it can be a challenging read because it includes a great range of different points and touches upon mythology, folklore, anthropology, philology (historical linguistics), and fantasy. The essay is divided into six sections. Tolkien begins the first section (entitled "Fairy-Story") with the question: "What are fairy-stories?" (Tolkien prefers the term "fairy-stories" to the more common "fairy tales.") He examines the origin of the term and attempts to define fairy-stories by giving examples of stories that do not fit into this genre.

In the second section, "Origins," Tolkien continues with exploring the origins of fairy-stories in mythology, folklore, and philology. His discussion refers to leading authorities of his time, including Andrew Lang, Max Müller, and various theories about the origin of myth (see Flieger, "'There Would Always Be a Fairy-Tale'"). Toward the end of that section he refers to language and the imagination. This is the point in the essay at which he seems to be talking for the first time not about fairy-tales, but about his own art: fantasy literature. He writes about the power of language and the way it affects not only our perception of the world but also our imagination:

> The human mind endowed with the powers of generalization and abstraction, sees not only *green-grass*, discriminating it from other things (and finding it fair to look upon), but sees that it is *green* as well as being *grass*. But how powerful, how stimulating to the very faculty that produced it, was the invention of the adjective. . . . The mind that thought of *light, heavy, grey, yellow, still, swift*, also conceived of magic that would make heavy things light and able to fly, turn grey lead into yellow gold, and the still rock into swift water. If it could do the one, it could do the other; it inevitably did both. When we can take green from grass, blue from heaven, and red from blood, we have already an enchanter's power—upon one plane; and the desire to wield that power in the world external to our minds awakes. It does not follow that we shall use that power well upon any plane. We may put a dead green upon a man's face and produce a horror; we may make the rare and terrible blue moon to shine; or we may cause woods to spring with

silver leaves and rams to wear fleeces of gold, and put hot fire into the belly of the cold worm. But in such "fantasy," as it is called, new form is made; Faërie begins; Man becomes a sub-creator. (*Tree and Leaf* 22–23)

This ability of the human mind to create an imagined world out of language is crucial to the genre of fantasy, and Tolkien elaborates his argument further on in the essay.

In the third section, "Children," Tolkien tackles the popular idea that children are the natural audience for fairy tales and rejects it, claiming that fairy tales are equally (if not mainly) valuable for adults. He speculates that one of the reasons why fairy tales are often restricted to the nursery is that we, adults, think that children (due to their lack of experience) are credulous and actually *believe* in fairy tales. Here, Tolkien is again talking about fantasy, the creation of a believable imaginary world. He writes:

> What really happens is that the story-maker proves a successful "subcreator." He makes a Secondary World which your mind can enter. Inside it, what he relates is "true": it accords with the laws of that world. You therefore believe it, while you are, as it were, inside. The moment disbelief arises, the spell is broken; the magic, or rather art, has failed. You are then out in the Primary World again, looking at the little abortive Secondary World from outside. (37)

Tolkien's terms "Primary" and "Secondary World" underpin Clute and Grant's definition above. Clute and Grant prefer the more general "this world" and "otherworld," but Tolkien's terminology is often reproduced by critics and is clearly related to the religious overtones of the term "sub-creator," which Tolkien uses to refer to the figure of the fantasy writer.

It is important to note here that "On Fairy-Stories" was written and delivered as a lecture at a crucial point in Tolkien's writing career. At the time, his children's fantasy *The Hobbit* (1937) had already been published and was hailed as a great success, while his own, private, somewhat difficult, visionary mythology (known today from *The Silmarillion*, published posthumously in 1977) had been rejected by his publishers, who—instead—had asked for a "sequel" to *The Hobbit* (Carpenter 187–88). While writing the first parts of this "sequel," which later became *The Lord of the Rings*, Tolkien realized that the story was growing, and, although it was still a fantasy work, it would not necessarily be suitable only for children. Tolkien's biographer, Humphrey Carpenter, shows that Tolkien's new fantasy work was very much in his mind when he was invited to give the Andrew Lang lecture at the University of St. Andrews in 1939. Thus, "On Fairy-Stories" became a platform to think about and justify the writing of the work that became his most celebrated creation. Tolkien used the lecture to develop his theory of "sub-creation." In the fourth section of the essay, "Fantasy," he claims that the writing of fantasy is the creation of a "Secondary World" and thus imitates God's creation of the "Primary" world. Man, therefore, can become a "sub-creator" because he himself is created, and thus has the natural impulse to imitate God's creative process. As Tolkien argued in his contemporary poem "Mythopoeia," in which he discussed the same idea (and from which he quoted an extract in "On Fairy-Stories"), "we make still by the law in which we're made" (*Tree and Leaf* 55).

After having claimed that fantasy is a "human right," the right to "sub-create," Tolkien dedicated the fifth section of "On Fairy-Stories" to the functions and uses of fantasy. As per the title of that section of the essay, fantasy offers "Recovery, Escape, Consolation." "Recovery" refers to "seeing things as we are (or were) meant to see them" (58) as part of God's creation, awe-inspiring and enchanting. Tolkien refers to the fact that we are too familiar with our own world and see everything as trite, while fantasy can allow us to recover "the potency of the words, and the wonder of the things, such as stone, and wood, and iron; tree and grass; house and fire; bread and wine" (60). "Escape" means breaking free from dull reality, from the prison of a gray and unimaginative world. Tolkien famously defended "escapism" by contrasting the desirable "Escape of the Prisoner" with the dishonorable "Flight of the Deserter" (61). "Consolation" refers to the consolation of the happy ending in fairy-stories, the "sudden joyous 'turn'" (68), the unexpected stroke of good fortune when everything seems to be going awry. Tolkien believed in the necessity of the happy ending in fantasy and coined the term "eucatastrophe" to express it. The possibility of "eucatastrophe" in the Primary World was linked in Tolkien's mind with God's providence and plan for final salvation, and he claimed that the ultimate "eucatastrophe" was witnessed in Jesus Christ's resurrection after the passion and crucifixion.

After the lecture, Tolkien felt that he had succeeded in proving that writing fantasy (or "fairy-tales for adults") was not only a worthwhile cause but also a writer's duty. Carpenter writes that after the delivery of "On Fairy-Stories," Tolkien "returned with a new enthusiasm to the story whose purpose he had justified" (191). *The Lord of the Rings* would not be a comic children's story, but an ennobled fairy tale for adults, aspiring to much higher ends than just to entertain: it would provide "fantasy," "recovery," "escape," and "consolation" in the way he defined and justified these notions in his lecture.

Tolkien's theorizing of fantasy is definitely religious and spiritual, and, more specifically, Christian. This is significant when considering fantasy works before and after Tolkien: they often express or reflect a spiritual (not always Christian) and philosophical understanding of life and art. Tolkien's defense of "escape" outlined above is not only associated with the idea of escaping from a trite, everyday, unimaginative world, but also escaping from constraints that "reality" imposes on us. He thus examines fantasy as a vehicle of satisfying impossible desires: the desire to converse with other living creatures, such as animals; the desire to fly like a bird; and "the oldest and deepest desire, the Great Escape: the Escape from Death" (68). Significantly, death and immortality are recurring themes in fantasy literature as well. Tolkien's use of the term "eucatastrophe" adds a further religious and spiritual dimension to his theory of fantasy, but it also introduces a major structural element into the plotlines of fantasy. Clute's and Grant's definition of fantasy also includes a delineation of the main narrative pattern that most fantasy literature follows:

> A fantasy text may be described as the story of an earned passage from *bondage*—via central *recognition* of what has been revealed and of what is about to happen, and which may involve a profound metamorphosis of protagonist or world or both—into the eucatastrophe, where marriages may occur, just governance fertilize the barren land, and there is a *healing*. (338–39; emphasis original)

The three structural stages that Clute and Grant outline (bondage, recognition, and healing) are easy to see when applying them to specific examples of fantasy literature texts. Most works of fantasy seem to start with a sense of something being wrong in the "secondary" world, the stage of "bondage." Taking again *The Lion, the Witch and the Wardrobe* as an example, one would think of the moment when Lucy walks into Narnia through the wardrobe and finds out from Mr. Tumnus that the White Witch has condemned the land to eternal winter. In various works the stage of bondage is expressed by the "secondary" world undergoing a "*thinning* of texture, a fading away of beingness" (Clute and Grant 339; emphasis original), which is usually caused by a dark lord (male or female) whose attempts to take over the land have succeeded or are threatening to succeed. "Recognition" refers to the moment when the hero or heroine realizes that bondage is at work and sees what needs to be done to avert it or reverse it. In *The Lion, the Witch and the Wardrobe*, this moment occurs when Lucy, Susan, Peter, and Edmund decide to fight on the side of the lion, Aslan. The stage of "healing" represents the final resolution, the happy ending that most fantasy works share (Tolkien's "eucatastrophe") when the wrongness that created the bondage has been addressed and the dark lord defeated.

Although Tolkien only analyzed and discussed the last stage of the three described above, *The Lord of the Rings* follows all three stages of this pattern very closely. Attebery has claimed that *The Lord of the Rings* is our "mental template" for defining fantasy (14). Attebery draws on "fuzzy set" theory, which comes from mathematics and the study of logic, to justify this belief. According to this theory, categories are defined "not by boundaries but by a center" (12). Instead of outlining a series of criteria or shared qualities for inclusion in a category, "fuzzy set" theory uses a principal, prototypical example as the center of the category and ranks other possible candidates in terms of their proximity or distance from the center. Attebery explains:

> A book may be a classic murder mystery, like Dorothy Sayers's *Strong Poison*, or more or less a mystery, like her *Gaudy Night*, or somewhat of a mystery, like Mark Twain's *Pudd'nhead Wilson*, or similar to a mystery in some respects, like *Crime and Punishment*. The category has a *clear center* but *boundaries that shade off imperceptibly*, so that a book on the fringes may be considered as belonging or not, depending on one's interests. (13–14, my italics)

Attebery goes on to argue that if we look at the genre of fantasy as a "fuzzy set," then the center from which fantasy "radiates" is *The Lord of the Rings*. He also points out that Tolkien's fantasy is not necessarily in the position of the "center" because it is the best fantasy ever written. Rather, he insists that *The Lord of the Rings* is the "center" of the "fuzzy set" we call fantasy because:

> When *The Lord of the Rings* appeared, we had a core around which to group a number of storytellers who had hitherto been simply, as Northrop Frye suggests, "other writers" belonging to no identified category or tradition. . . . Tolkien's form of fantasy, for readers in English, is our mental template, and will be until someone else achieves equal recognition with an alternative conception. One way to characterize the genre of fantasy is the set of texts that in some way or other resemble *The Lord of the Rings*. (14)

Attebery continues in order to refine further the role of *The Lord of the Rings* as a "core" text for fantasy. He argues that we tend to define as "fantasy" those works that resemble *The Lord of the Rings* in three fundamental ways: content (a narrative that breaks from realism); structure (a plot that "begins with a problem and ends with resolution" [15]); and reader-response (a text that creates an effect of "wonder" upon the reader).

III. Fantasy before and after Tolkien: The Roots and the Branches

Both Attebery's "fuzzy set" approach and Clute's and Grant's more traditional "stages" of fantasy stem from "On Fairy-Stories" and *The Lord of the Rings* as a prototypical work for defining fantasy. It is important, however, to note that there were precursors of the fantasy genre long before Tolkien. There are two schools of thought in terms of the historical development of fantasy literature. Some scholars (Brian Stableford, Neil Barron) take the view of a "long" history of fantasy. They argue that it goes back to the beginning of time, since they claim that the first texts of fantasy literature are ancient myths, legends, and folktales. If we take into consideration only certain formal elements, such as the acceptance of fantastical elements as "true" and the structure of bondage-recognition-healing, then some mythological texts such as Homer's *Odyssey*, for example, could potentially qualify as fantasy. Odysseus journeys from one magical island to the other and encounters a giant, one-eyed Cyclops, evil witches, and half-bird, half-woman sirens. There is a sense of wrongness at the beginning; Odysseus does eventually reach a point of recognition, and eucatastrophe is achieved with his return to Ithaca. The anonymous Anglo-Saxon epic *Beowulf* and several of the medieval Arthurian romances could also potentially fulfill the structural and formal criteria and work as fantasy texts.

However, reading these texts as fantasy ignores their historical and cultural context. A number of other scholars (Le Guin, Clute and Grant, Tom Shippey "Influence," C. W. Sullivan) have rather outlined a "short" history of fantasy, dating its origins to the nineteenth century as a reaction against the dominance of the realist novel. Ancient and medieval texts that draw on myth and folklore, such as the Greek and Roman epics and tragedies, or medieval romances, come from a time when narratives with fantastic elements were very widespread. Both fantasy and "the fantastic" (the two categories are less easily distinguishable before Tolkien established the "rules" of fantasy) come from a time when realistic representation had been elevated to the most important element in literature and the arts. Richard Mathews argues that "the literary paths of realism and fantasy began to diverge in the 1600s as new systems of learning from the Renaissance brought about a rejection of superstition in favor of science and reason" (2). The literary response to the Renaissance and the Enlightenment was the rise of the realistic novel. Fantasy and "the fantastic" started to emerge in the nineteenth century as a counterreaction, when the aesthetics of realism became established and the realistic novel reached its peak. There were supernatural elements in literature before the Victorian period, such as in the gothic novel, or the visionary imagery of the Romantic poets. Both of these genres were also, partly, counterreactions to the rise of science and rationality. But fantasy as we know it today began and developed as an "underside" to the dominance of the Victorian realist novel.

When one thinks of the Victorian roots of fantasy, the texts that tend to come to mind most readily are children's books. There was fantasy literature for adults at that time, but many of the relevant texts became part of the canon of fantasy later on. A major role in that process was played by the Ballantine Adult Fantasy Series published from May 1969 to April 1974 in response to the growing popularity of *The Lord of the Rings*. The series editors were keen to find new authors of fantasy or rediscover older ones. A total of seventy titles were released in the series, many of which were reprints of older fantasy works, often out of print for years (see Anderson). The series included a great number of Victorian fantasy works that had been largely neglected by critics and readers alike and were sinking into oblivion. Here we can see Attebery's idea of *The Lord of the Rings* as the "center" of a "fuzzy set" in practice: as a model or compass for selecting and classifying older works as fantasy.

Two authors that figure prominently in the Ballantine series and who have been credited by most scholars as the forefathers of the fantasy tradition are George MacDonald and William Morris. MacDonald wrote both fairy tales for children and fantasy romances for adults, but he was also one of the first fantasy writers to attempt to theorize fantasy literature. His essay "The Fantastic Imagination" (1893) anticipates many of Tolkien's ideas in "On Fairy-Stories." MacDonald pointed out, like Tolkien, that fantasy might require the "child-like" characteristics of desiring wonder and "suspending disbelief," but he also insisted that fantasy is not specifically for children. He came very close to Tolkien's idea of a "secondary" world with its own consistent laws and rules, as well as Tolkien's analogy between the creation of a fantasy world and God's creation of the "primary" world:

> The natural world has its laws, and no man must interfere with them in the way of presentment any more than in the way of use; but they themselves may suggest laws of other kinds, and man may, if he pleases, invent a little world of his own, with its own laws; for there is that in him which delights in calling up new forms—which is the nearest, perhaps, he can come to creation. . . . His world once invented, the highest law that comes next into play is, that there shall be harmony between the laws by which the new world has begun to exist; and in the process of his creation, the inventor must hold by those laws. The moment he forgets one of them, he makes the story, by its own postulates, incredible. (314–15, my italics)

MacDonald's most important works in terms of the emergence of the fantasy genre are two fairy tales for adults and two works of children's fantasy. *Phantastes: A Faerie Romance for Men and Women* (1858) follows its young protagonist, Anodos, into Fairyland, to pursue a quest that begins as a love interest but ends as a much more spiritual journey, during which the young hero moves through an enchanted landscape, described beautifully and with powerful emotion. *Lilith* (1895) concentrates more on the "dark" side of fairyland. The main hero, Mr. Vane, moves through a terrifying, nightmare landscape, dominated by Lilith (inspired by the female demon of Jewish tradition). Both novels use portals to enter the secondary world, and they present us with the dual nature of fairyland: one beautiful and melancholy, and one terrifying and nightmarish. MacDonald opened the way for renegotiating the traditional fairyland of folklore into a world with its own internal laws and rules. His children's books *The Princess and the Goblin* (1872) and *The Princess and Curdie* (1880) are equally important for the nascent fantasy genre, not least because they introduced the goblins: the intrinsically evil, monstrous "others" often found in fantasy. Tolkien's orcs were called "goblins" in *The Hobbit*, and Tolkien acknowledged his debt to MacDonald (*Letters* 185). Lewis praised MacDonald, calling him "the master," and said that his imagination was "baptized" through *Phantastes* (181).

If MacDonald exemplifies the roots of fantasy in the Victorian interest in folklore and the literary fairy tale, then Morris represents the kindred interest in medievalism and the rediscovery of northern European mythologies. Morris was fascinated with the Middle Ages as a "better" place than Victorian modernity, and he was interested in Old Norse and Germanic myths and legends. His contributions to early fantasy included prose romances taking place in invented worlds with a vaguely medieval atmosphere, such as *The Wood beyond the World* (1894) and *The Well at the World's End* (1896), and northern-world works taking place in imagined Germanic societies—for example, *A Tale of the House of the Wolfings* (1889) and *The Roots of the Mountains* (1889). The former two novels are set in a pseudomedieval imaginary world full of supernatural powers and enchantment, following the quests of two young heroes. The latter two romances are set in northern Europe in the early medieval period and depict (historical) wars of idealized Goths against the Romans and the Huns. Morris's idealization of the

Germanic world, following the pattern of the Old Norse sagas in interspersing prose with verse and including elements of enchantment and supernatural occurrences, was a major influence on Tolkien's fantasy. By attempting to revitalize the medieval romance genre, Morris gave fantasy some of its most enduring elements: preindustrial, "medieval" settings; complex narratives with multiple characters and subplots; and a focus on northern European mythologies (as opposed to the Classical motifs that English literature had used for centuries before).

Fantasy writers after Tolkien had an established tradition to write within but also to rebel against. Shippey has shown that the "rules" of Tolkienian fantasy dominated many twentieth-century texts. In this context, he has discussed Terry Brooks's epic fantasy novel *The Sword of Shannara* (1977, followed by numerous other *Shannara* books) as a rewriting and Stephen Donaldson's *The Chronicles of Thomas Covenant the Unbeliever* series (1977–79) as a revising of *The Lord of the Rings* (*Author* 319–22, "Influence" 378–82). Nevertheless, some of the most mature and original contributions to modern fantasy have come from writers who stretched the limits of the genre and forced it into more adventurous territories. Significantly, such noteworthy writers have also continued the trend of theorizing and critically reflecting on the function, aesthetics, and cultural impact of fantasy. Works such as Le Guin's *Earthsea* trilogy (1968–72; expanded in the 1990s and 2000s) demonstrate that fantasy has come of age and has the power to produce original contributions.

Le Guin's Earthsea is a fully fledged secondary world, with its own history, languages, and traditions, but this is a very different world to the "European" flavor of Tolkien's Middle-earth, and the similar landscapes of much other fantasy. Earthsea is an archipelago of islands, and most of the heroes of its stories are copper-brown in complexion. The spiritual undertones of the cultures of Earthsea are Eastern, reflecting Le Guin's Taoist leanings. The peoples of Earthsea are not distinguished so much in terms of their linguistic and cultural history but rather in terms of anthropological observation: they display elements and traditions of tribal societies rather than the strict hierarchies of Tolkien's pseudomedieval world. At the same time, Le Guin has published critical work that offers a wealth of theoretical explorations of fantasy. Some of her best essays, collected in *The Language of the Night*, have commented on the power of fantasy to reach diverse audiences and inspire "crossover" reading, respond to the anxieties and concerns of its times, and foreground the Jungian motif of the journey to self-knowledge.

IV. Fantasy, Reality, and Myth

The success of fantasy has often perplexed critics and the literati. When *The Lord of the Rings* topped several polls and surveys as the best book of the twentieth century, the reaction of the literary world was horror (see Shippey, *Author* xx–xxiv, 305–9). The reason is that many critics see fantasy as "reactionary," conservative, escapist, nostalgic of a "golden past," and reproducing dominant ideology. This attitude is typified by Rosemary Jackson's seminal work *Fantasy: The Literature of Subversion* (1981). She recognizes the power of "fantastic" literature to subvert and challenge established norms and ideology, but she argues that the subcategory of fantasy requires "passive" readers who are not encouraged to take any action or effect change in the real world. Jackson accuses fantasy works of "utopianism," which:

> does not directly engage with divisions or contradictions of subjects *inside* human culture: their harmony is established on a mystical cosmic level. . . . Whereas fantasies (of dualism) by Mary Shelley, Dickens, Stevenson, etc., interrogate the cost of constructing an ego, thereby challenging the very formation of a symbolic cultural order, romances (of integration) by Le Guin, Lewis, White, etc., leave problems of social order untouched. . . . The current popularity of J. R. R. Tolkien's *The Hobbit* and *The Lord of the Rings* indicates the strength of a romance tradition supporting a ruling ideology. (154–55; emphasis original)

However, other critics have focused on the power of fantasy to actually engage with the fears, anxieties, and concerns of reality. Charles Kingsley's *The Water-Babies* (1863) was an early fantasy work that did initiate real political change in Victorian society by portraying child abuse and death within the framework of fantasy. The plight of Tom the chimney sweep played a decisive role in the passing of the Chimney Sweepers Regulation Act a year after its publication (Prickett 150). This novel also addressed the Victorian uneasiness with the relationship between religion and science by attempting to reconcile a religious understanding of the world with Darwin's theory of evolution (see Beatty and Hale, Chassagnol). At the same time, Tom Shippey ("Post-War," "Orcs") has repeatedly discussed Tolkien as a postwar writer, who engaged with twentieth-century concerns of world war and the origins of evil, akin to the imaginative responses of William Golding and George Orwell. Also, Patrick Curry has explored Tolkien's work via the lens of ecocriticism and has argued that Tolkien's idealistic environmental vision (e.g., the rural paradise of the Shire, the animism of the Ents, etc.) in an industrialized world can be aligned with Frazer Harrison's idea of "radical nostalgia," allowing the formation of a new bond with the earth that can have real political power. Bearing these scholarly discussions in mind, fantasy literature can be fruitfully compared to myth, legend, and other genres of folk narratives.

The relationship between folk narratives and fantasy literature is not difficult to establish. Although, as discussed above, ancient myths and legends are not part of fantasy literature, there are obvious similarities between the two genres in terms of setting (usually primordial times, premodern societies, and preindustrial landscapes); characters (e.g., deities, heroes, wizards, dragons, elves, spirits, talking animals, etc.); and motifs (e.g., cosmogony stories, tales of falls from grace, messianic prophesies of delivery, evil stepmothers, orphan heroes who do not know their origins, etc.). Historically, fantasy literature has mined the myths, legends, and folklore of different cultures and traditions but has used this material creatively, reshaping it to fit new contexts. Morris was very familiar with material from Old Norse mythology and used it extensively, especially the Volsunga Saga (mid-thirteenth century). Arthurian legends, mostly known from medieval romances, were also an important source for both Morris and the other "forefather" of fantasy, MacDonald. Early fantasists drew freely from the world, characters, and motifs of folktales and fairy tales, as did one of the first American fantasy writers at the turn of the twentieth century, Frank Baum. Tolkien, Lewis, and many other fantasy writers during the twentieth century also relied on motifs and characters from medieval and ancient mythological texts.

However, successful fantasy writers have managed to transform this material and create their own imaginative inventions that respond to reality. There are plenty of examples of such "mythical" invention. Tolkien's Middle-earth is full of elves and dragons of northern European mythology, but some of his most memorable characters, like the Ents, are his own original creations. The treelike Ents succeed in expressing contemporary feelings of discontent with industrialization and the destruction of nature in a much more vivid and emotionally engaging way than much realistic fiction, however eco-conscious. To take a more recent example, some of the most interesting characters of the Harry Potter mythology are new "monstrous" or magical creatures that seem to have an equally symbolic or metaphorical status. J. K. Rowling's Dementors are soul-sucking creatures that seem to personify conditions of mental illness such as depression. Her Thestrals are winged horselike beings that can be seen only when one has witnessed, and accepted, death. Fantasy's fundamental theme of good versus evil has been central since the beginnings of the genre, but in the twentieth and early twenty-first centuries, fantasy has become increasingly interested in the origins of evil, in a world in which "evil" as a notion and a reality is not straightforward and unproblematic to understand.

Numerous other examples of characters and plotlines from different fantasy writers could be listed here. It seems to me, therefore, that fantasy literature and myth, legend, and folklore can be more fruitfully compared not in terms of form or structure, but in terms of function. Myth is an imaginative, but also economical, way of thinking about the world and fundamental questions of human existence and has been a feature of many cultures and societies around the world during different historical periods. Mary Beard, a professor at Cambridge University and a guest on the radio program *In Our Time*, in an extremely approachable and lucid discussion of the function of myth, has suggested that we should be thinking of myth as a verb ("to myth"), as a process that allows different societies to express their worldviews, beliefs, fears, and anxieties, not by attempting a scientific "explanation" or using empirical methods, but by telling a story. Laurence Coupe, drawing on the work of philosopher Paul Ricoeur, has similarly examined myth as a tool to explore and understand reality via a symbolic, metaphorical way of thinking (Coupe 8–9). Citing Jewett and Lawrence, Coupe agrees that "the belief that humanity has successfully transcended the need for mythical forms" is itself a myth, "the myth of mythlessness" (12). Fantasy addresses this need directly: it can be seen as a "mythical form" of engaging with reality.

The spiritual, metaphysical, and philosophical concerns of fantasy provide a locus for literature to explore questions that have become unfashionable in "mainstream" realist fiction, such as death and immortality, the origins of evil, and other existential questions that have traditionally been treated by religious or mythological texts in different societies. It is not an accident that many writers of fantasy have a religious (not always Christian) or spiritual understanding of the world, or at least a philosophical viewpoint. As we saw above, Tolkien's theorizing of fantasy is based on Christian ideas, but Le Guin's Earthsea has Taoist leanings, while Philip Pullman's work, although self-proclaimed as atheist, has clear spiritual and philosophical resonances. Most importantly, these writers engage with the real world not by attempting to imitate it in a realistic way, but by creating an otherworld (or fantastic intrusions to the primary world) with similar concerns and anxieties, but with mythical, metaphorical, symbolic ways of thinking about them and resolving them. At the same time, the reception of myth has always been a process involving revising, rewriting, and adapting to suit different purposes, and fantasy literature can be seen as part of that tradition. Fantasy, therefore, can be seen as the prime location for modern mythopoeia (myth-making): the reincarnation of one of the older forms of storytelling, which endures in this adapted form.

Notes

1. I am grateful to Carmen Casaliggi and John D. Rateliff who read this essay in draft and made valuable suggestions.

Works Cited

Anderson, Douglas A. "The Mainstreaming of Fantasy and the Legacy of *The Lord of the Rings*." The Lord of the Rings *1954–2004: Scholarship in Honor of Richard E. Blackwelder*. Ed. Wayne G. Hammond and Christina Scull. Milwaukee, WI: Marquette UP, 2006. 301–15.

Armitt, Lucie. *Fantasy Fiction: An Introduction*. New York: Continuum, 2005.

Attebery, Brian. *Strategies of Fantasy*. Bloomington: Indiana UP, 1992.

Barron, Neil, ed. *Fantasy Literature: A Reader's Guide*. New York: Garland, 1990.

Beard, Mary. Interview. "The Greek Myths." *In Our Time*. BBC Radio 4, London. 13 Mar. 2008.

Beatty, John, and Piers J. Hale. "*Water Babies*: An Evolutionary Parable." *Endeavour* 32.4 (2008): 141–46.

Carpenter, Humphrey. *J. R. R. Tolkien: A Biography*. London: Allen, 1977.

Chassagnol, Anne. "Darwin in Wonderland: Evolution, Involution and Natural Selection in *The Water Babies* (1863)." *Miranda* 1 (23 Mar. 2010).

Clute, John, and John Grant, eds. *The Encyclopedia of Fantasy*. London: Orbit, 1997.

Cornwell, Neil. "Fantastic, The." *The Literary Encyclopedia*. 18 July 2002. Web. 7 Mar. 2012.

Coupe, Laurence. *Myth*. London; New York: Routledge, 2009.

Curry, Patrick. *Defending Middle-Earth: Tolkien: Myth and Modernity*. London: HarperCollins, 1997.

Flieger, Verlyn, and Douglas A. Anderson, eds. *Tolkien on Fairy-Stories*. London: HarperCollins, 2008.

_____. "'There Would always Be a Fairy-tale': J. R. R. Tolkien and the Folklore Controversy." *Tolkien the Medievalist*. Ed. Jane Chance. New York: Routledge, 2003. 26–35.

Gamble, Nikki, and Sally Yates. *Exploring Children's Literature: Teaching the Language and Reading of Fiction*. London: Chapman, 2002.

Jackson, Rosemary. *Fantasy: The Literature of Subversion*. London: Methuen, 1981.

James, Henry. The Turn of the Screw: *Authoritative Text, Contexts, Criticism*. Ed. Deborah Esch and Jonathan Warren. New York: Norton, 1999.

Jewett, R., and Lawrence, J. S. *The American Monomyth*. New York: Doubleday, 1977.

Le Guin, Ursula K. *The Language of the Night: Essays on Fantasy and Science Fiction*. New York: HarperCollins, 1992.

Lewis, C. S. *Surprised by Joy*. New York: Harcourt, 1955.

MacDonald, George. *A Dish of Orts: Chiefly Papers on the Imagination, and on Shakespeare*. London: Low, 1893.

Mathews, Richard. *Fantasy: The Liberation of Imagination*. London: Routledge, 2002.

Mendlesohn, Farah. *Rhetorics of Fantasy*. Hanover, NH: Wesleyan UP, 2008.

Prickett, Stephen. *Victorian Fantasy*. Waco, TX: Baylor UP, 2005.

Shippey, Tom. *J. R. R. Tolkien: Author of the Century*. London: HarperCollins, 2000.

_____. "Literature, Twentieth Century: Influence of Tolkien." *J. R. R. Tolkien Encyclopedia: Scholarship and Critical Assessment*. Ed. Michael D. C. Drout. New York: Routledge, 2007. 378–82.

_____. "Orcs, Wraiths, Wights: Tolkien's Images of Evil." *J. R. R. Tolkien and His Literary Resonances: Views of Middle-earth*. Ed. George Clark and Daniel Timmons. Westport, CT: Greenwood, 2000. 183–198.

_____. "Tolkien as a Post-War Writer." *Proceedings of the J. R. R. Tolkien Centenary Conference 1992*. Ed. Patricia Reynolds and Glen H. GoodKnight. Milton Keynes, Eng.: Tolkien Society, 1995. 217–36.

Stableford, Brian. *Historical Dictionary of Fantasy Literature*. Lanham, MD: Scarecrow, 2005.

Sullivan III, C. W. "High Fantasy." *International Companion Encyclopedia of Children's Literature*. Vol. 1. Ed. Peter Hunt. London: Routledge, 2004. 436–46.

Todorov, Tzvetan. *The Fantastic: A Structural Approach to a Literary Genre*. Trans. Richard Howard. New York: Cornell UP, 1973.

Tolkien, J. R. R. *The Letters of J. R. R. Tolkien*. Ed. Humphrey Carpenter with the assistance of Christopher Tolkien. London: Allen, 1981.

_____. *Tree and Leaf*. London: HarperCollins, 2001.

Rethinking the Fantastic and Related Modes: New Perspectives from Spatial Theory_____

Amaryll Chanady

In this chapter, I wish to return to some of the basic distinctions made in the past four decades between the fantastic and related literary modes such as fantasy, the marvelous, and magic realism, using a post-structuralist approach focusing on recent theories of space. Although the narratological distinctions made by theoreticians such as Tzvetan Todorov are still essential to our understanding of the different ways in which nonrealistic literature can be analyzed, interdisciplinary spatial theory can give us a broader perspective on the social and cultural dimensions of the various modes. As Edward Soja, one of the foremost contemporary theoreticians of space, remarked: "At the turn of the twenty-first century, there is a renewed awareness of the simultaneity and interwoven complexity of the social, historical, and spatial dimensions of our lives . . ." (7). Rather than reconfirming or refining generic distinctions in merely semiotic (concerning the study of sign systems) or structural terms, a spatial approach will show us how the evolving literary treatment of nonrealistic subject matter also illustrates different ways of conceptualizing cultural difference and our relation to knowledge. Spatial theory does not limit itself to studying specific spaces as objects, but as "modes of understanding and explaining" (Soja 4) our world. Whereas semiotics and structuralism provide us with a description of literary forms and conventions, spatial theory gives us a broader explanatory model.

A parallel may be drawn with Michel Foucault's analysis of certain spatial structures of modernity, such as the prison or the factory, which he considers indispensable for our understanding of what he calls the "genealogy" (*Discipline & Punish* 29), or emergence and development, of the modern soul. He is interested not in the minute description of institutions and spatial structures as such, but in the general social, political, and economic conditions that give rise to particular institutions and the way in which these institutions reflect our changing society. In an analogous way, spatial theory, rather than making us aware of the intricacies of the craft of writing, will shed light on the social conditions necessary for the emergence of the fantastic and its connection with our comprehension of the world.

In order to illustrate the contributions of spatial theory to our analysis of the fantastic, I will discuss Washington Irving's well-known short story "Rip Van Winkle." Not only was this text published in 1819, a period of modernity associated with the apogee of the fantastic as defined by the major structuralist critics of the 1970s, but it is also, in spite of its apparent simplicity, an ideal example of this frequently complex and ambiguous literary mode that is not always easy to distinguish clearly from related nonrealistic forms of writing. The discussion of this short story in terms of spatial theory will give us additional insights into some of the differences between these modes, several of which are suggested but not fully developed in Irving's tale.

There continues to be widespread debate about the definition of the fantastic and related terms. "Fantastic" is often used as a synonym for "fantasy" or any kind of nonrealistic writing, and literary works considered as fantastic by some are seen as magical realist by others. As for magical realism, many critics associate it with a cultural setting in which different worldviews coexist (Western and non-Western), while others consider it as a universal mode. Although we can in no way claim that we have now arrived at a definitive terminology, most critics would agree that there are significant differences between these literary modes. A fairy tale (the marvelous), for example, can hardly be put in the same category as the novel *One Hundred Years of Solitude* by the Colombian writer Gabriel García Márquez (magical realism). I will therefore start with a rapid presentation of my understanding of the main characteristics of the fantastic as opposed to those of fantasy, the marvelous, and magical realism.

While the term "marvelous" designates a mode in which the supernatural is fully accepted and which is generally associated with simple oral or written narratives such as the fairy tale and many kinds of children's literature, fantasy includes any kind of writing that gives free rein to the imagination, including science fiction and improbable adventure stories. There is thus considerable overlap between these two terms. The marvelous, however, is generally associated with a particular literary genre or mode, while fantasy, as aptly observed by Neil Cornwell, "denotes a wider concept—be it called a 'mode,' an 'impulse' of equivalent value to mimesis, or a trans-generic literary quality ever present to some degree" (31). As for magical realism, it involves the sustained development of a relatively realistic and complex fictional world in which the supernatural also exists. The natural and the supernatural, in other words, are juxtaposed without creating a contradictory or impossible world. The supernatural can be associated with the beliefs of a non-Western culture (anthropological magical realism), but this is not always the case. Critics still disagree whether the term *magical realism* should be reserved for mainly non-Western literature in which equal treatment is given to native beliefs and Western observations of reality linked to rational and empirical understanding, or whether any sustained development of the natural and the supernatural should be considered magical realist.

In the fantastic, on the other hand, the supernatural is presented as problematic, since it intrudes in a rational world from which it has been banished as superstition. The major contribution of French structural theory to our understanding of the fantastic is the emphasis on the specificity of the fantastic as opposed to the marvelous and other forms of nonrealistic writing. Todorov's classic study distinguishes among three literary genres: the marvelous, in which the supernatural is accepted; the uncanny, in which it is only suggested; and the fantastic, in which the reader hesitates between a supernatural and a natural explanation of the events (25–26). He also stresses the historicity of the mode, which emerged at the end of the eighteenth century when a dominant rational worldview clashed with older superstitions that had not yet entirely disappeared. The fantastic is thus not a synonym of fantasy writing in general, but a specific literary genre with identifiable conventions. I prefer to use the term "mode," which denotes a particular form and style of writing that can be found in several different genres, such as the short story or the novel, but not in the lyrical poem. As for the uncanny, I do not consider it as a specific genre, as does Todorov, but rather as a feeling or an atmosphere that can exist in literature as well as in the real world, and that is an essential element of the fantastic. In my book on the fantastic and magical realism, I identified three main criteria to distinguish the fantastic in the narrower sense (in other words, not as a synonym of fantasy writing in general) and magical realism, with which it has often been confused: the presence of the supernatural in a largely realistic world (32–68); the antinomy or "simultaneous presence of two conflicting codes" (12) seen as problematic in the fantastic, since its world is ruled by reason, but fully accepted in magical realism, in which several belief systems coexist (69–120); and "authorial reticence," or the deliberate withholding of explanations, which maintains uncertainty in the fantastic but presents several worldviews directly and as equally valid in magical realism (121–60).

Even though these criteria do not allow us to establish a strict classification of the infinite variety of nonrealistic texts, they are still useful as general guidelines. Modern spatial theory, however, shows us that these distinctions are not based on arbitrary structural precepts. The most important and influential French theoretician of space, Henri Lefebvre, emphasized the intimate connection between space and social organization, which influence each other. He also helped us understand the complexity of space by identifying three spatial categories: perceived, conceived, and lived space (38–39). Perceived space (which he also calls spatial practice) is the concrete spatial configuration of our world—the shape of cities, buildings, and highways—as we see it in our everyday lives and as it influences our actions. Conceived space (also called the representation of space) is the rationally organized space of urban plans and architectural models, as well as the analytic space of geography and geometry. This type of space is associated with dominant institutions of learning and power.

As for lived space, it concerns our everyday experience of the world and combines concrete perception, the individual appropriation and adaptation of different models of conceived space, and personal memories and emotions. This space is associated with the private sphere, as well as with marginalized experience and older cultural traditions. Another important and related distinction made by Lefebvre is that between absolute space, which concerns our natural connection with our concrete surroundings, and the abstract space of modernity, which is the result of the rational organization and understanding of our world that is rapidly engulfing every facet of our experience (48–49). These concepts will allow us to rethink the fantastic as a literary mode closely connected to the increasing rationalization of space in Western modernity, while related nonrealistic modes emerge in very different cultural and historical contexts.

The fantastic can thus be seen to illustrate the desire of the rational subject of modernity to subjugate the entire world through abstract models in order to organize it efficiently and understand it scientifically, and the resulting uneasiness is produced by situations that cannot be reduced to these explanatory models. The supernatural contradicts our rational knowledge of the world and is therefore considered unacceptable. The resulting antinomy between a rational worldview and events that appear to be supernatural leads to what Todorov calls hesitation (26) on the part of a narrator who is confronted with the inexplicable (according to the laws of physics). In other words, the narrator-observer hesitates between an unsatisfactory natural explanation and one based on what I called the "code of the supernatural" (Chanady 13) known by the narrator but rejected as superstition. In terms of Lefebvre's spatial distinctions, we could say that in the fantastic, the conceived space of reason collides with the lived space of the individual, which is connected to several cultural codes, including past beliefs and superstitions. Irrational terrors are often situated in specific spaces, such as castles, dungeons, dark ancestral mansions, impenetrable forests, or foreign countries, in order to exclude them symbolically from the enlightened world of modernity. These spaces are considered to be uncanny and illustrate the return of the repressed in a familiar world of reason. The fantastic frequently has an important psychoanalytical dimension, such as in Edgar Allan Poe's short story "The Tell-Tale Heart" (1843), in which the protagonist, who insists on the rational nature of his actions (he proceeds "wisely" and with "foresight," proud of his "sagacity" [800]), hears the heartbeat of a murdered and dismembered old man under the floorboards. In this case, the supernatural is not situated in foreign or isolated places, but in the midst of our everyday surroundings, symbolically located beneath the room to symbolize the hidden nature of the unconscious and repressed guilt.

The spatial distancing of the site of supernatural occurrences in many fantastic narratives is connected with a much longer history of spatial distinctions, such as that between sacred and profane spaces, which have not entirely disappeared in modernity. This led French philosopher Michel Foucault to develop his theory of *heterotopia*, which is a differently organized space existing within society but visibly separated from it. He considers hospitals, asylums, prisons, ships, and fairgrounds as examples of heterotopias, defined as "counter-sites" in which "all the other real sites that can be found within the culture, are simultaneously represented, contested, and inverted" ("Of other Spaces" 24). In other words, they are deforming mirrors of the larger society. According to Foucault, these spaces exist in every culture and may have several different functions. They often involve the juxtaposition of several incompatible sites (the theater, for example, opens up different spaces, since both the space of the living-room and that of the town square can be represented on the same stage), and they contain different slices of time or "heterochronies" (26; from "hetero" or different, and "chronies" meaning times), as in the case of museums' accumulation of artifacts from different epochs. Finally, they have a restricted access (either physical or social) and involve either illusion or compensation in an alternate world more satisfactory than our own.

Whereas Foucault's modern heterotopias are part of a heterogeneous but rationally constructed and understood social space, the heterotopias of the fantastic (such as haunted castles) cannot be integrated within the rational space of modernity and are thus frequently expelled to its margins. In magical realism, on the contrary, the modern desire of absolute mastery of space is replaced by a differential view of space, in which no single explanatory model exists. Reality, rather than being seen as something objectively knowable by universal laws, is seen as a mental and social construction that varies according to personal and cultural determinations. Since no single model is considered absolute, there can be no logical contradiction between different perceptions of space. Space in magical realism is not merely heterotopic, involving different spaces juxtaposed within the same rational and spatial model, or, in the case of the fantastic, placed on its spatial margins and contradicting it. Rather, space in magical realism is differential, in that the same space is understood differently according to very diverse cultural and cognitive models. In the fantastic, contradictory views of space can also coexist within the same physical space and are thus not heterotopic (belonging to different locations, or sites) but merely incompatible. Whereas magical realism can be linked to a relativistic and postmodern understanding of reality, the marvelous belongs to a premodern worldview in which the natural and the supernatural do not enter into conflict. As for fantasy literature (meant to be understood in a broad sense, as opposed to the fantastic), it creates an autonomous fictional world in which the laws of reason and nature do not hold.

Both Lefebvre's and Foucault's theories of space are primarily concerned with the connections between space and social organization. Lefebvre's category of lived space, however, also opens up the question of the individual's relation to place, and this involves memory and emotions. Foucault distinguishes between this "internal" space and the "external" space of social organization ("Of other Spaces" 23), in which he situates heterotopias. There is a certain parallel between this opposition and that between "place," understood not simply as a site or geographical emplacement, but as a site that has a particular psychological and cultural relevance to a group or an individual and has been appropriated by the imagination, and "space" as a more neutral term denoting geometric and geographical specifications. Place, in other words, concerns the relations between people and location, whereas space concerns measurement. Place, however, cannot be separated from space, since it includes spatial perception and practice. Phenomenology (a method for approaching concrete experience) has analyzed the complex relationship between individuals and space, but generally without discussing its political or social dimensions (for an excellent overview of phenomenological theories of place and space, see Casey). Since this chapter is interested primarily in spatial theory as relevant to the fantastic in its social and cultural dimension, I will concentrate on the phenomenological aspect of space as it intersects with this.

Linked to the experiential or phenomenological aspect of space is the line of inquiry opened up by Michel de Certeau in his investigation of what he calls the "spatial practices" (91), which include everyday activities and our resulting physical as well as emotional relationship to space. He makes two important advances. First, he introduces the concept of movement into our understanding of space, starting with the distinction between the "tour" (or "path") and the map, in which the former denotes a person's movement through space, while the map illustrates the product of knowledge, inevitably linked to power (121). Whereas the tour or itinerary is fluid, the map is static, and whereas the map is associated with hegemonic social organization, personal spatial practice (this concept is derived from that of the tour) illustrates the individual's deviation from imposed models and thus a relative degree of freedom from highly organized disciplinary society. The emphasis on movement adds an essential dimension to the fantastic, which thus involves not only a static mapping of the world, but also the representation of change and displacement. De Certeau's distinction also introduces the concept of the "delinquent" act, which takes place "not on the margins but in the interstices of the codes that it undoes and displaces" (130). The deviant movement of the "delinquent" (which he understands not in the commonly accepted meaning of minor criminality, but as a transgression of hegemonic models) is his answer to Foucault's theory of the disciplinary society, since it opposes an "individual mode of reappropriation" to Foucault's "collective mode of administration" and institutional power (96). The individual, in other words, is not entirely programmed by the dominant social and spatial structures, but has a considerable amount of liberty to act in unforeseen ways and adapt the system to personal needs, wishes, and desires.

These concepts from spatial theory allow us to reread "Rip Van Winkle" as a particularly complex fantastic story. Before returning to spatial theory, I will briefly discuss it in terms of the major structural criteria of the fantastic. Irving's tale describes the transformation of a small, isolated village by the Hudson River after the proclamation of the United States' independence, thus introducing a relatively realistic historical setting, albeit presented in a humorous and ironic tone. The supernatural intervenes when the protagonist, Rip, wandering through the Catskill Mountains on a squirrel-hunting excursion after escaping from his duties as husband, father, and home-owner, meets the ghosts of the founders of the former Dutch colony of New Netherland (now known as the states of New York and New Jersey). This plunges him into an inexplicable twenty-year-long sleep spanning the years of war and struggle for independence from the British Empire, which had succeeded the earlier Dutch colony. The two dimensions (the natural and the supernatural) are presented as contradictory.

As Rip wanders up the mountainside, many terms signal the presence of the supernatural and create an atmosphere of foreboding. The mountains, already described at the beginning as "fairy mountains" with "magical hues" shrouded in "gray vapors" (55–56), become the scene of a supernatural occurrence. As Rip comes to an isolated ravine, lying in deep shadows from the surrounding steep cliffs and described as "wild, lonely, and shagged" (63), he sees a crow and hears a mysterious voice calling his name. Like the protagonist of traditional fantastic stories, he is afraid. Even his dog expresses fear. When he sees a "strange figure" climbing up the rocks, he again reacts like the protagonist of a classic fantastic story by trying to find a rational explanation and supposing that the man is simply someone from the village.

The entire episode in which Rip accompanies the mysterious stranger, helping him carry a keg of liquor to a hidden clearing in which old men dressed in "quaint outlandish fashion" (65) play at nine-pins, is described as uncanny ("strange and incomprehensible" [65]) and terrifying ("his heart turned within him, and his knees smote together" as he obeys their instructions to serve them drinks "with fear and trembling" [66]). His awakening in bright sunshine in perfectly normal surroundings constitutes another frequently used device of the fantastic, since it suggests the rational explanation that everything had been a dream. This, however, is rapidly contradicted by the absence of the dog, the rust on Rip's gun, his stiff joints, his long beard, the fact that he recognizes nobody when he returns to the village, as well as the community's transformation into a larger agglomeration. He wonders whether he is "bewitched" (69), while many inhabitants of the village consider him deranged. The narrator never provides a final explanation of the apparently supernatural events, and the reader is left with several possible explanations, none of which is satisfactory. Antinomy and contradiction are thus maintained throughout the entire story.

Although a narratological reading of the story allows us to conclude that it is a perfect example of the fantastic, in which the antinomy between the natural and the supernatural is never resolved, a spatial approach taking into consideration the intersection between society, history, and space will question this simple generic identification and description. The encounter with the ghosts of the Dutch ancestors occurs in a wild and isolated part of the mountains, in which hunting, drinking, and bowling are the principal activities, thus making it an obvious heterotopia with respect to the village, in which the inhabitants toil on their farms and only a few adults do not respect the dominant work ethic—the owner of the inn, the schoolmaster, and Rip. Like Foucault's heterotopia, it is difficult to access and involves a different organization of time (bowling as leisure-time, and hunting and fishing as activities that do not follow the strictly organized timetable of the disciplinary society). It also introduces us to a different epoch, since the supernatural bowling party corresponds to a former period of colonization of the region by the Dutch, whereas Rip's hunting expedition, which brought him to the ravine, signals an even earlier state of society in which hunting and fishing, instead of farmwork, nourished the inhabitants. The supernatural is thus set on the spatial margins of society and refers to former times.

As for the village, the changes brought about by independence alter its organization and perception of social and political space. Whereas the small community had been a Dutch colony and then an isolated part of the British Empire, in which newspapers were received many months after their publication, and in which the lived space of the inhabitants was limited to their immediate environs, the emergence of the independent republic of the United States brings about its integration into a larger national space. The small face-to-face community in which all the inhabitants knew one another in a limited space bounded by natural barriers and geographic isolation is transformed into part of a larger national society of anonymous individuals in which strangers are encountered on a regular basis. Commercial travelers draw the village into a larger economic network, while the representatives of the two parties fighting to win the elections include the inhabitants in a national political space. These changes represent the village's entry into a more fully developed modernity within a nation state. Not only is the conceived space of a juxtaposition of small outposts of a distant colonial power transformed into the imagined national space of the United States; the lived space of the village's inhabitants is also profoundly modified to include elements intruding from outside its former borders, leading to the consternation of many villagers. This is symbolized by the death of Dame Van Winkle after her encounter with a New England salesman. As for Rip's disarray after returning to the changed village after twenty years, it is produced by his encounter with elements belonging to a national space (elections, Congress) that are incomprehensible to him. Even the people have changed, as a "busy, bustling, disputatious tone" replaces the "accustomed phlegm and drowsy tranquility" (70) of the former community. The changed status of the village is illustrated by visible changes to the central village square, in which the shade-giving tree of the past has been replaced by an American flag flying from a pole, the portrait of King George by that of George Washington, and the sleepy village inn by the hotel.

The social and spatial changes in the village bring about a corresponding change in the status of the supernatural. Rip's encounter with the Dutch ghosts and his long sleep are presented at the beginning of the story as a profoundly disturbing experience befalling a rational individual confronted with the inexplicable, just as in a classic fantastic story. Understandably, it is set on the spatial margins of a small fragment of a colony, in an untamed space not yet integrated into the social space of the village. After his return, immediately following the independence of the former colony, the supernatural is transformed into the subject of oral lore, as Rip becomes a village patriarch spending his days in the square telling his tale to all who will listen. His frightening experience with the supernatural in the mountains becomes part of the cultural heritage of the modernized village and is symbolically situated at the center, in the village square, and is thus domesticated by its setting among other social, political, and commercial activities. Rip's new position as storyteller, accepted by everyone owing to his advanced age and consequent exemption from political, domestic, and commercial activity, contrasts strongly with his position at the beginning, even in spatial terms. Whereas he fled his house and farm whenever possible to wander around the village, play with other people's children, help his neighbors on their farms, and go fishing, ending up in the mountains in a symbolic flight from the organized space of the village with its work ethic and its division of activity according to the individual spaces of private property, he is integrated at the end. The former Rip can be seen as "delinquent" in his spatial practice, since his activities are not confined to the spatial enclaves of his own house and farm but take place in what de Certeau called the "interstices" (130) of disciplinary society. In his old age, however, his idleness is no longer seen as a transgression, as he sits in the village square telling tales and strolls through the streets talking to children in his newly acquired function as the community's living memory. It is not simply a matter of physical movement through space, but also of the way in which the same movement (sitting in the square or strolling) is constructed differently according to social considerations. Rip's spatial and social integration coincides with the integration of the supernatural as mere legend, and the valorization of myth in a modernized society from which past beliefs have been largely eradicated.

A particularly significant passage relates the disappearance without trace of the opening into the clearing in which Rip had encountered the ghosts. Occurring after his awakening from his long sleep, this pro-longs the uncertainty of the status of the supernatural events, since we wonder whether or not he had been dreaming. However, the incident is even more interesting in spatial and cultural terms. The untamed and uncivilized spatial margins of the former village have been en-tirely transformed, as the sacred space of the supernatural has become simply nature. There is no longer a place for supernatural beliefs in a modern nation state, and a genuine fear of the unknown has been re-placed by its transformation into folklore. To use Lefebvre's terms, the former absolute space, which allowed the natural and the supernatural to coincide, has now been completely eliminated by the abstract space of modernity, while Rip's incursion into the mountains corresponded to an intermediate stage in which the supernatural was feared but no longer accepted, as in the classical examples of the fantastic. In the new nation, the supernatural has been fully domesticated as myth, in-stead of being seen as a frightening other dimension of reality. Irving's story is thus a complex example of the transformation of the status of the supernatural, and of the corresponding changes undergone by the fantastic mode. The lived space of Rip and his listeners in the center of the village after independence no longer represents a contradiction between dominant explanatory models and earlier beliefs in the supernatural, but a heterotopic space of leisure and oral traditions existing within society. It is a space in which time is organized differently (it does not contribute to economic activity) and opens up into a former period of history (by integrating the past as memory). By becoming a space of storytelling, the village square also opens up to different, incompatible spaces (this is the fourth criterion of the heterotopia as defined by Foucault; "Of other Spaces" 25), since it is a "space of illusion" that "mirrors, contradicts, and exposes the workings of the rest of society" (27). Space is, however, not presented as a static mapping of society. The village square as a heterotopia of illusion is closely connected to Rip's former "delinquent" practice of space, both within and outside the village, including his two different incursions into the uncanny ravine in the mountains, in which the first brought him into contact with the supernatural, and the second (after his awakening) showed him that the past and the supernatural had irremediably disappeared.

At this point, I wish to return to my third criterion of the fantastic, authorial reticence, which is also shared by magical realism. Whereas in the fantastic, this withholding of information maintains the tension between the natural and the supernatural, which is neither confirmed nor disproved, reticence in magical realism gives the reader access to different beliefs without ethnographic distancing and without narrative commentary that could discredit the supernatural. Different worldviews are juxtaposed without contradiction, in the absence of a desire for a universal explanatory paradigm. At the end of Irving's story, the narrator informs us that although many villagers doubt the veracity of Rip's account, the old Dutch inhabitants believe it. In the postscript, he introduces us to the beliefs of the Amerindians, for whom the mountain was the "abode of spirits" (77). Although he uses the term "fable" in the first sentence, the subsequent description of indigenous beliefs il-lustrates a sympathetic identification with their worldview. This direct presentation, without any explanatory or discrediting comment, fore-shadows the writing of one of the major exponents of anthropologi-cal magical realism, the Nobel Prize–winning novelist Miguel Ángel Asturias, who presented the beliefs of the Guatemalan Amerindians in a direct and sympathetic manner, set in a relatively realistic world.

Returning to spatial theory, we can then make distinctions be-tween several types of space that allow us to understand the fantastic in broader cultural terms and contrast it with related modes. The het-erotopic space of the margins of modernity, the untamed space of the wild mountains described at the beginning of Irving's tale, contrasts with the civilized space of the village and contradicts its organization and understanding of reality. This leads to the consternation of a ra-tional character faced with an apparently supernatural event that does not correspond to dominant belief systems. We can thus call the wild and isolated part of the mountains a contradictory heterotopia, which exists on the margins of a society in which ancient beliefs have not entirely disappeared but remain part of the cultural imaginary in spite of their rejection as superstition. At the end of the story, however, the supernatural is expelled from an actual physical location (since the entrance to the uncanny clearing in the mountains disappears) and displaced to the center of the village square, where it is transformed from an alternative and contradictory way of explaining reality to a purely fictional construct, at least for most of the villagers. The square is also a heterotopia in terms of social organization, since its users do not participate in commercial and political activities, but not in terms of cognitive models, since the supernatural stories told there are not generally believed. The supernatural thus disappears as an ontological dimension (in other words, it is not considered as really existing) as it is spatially displaced from the natural margins to the social center. In a final move, the story (with its postscript) creates what I will call a fully differential space, in which a single location (the natural surroundings of the village) is constructed differently according to diverging belief systems: that of most members of modern society, that of the older Dutch inhabitants, and that of the Amerindians. This differential space is not contradictory, since no single model is considered to be absolute, even though the belief systems are antinomic, since they correspond to different cognitive laws. This is the space of magical realism, which is suggested but not fully developed in Irving's fantastic tale.

In conclusion, we can define the fantastic as a contradictory way of representing the world in which dominant rationality enters into conflict with residual belief in the supernatural in an unsuccessful attempt to subject our spaces of experience to a totalizing grid of interpretation. This grid, linked to what Lefebvre called abstract space and to what he described as the "conceived space" of dominant scientific forms of knowledge, is unable to eradicate entirely the stratified nature of space in which former belief systems coexist with newer ones in the same cultural milieu. In other words, spaces seen as knowable may at the same time be linked to occult forces. This may occur in a specific contradictory heterotopia on the margins, or within civilized space itself. The resulting perplexity expressed by a fictional character faced with contradictory attitudes toward lived space leads to the uncertainty considered by many critics as a major defining characteristic of the fantastic. Our desire for the cognitive mastery of space, in other words, is continually thwarted by our own cultural past as well as by newer discoveries not yet integrated into our habitual mapping of reality. The marvelous, on the other hand, is not linked to a rational mapping of the world. In its various guises, this literary mode illustrates the free rein of the imagination in which supernatural beings are simply part of the fictional world and is thus linked to the broader category of fantasy, while oral forms of the marvelous, such as fairy tales and myths, characterize a premodern world not wholly explained by reason.

In the anthropological version of magic realism, a more recent mode combining a realistic depiction of society with belief in the supernatural by non-Western cultures, or specific groups within Western society, the natural and the supernatural coexist without tension. Again, this mode illustrates a particular conception of cultural space, one in which the nonrational belief systems are no longer those of the character's own cultural past, but that of different cultures within our society. The differential construction of space is thus not ambiguous and contradictory, since it does not enter into conflict with our desire to gain absolute mastery of space. On the contrary, magical realism is an attempt to integrate various worldviews in a differential representation of space seen as inclusive and heterologic.

Works Cited

Casey, Edward S. *Getting Back into Place: Toward a Renewed Understanding of the Place-World*. 2nd ed. Bloomington: Indiana UP: 2009.

Chanady, Amaryll. *Magical Realism and the Fantastic: Resolved Versus Unresolved Antinomy*. NY: Garland, 1985.

Cornwell, Neil. *The Literary Fantastic: From Gothic to Postmodernism*. NY: Harvester Wheatsheaf, 1990.

De Certeau, Michel. *The Practice of Everyday Life*. Trans. Steven Rendall. Berkeley: U of California P, 1984

Foucault, Michel. *Discipline & Punish: The Birth of the Prison*. Trans. Alan Sheridan. NY: Vintage Books, 1995.

_____. "Of other Spaces." *Diacritics: A Review of Contemporary Criticism* 16.1 (1986): 22–27.

Irving, Washington, "Rip Van Winkle." *Washington Irving's Sketch Book*. 1919. New York: Avenel, 1985. 53–80.

Lefebvre, Henri. *The Production of Space*. Trans. Donald Nicholson-Smith. Malden, MA: Blackwell, 1991.

Poe, Edgar Allan. "The Tell-Tale Heart." *The Unabridged Edgar Allan Poe*. 1843. Philadelphia: Running, 1983. 799–803.

Soja, Edward W. Postmetropolis: *Critical Studies of Cities and Regions*. Malden, MA: Blackwell, 2000.

Todorov, Tzvetan. *The Fantastic: A Structural Approach to a Literary Genre*. Trans. Richard Howards. Cleveland, OH: P of Case Western Reserve U, 1973.

Never Take a Psychic to a "Bad Place": The Haunted House in Modern American Horror Fiction[1]

Bernice M. Murphy

In *The National Uncanny: Indian Ghosts and American Subjects* (2000), Renée Bergland observes that "in another context, setting out to build a haunted house would be absurd. However, in America, where every white house displaces an Indian one, . . . it may be inevitable . . ." (60). Nowhere in popular culture is this relationship between the nation's often disagreeable past and sometimes deliberately amnesiac present more strikingly articulated than in the horror and the gothic genres, in which the past literally refuses to stay buried, and the only thing more unsettling than terrifying external threats are those that come from within. And nowhere in horror and the gothic are these elements dramatized so effectively as in the haunted-house story.

Many of the best-known American haunted-house narratives—such as *The Amityville Horror* (book: 1977; film versions: 1979; 2005), *Poltergeist* (1982), *The House of Leaves* (2000), or more recently, *Paranormal Activity* (2007) and *Insidious* (2011)—are about ordinary people being terrorized in their own homes. As such, they share the same basic plot. As Dale Bailey suggests in *American Nightmares: The Haunted House Formula in American Popular Fiction* (1999), one of the reasons why an allegedly "true" story such as *The Amityville Horror* is so useful for critics (and so attractive to readers and movie audiences) is because it adheres to our expectations of what a haunted-house story should be. Bailey outlines these conventions as follows:

Formula for the Haunted House Tale

Setting: a house:
1. with an unsavory history
2. with an aristocratic name

3. disturbed by supernatural events usually unrelated to human ghosts

Characters:
1. a middle-class family or family surrogate, skeptical of the supernatural, who move into the house
2. knowledgeable helpers who believe in the supernatural
3. an oracular observer who warns of danger

Plot: dual structure:
1. an escalating series of supernatural events that isolates the family physically and psychologically
2. the discovery of provenance for these events

Climax:
1. the escape of the family and the destruction of the house

or

1. the escape of the family and the continued existence of the house
2. a twist ending that establishes the recurring nature of evil

Themes:
1. class and gender conflict
2. economic hardship
3. consequences of the past (especially unpunished crimes)
4. Manichean clash of good and evil
5. clash of scientific and supernatural world views
6. cyclical nature of evil (Bailey 56)

The protagonists in these stories may have some vague idea that their new residence has an unsavory history or "odd" reputation, but they certainly do not actively seek out the supernatural/paranormal.[2] Rather, such events happen to them despite their longing for a "normal" life. Sometimes, these characters are being punished for ignoring or not respecting the history of the land upon which their home is built—a plot development that obviously brings to mind the contested history of the American continent itself (which both *Poltergeist* and

Amityville's haunted burial grounds strongly evoke). Occasionally, demonic or occult activity is to blame, as in *Paranormal Activity* and *Insidious*. More rarely, it is a cursed architect (*The House Next Door*) or evil necromancer (*The Haunting in Connecticut*; 2009). However, while the protagonists of these kinds of stories often bear at least some of the blame for what is happening to them, the fact remains that they are unwilling victims. They did not set out to move into a haunted house: rather, they did so by mistake, and it is an error that will cost them their financial, physical, and psychological safety.

The novels that I will discuss here dramatize the *other* kind of haunted-house story—that in which our protagonists actively seek contact with the supernatural forces that will later engulf them, and in which they display a heightened sensitivity to the uncanny, rendering them dangerously vulnerable. These characters are not being terrorized in their own homes: they are investigators trying to figure out whether the location they have arrived in is truly haunted or not. As we shall see, sometimes it is even suggested that they have helped create the very haunting that they are looking for.

This chapter will discuss novels by three of the most influential American horror authors of the twentieth century: Shirley Jackson (1916–65), Richard Matheson (b. 1926), and Stephen King (b. 1946). King, the most famous and commercially successful horror author of modern times, was greatly influenced by the work of the horror and fantasy writers he read while growing up in the 1950s and 1960s and, in particular, by Jackson and Matheson. The similarities—and differences—between King and his predecessors can be seen very much at work in the three novels each has written with the same basic premise: an individual (or group of individuals) with psychic powers enters a house (or in the case of King's *The Shining*, a hotel) that is reputed to be haunted—with devastating consequences.

Before analyzing the texts themselves, however, it is important to outline the reasons why the haunted-house story continues to exert such a strong fascination for readers and moviegoers. There is something about the idea of our homes being invaded by the unknown that raises the hackles of even the most hardened skeptic. There are few among us who can deny never having suppressed a momentary shudder at entering an unfamiliar room in total darkness or upon hearing someone— or something—moving around in the attic above us in the dead of night. Hardly surprising, then, that from its earliest manifestations, the gothic—the literature of unease—has been intimately associated with architecture. Indeed, it was Gothic architecture that indirectly inspired the writing of the text that kick-started the literary manifestations of the genre in the first place. As Devendra Varma noted in 1976, Horace Walpole's novel *The Castle of Otranto* (1764) "opened the floodgate of 'Gothic' tales" (12). By making the castle the centerpiece of his gothic tableaux, Walpole had ensured that "the principal engine of the gothic plot would be an inlaid system of architectural contraptions, acoustical effects installed throughout the gothic castle . . . where inanimate objects behaved in human ways" (Franks 7). It was not until the genre was transported to the radically different social and political landscape of the United States that it would undergo a major change of direction and the architecture that propped up the form would undergo a major overhaul. As Teresa Goddu observes in *Gothic America*, the "howling" wilderness, isolated settlements, and, later, fledgling cities of colonial America "would not support the entirely old-world structures of castles, abbeys, ancient ruins, and underground passages associated with the European Gothic, nor the specific cultural context under which they had been deployed" (4). As Richard Davenport Hines has noted, in order to overcome these impediments, traditional European settings and concerns were replaced with homegrown ones and the family home replaced the castle as the central source of terror (267).

However, as the American gothic would so often demonstrate, home is not always the safest place to be. A significant early example of this trend is found in *Wieland* (1798) by Charles Brockden Brown, which tells the story of a man urged by mysterious voices to murder his entire family and, as Peter Kafer has suggested, anticipates *The Shining* by almost two hundred years (Kafer xvii). Nathaniel Hawthorne also replaced the castles of the European gothic with the family home. His novel *The House of the Seven Gables* (1851) is set in a crumbling mansion that successfully acts as a native substitution for the hackneyed settings of the European gothic. As in many haunted-house narratives to follow, the plot hinges upon the usurpation of land, a device that takes on renewed significance when one again considers that the US nation was built on land wrested from the sitting tenants. In Edgar Allan Poe's story "The Fall of the House of Usher" (1839), the link between family and house is rendered even more significant by its depiction of a family and a house that "actually share a single, indissoluble identity" (Hines 267). This use of architecture symbolically to parallel the mental state of those who reside within—as seen at work in Brown and Poe—is an approach that would be used again and again in the American gothic.

The story to which the three novels discussed here owe most is Henry James's 1898 novella "The Turn of the Screw," one of the most influential and important tales of the supernatural ever written. James authored many supernatural tales and had several acquaintances who, like his brother William, were active in the "SPR," or "Society for Psychical Research." The purpose of the society, established in 1882, was to investigate "that large body of debatable phenomena designated by such terms as mesmeric, psychical, and spiritualistic," and to do so "in the same spirit of exact and unimpassioned enquiry which has enabled Science to solve so many problems" (Gauld 137). In other words, they wanted to apply rational and scientific methods to supernatural and spiritual mysteries. As Martha Banta notes in *Henry James and the Occult* (1973), the author was fascinated by this research, and it is likely that it influenced the manner in which he depicted the supernatural in his own work. In his later tales, he tends to use "modern, recognizably nineteenth-century settings, and . . . his apparitions tend to appear only to people sensitive enough to be capable of perceiving the ghostly" (Banta 119). This development plays a major role in *The Turn of the Screw* as well as in the texts I will discuss shortly.

Having taken up a position as governess to two young children living in a comfortable country house, James's "young, untried, nervous" narrator who has clearly lived a sheltered existence as a clergyman's daughter, soon comes to the conclusion that her new home is haunted by the ghosts of her predecessor and her employer's valet (James 5). What's more, she believes that her young charges are being malignly "influenced" by the spirits and that it is her duty, as self-appointed heroine, to save them. To the governess, as to the reader, the possibility that there are no ghosts at all is actually much more disturbing than the chance that there are: after all, her belief in their reality ultimately results in the death of one of her charges.

This idea that supernatural forces are particularly attracted to those "sensitive" enough to perceive them is also dramatized in Shirley Jackson's *The Haunting of Hill House* (1959). Jackson was inspired to write the novel by the story of nineteenth-century psychic researchers who rented a supposedly haunted house and recorded their impressions. What fascinated her in particular were the dynamics that existed between the researchers themselves:

> They thought they were being terribly scientific and proving all sorts of things, and yet the story that kept coming through their dry reports was not at all the story of a haunted house, it was the story of several earnest, . . . misguided people, with their differing motivations and backgrounds. I found it so exciting that I wanted more than anything to set up my own haunted house, and put my own people in it, and see what I could make happen. (*Come Along With Me* 200)

Jackson carried out a great deal of research into the paranormal before settling down to write the novel. She also began to look for "odd" houses and was rewarded by a sighting of a building in New York that was so disagreeable that it gave her nightmares for weeks afterward. It turned out that the building was actually a burnt-out shell, in which nine people had recently perished. Another house, glimpsed in a magazine, had an indescribable "air of disease and decay": in a bizarre coincidence, she discovered that it had been built by her great-grandfather. The instinctive revulsion she felt toward these buildings informed her creation of Hill House: as she explained, "It seemed clear to me that what I had felt . . . was an excellent beginning for learning about how people feel when they encounter the supernatural" ("Experience and Fiction" 202).

The plot of *The Haunting of Hill House* is simple. Dr. John Montague, an academic interested in the paranormal, assembles a small band of psychically sensitive researchers in a notorious house. Though he contacts many potential subjects, only two respond positively: shy introvert Eleanor Vance and sophisticated, sexually ambiguous artist Theo. Theo has been recruited because she is a telepath, while Eleanor's presence is as a result of the fact that her childhood home was pelted by a shower of stones, an incident that Montague believes to be a result of latent telepathic abilities. It has often been suggested that telekinesis may be responsible for many outbreaks of so-called "poltergeist" phenomena, which are often associated with adolescent girls. Eleanor was twelve—on the verge of puberty—when this incident occurred, and the question of to what extent she may or may not be responsible for what takes place in Hill House is the central mystery of the narrative. Accompanying the women and Dr. Montague is playboy Luke Sanderson, who has been ordered to accompany them by his aunt, the owner of the property. Food and housekeeping services are provided by a couple from the town, who have a healthy fear of the house. Tellingly, they have looked after Hill House for many years, while Dr. Montague's group lasts barely a week before tragedy strikes.

With the aid of his research subjects, Dr. Montague hopes scientifically to prove the existence of ghosts. Jackson establishes from the very outset that, despite outward appearances of solidity, Hill House is "not sane," that it has existed for too long under conditions of "absolute reality," and that it holds "darkness within" (*Haunting* 1). As will again be the case in *Hell House* and *The Shining*, the house singles out the most vulnerable member of the group for special attention, in this case Eleanor. The relationship between Eleanor and Hill House is therefore the heart of the novel, just as it is the relationship between Jack Torrance and the Overlook hotel that provides the narrative impetus of King's novel, while the Belasco house in Matheson's novel targets Florence Tanner.

Eleanor has up until now lived a life of intense loneliness, yet holds fast to "the belief that someday something would happen" (2). She views the impulsive decision to go to Hill House as the first step toward independence and spins constant fantasies of settlement in a house of her own. These musings serve as a portentous foreshadowing of her final acceptance of Hill House. Although it has been established that the house is "arrogant and hating, never off guard," it is not long before Eleanor begins to experience a strange sense of belonging (35). Soon, the "vile" house becomes "charming," and the malign residence, as in the other novels that will be discussed here, begins to take control of its most susceptible inhabitant. A mysterious rapping late at night reminds Eleanor of the resentful years spent caring for her mother, whose demands irreparably stifled her emotional development. An eerie message written in what may be blood appears on the wall: "HELP ELEANOR COME HOME" (146). Whether it is a message from her dead mother, the house, or her own subconscious is left up to the reader. Eleanor has already decided: "I am the one chosen" (147). The universe contracts until all that is left is her new home—"I can't picture any world but Hill House" (151). This kind of contraction also takes place in *Hell House* and *The Shining*: to those singled out by the dark forces that inhabit these places, they become everything. As Benjamin Tanner ruefully says toward the end of Matheson's novel, "We have our own world here" (178). Similarly, the Overlook hotel gradually becomes the only thing that matters to Jack Torrance.

In another soon to be familiar development, Eleanor's increasing isolation from her companions parallels her growing affinity with the house. She listens intently to sounds only she can hear, creeps about the corridors at night, and knocks on the doors and walls—replicating the mysterious events of previous nights. As she climbs the rickety old library stairs (scene of a previous suicide), her descent into a fantasy world is complete: she joyfully thinks: "I am home, I am home," and envisions herself as a fairy princess awaiting rescue from atop a tower (232). This desperate act prompts her dismissal from the house by Dr. Montague and the others, despite her cries that she has nowhere else to go. She finally surrenders what is left of her free will and identity and succumbs to the malign embrace of Hill House by—perhaps intentionally, though we cannot be sure—driving her car into a tree in the driveway. The horrifying truth of Eleanor's fate is made clear when she experiences a moment's panicked clarity—"Why am I doing this? Why? Why don't they stop me?" (246). The final paragraph is identical in almost every aspect to the famous opening lines of the text, which read as follows:

> No live organism can continue for long to exist sanely under conditions of absolute reality; even larks and katydids are supposed, by some, to dream. *Hill House, not sane, stood by itself* against its hills, holding darkness within; it had stood so for eighty years and might stand for eighty more. Within, walls continued upright, bricks met neatly, floors were firm, and doors were sensibly shut; silence lay steadily against the woods and stone of Hill House, and whatever walked there, walked alone. (3, my italics)

Almost identical, that is, except for the chilling implications of the change made to the sentence highlighted above in italics, which now reads, "Hill House *itself,* not sane, stood against its hills . . ." (246, my italics). Hill House still stands, in other words, but it may no longer be alone.

As in James's novella, it is left up to the reader to decide to what extent the main protagonist is responsible for the supposedly supernatural occurrences that have taken place. Many of the events that occur in the house do seem intimately connected to Eleanor's troubled past and precarious sense of self, and could be perceived as manifestations of her latent telekinetic ability. That is not to say, however, that the active malevolence of Hill House is ever in any doubt. Constructed eighty years previously by a wealthy businessman named Hugh Crain, who "made his house to suit his mind" (*Haunting* 105), it has brought unhappiness to all those who reside within. While it may not have a dark past quite as chilling as that of the Belasco house, or the Overlook hotel, it is still, as Dr. Montague makes clear, "deranged" (70), and, in a clear foreshadowing of Eleanor's fate, "seemingly dislikes letting its guests get away" (67).

Though *Hell House* was published only thirteen years after *Hill House*, in it we can already see the evolution of the horror novel that would pave the way for the publishing boom of the 1970s and 1980s and the success of authors like King. As his entry in the *Encyclopedia of Science Fiction* observes, Richard Matheson was from the 1960s onward recognized as one of the most significant modern creators of terror and fantasy in both fiction and film (Clute and Nicholls 585). His best-known horror/science fiction novels—*I Am Legend* (1954), *The Shrinking Man* (1956), and *A Stir of Echoes* (1958)—were all written in the 1950s, and Matheson has not written much in this vein since *Hell House* appeared in 1971. It stands therefore as a kind of bridge between the restrained ambiguity of Jackson's work and the gleeful excesses of King.

The basic setup is almost identical to Jackson's. Dr. Lionel Barrett, a physicist with a sideline in parapsychology, is asked by a dying newspaper baron to investigate rumors of paranormal activity in "the Belasco house in Maine," built in 1919, in order to find out whether there really is life after death. He has one week and will be paid $100,000 if successful. "Hell House" is, as Barrett informs his wife Edith, "the Mount Everest of Haunted Houses" (Matheson 15), and two previous expeditions to it resulted in the death, suicide, or insanity of those involved. Like Hill House, it is a New England mansion built by a wealthy man who wanted to create his own private world.[3] However,

Hugh Crain's eccentricities have nothing on the sheer malevolence of Emeric Belasco, the six-foot-five "roaring giant" (55), who used his inheritance to bankroll a succession of depraved gatherings that culminated in acts of unthinkable sexual and moral perversion (57). Perhaps deliberately, they evoke the debauched revels of Poe's "The Masque of the Red Death" (1842) as well as the unsavory carousing in the Overlook hotel's murky past:

> Visualize twenty to thirty people set loose upon each other mentally—encouraged to do whatever they wanted to one another, no limits but those of the imagination. . . People stayed here months, then years. The house became their way of life. A way of life that grew a little more insane each day. . . Debauchery became the norm. Brutality and carnage became the norm. (58)

By 1929, things had degenerated so much that "everyone but Belasco was at an animal level, rarely bathing, wearing torn, soiled clothes, eating and drinking anything they could get their hands on, killing each other for food and water, liquor, drugs, sex, blood, even for the taste for human flesh, which many of them had acquired by then" (58). When the relatives of some of his guests broke into the house later that year, everyone was dead—and there was no trace of Belasco.

Barrett's team consists of world-weary psychic Benjamin Franklin Fischer, "lone survivor of the 1940s debacle"—a previous expedition intended to discover the "truth" behind Hell House (11), and Hollywood-actor turned spiritualist Florence Tanner, the most psychologically vulnerable member of the group. In their own ways, both Florence and Barrett repeat the mistake made by James's governess. They see themselves as the heroic individuals who will finally vanquish the dark forces that dwell within. The only real difference lies in their approach: Barrett wants to best Hell House with science, while Florence—who sees her abilities as a gift from God—believes that love will do the trick. Many of the novel's most dramatic supernatural incidents revolve around Florence, who, like Eleanor, and later, Jack Torrance, has laid herself open to supernatural influence. Even more than Dr. Montague, Barrett allows his faith in science to blind him to the true nature of the house. His obsession with his specially built machine, the "Reversor" (which will reverse the electromagnetic radiation he believes to be responsible for paranormal activity), overrides his sense of responsibility. Like Florence, he allows powerful preconceptions to override good sense. The two clash repeatedly, in an obvious reflection of the scientific/religious divide over the true nature of the "afterlife."

As the name suggests, Hell House has occult connections, and soon after their arrival, the investigators discover a satanic chapel that functions as a vile parody of the Christian place of worship (36). The scene anticipates the vandalized Catholic churches described in William Peter Blatty's *The Exorcist* (1972). Furthermore, Belasco is repeatedly likened to Satan. One of the things that most differentiates Matheson's novel from Jackson's is the graphic depiction of sexualized violence. Admittedly, Matheson's 1950s novels often had a notable strain of sexual sadism running through them, but *Hell House* was his most extreme novel to date, and its focus upon sexual violence and physical suffering anticipates the increasingly graphic nature of post-1970 American horror in both film and fiction. There is no place here for the delicate ambiguity of James and Jackson: the protagonists are repeatedly placed in extreme physical peril, and repressed sexual desires—particularly those of the female characters, Florence and Enid—are graphically exploited by Belasco's monstrous dwelling.

While Barrett busies himself with looking for evidence to support his theories, Florence inadvertently projects her own secret longings onto the house, becoming obsessed with the idea of "saving" the spirit she believes to be Emeric's son. She only realizes that "there *was* no Daniel Belasco" (196, emphasis original) and that she has already become the unwitting conduit through which Belasco's will can express itself when his power has become too great to resist. As Barrett had earlier theorized, it is her abilities that have created many of the terrifying phenomena that the group has experienced. However, arrogance has blinded him to the fact she has also come tantalizingly close to unraveling the true secret of Hell House.

Despite the increasingly violent succession of paranormal assaults upon the group, Barrett is still foolish enough to think that he has almost succeeded in his quest. Although he reflects, "This time, four of them had entered Hell House, four would be safely out by tonight" (237), he is proven wrong. Florence is crushed by the "obscene" crucifix, just as she comes agonizingly close to isolating the real source of the house's power. Despite her death, Barrett turns on his "Reversor." "There was only one thing that mattered at this moment: his defeat of Hell House and the victory of his work" (239). In spite of his conviction that "Hell House has been cleaned" (266), he has been fooled, and he pays for it with his life. It takes Benjamin, the only member of the group who has managed to resist Belasco's influence, to put the pieces together. The entire house is in fact an extension of Belasco's depraved ego. After murdering his guests, he sealed himself into a lead-lined room (which resisted the Reversor's power) and, in a final, supreme act of will, deliberately starved himself to death. As Benjamin explains:

There's never been anything like it in the history of haunted houses: a single personality so powerful that he could create what seemed to be a complex multiple haunting; one entity appearing to be dozens, imposing endless physical and mental effects on those who entered his house—utilizing his power like some soloist performing on a giant, hellish console. (286)

When Benjamin and Edith finally penetrate Belasco's inner sanctum, they discover his final, most bizarre secret—he was a short man who so despised his diminutive stature that he had his real legs amputated and replaced with prosthetics. Benjamin realizes then that, by assaulting his hugely inflated ego, Belasco can finally be bested: "You weren't a genius. You were a nut, a creep, a deviate, a slob, a loser. *And a sawed off little bastard in the bargain!*" (298; emphasis original). Ultimately, though, as Florence had predicted, it is a moment of true compassion that vanquishes him; once Benjamin says, "God help you, Belasco" with genuine feeling, his power dissipates (236). The combined efforts of Barrett, Florence, Benjamin, and Edith may finally have resulted in victory, but it has come at considerable cost. Unlike the conclusion of *Hill House*, there is no room for ambiguity here: everything is neatly tied up, and the central mystery conclusively resolved.

The same can be said of King's *The Shining* (1977), which also concludes with a dramatic battle between good and evil. The Overlook hotel has a great deal in common with both Hell House and Hill House, not least the fact that it knows how to exploit the psychological vulnerabilities of those who spend time there. The Torrance family are not investigators in the same sense that Montague's group or Barrett's group are, but Jack Torrance is there to do a job (to serve as caretaker during the winter months) and soon becomes fixated upon exploring the dark history of his new residence. Furthermore, although their stay in the Overlook is longer than that of Jackson's or Matheson's characters, like them, the Torrance family is completely isolated from the rest of the world during its stay. The Torrances also bring with them a powerful psychic, in the form of their young son Danny. However, though there are certainly rumors, The Overlook is no long-abandoned "pest hole" like Hell House and in fact during the summer months operates as a successful hotel. The horror here seems to be activated by a very particular set of circumstances—crucially, the presence of individuals uniquely placed to respond to and, indeed, stimulate its malign influence.

In *On Writing*, King admits that his portrait of Jack Torrance included an element of autobiography (89). Like recovering alcoholic Jack Torrance, for many years he too struggled to overcome a dependency on drink and drugs. Present as well were some of his feelings about the stresses of being a parent. What we have in this novel then is a narrative that combines the "psychic investigators entering a haunted house" story with the "middle-class family in peril" formula described by Bailey. Jack Torrance has come perilously close to losing everything even before the story proper begins: an aspiring writer who once worked in a private academy, his inner demons led him to start drinking heavily, a downward spiral that resulted in his assault of a student and his young son. Jack sees the chance to spend the winter at the Overlook as an opportunity to work on his writing, salvage his marriage with his wife Wendy, and repair his relationship with Danny. Before long, however, his already shaky mental stability begins to crumble, and the story moves toward a violent climax in which Jack loses all sense of reality and tries to murder those whom he loves most. In one of King's less subtle touches, the pressure building up in the hotel's temperamental boiler parallels Jack's increasingly unstable mental state: by the final section of the novel, both are primed to explode (and do). In a plot development that owes much to the novels already discussed, it is strongly suggested that whilst the Overlook (like Hill House) is a place "Born Bad" in which any number of unpleasant incidents have occurred over the years, the events experienced by the Torrance family also have much to do with Danny's abilities. The scope of his powers is revealed when Danny is introduced to the hotel's cook, Dick Halloran. Dick has psychic abilities himself—a talent he refers to as "the shining"—and he immediately recognizes that the child is similarly gifted. The relationship between the two becomes increasingly more important as the novel progresses. When Jack is finally taken over by the hotel's evil forces, the only outside help Wendy and Danny receive comes from Dick, who responds to the boy's terrified telepathic cries for help.

Danny seems to possess almost the full complement of psychic powers. He can read minds (even if, as a young child, he is often unable to figure out what adults actually mean), touch objects, or enter rooms and see terrifying visions of the past (as when he sees blood spatter in the room where a previous guest shot himself), and his "imaginary" friend Tony—who is actually a future version of himself—provides him with harrowing glimpses of the future. Although his parents and doctors try to find a medical rationale for his fugue states and cryptic pronouncements, Danny soon realizes that his powers may be the only thing that can save them from what the Overlook has in store. The trouble is they may well be the catalyst for these events as well. As Wendy reasons toward the end of the novel:

> Danny might be the one the hotel really wanted, the reason it was going so far . . . maybe the reason it was *able* to go so far. It might even be that in some unknown fashion it was Danny's shine that was powering it, the way a battery powers the electrical equipment in a car . . . the way a battery gets a car to start. If they got out of here, the Overlook might subside to its old semi-sentient state, able to do no more but present penny-dreadful horror slides to the more psychically aware guests who entered it. (*Shining* 412)

In other words, Danny himself is inadvertently responsible for the hotel's rapidly increasing power. However, he may not be the only one. As the novel progresses, it becomes obvious that Jack too possesses psychic ability, and that it is this facility, combined with memories of his own abusive father, addiction issues, and frustrated creative powers, that makes him easy prey for the "the management"—the evil forces that ultimately control the hotel.

Throughout, the novel alternates mostly between Danny's perspective and Jack's (King is not all that interested in Wendy), as the child becomes more and more terrified by his horrifying visions of past and future events in the hotel, and Jack falls further under its spell. Earlier, Jack had observed with some contempt that the Overlook's officious manager "referred to the hotel in the unmistakable tones of infatuation" (108), but as the weeks pass, and he spends more time poring over old scrapbooks that detail the hotel's checkered history, he too becomes obsessed. Jack rationalizes this by telling himself that he will be able to write a history of the hotel that also says something very pertinent about the course of twentieth-century American history. As he puts it, the Overlook, which has variously been associated with gamblers, bootleggers, crooked politicians, and shady businessmen, may serve as "an index of the whole post–World War II American character" (205).

Significantly, Jack finds the scrapbook that first piques his interest in the hotel basement. In his influential meditation on the significance of the house and the home, *The Poetics of Space* (1958), Gaston Bachelard characterizes the cellar as "first and foremost the dark entity of the house, the one that partakes of subterranean forces. When we dream there, we are in harmony with the irrationality of the depths" (18). The same is true here. When Wendy asks him why he has been spending so much time down there, Jack jokingly replies, "Trying to find where the bodies are buried, I suppose" (*Shining* 181), but he is not as far removed from the truth as he thinks. Once he gets pulled into the "irrational depths" in which the real character of the place manifests itself, there can be no way out. While his wife and child cower in their quarters, Jack is granted his wish to experience the Overlook as it once was, and he socializes with long-dead guests (383). The hotel's shadowy past has literally come back to life, and his fate has been decided by the sinister powers that be. As Jack's homicidal predecessor Grady says to him, "You're the caretaker, sir. . . . You've *always* been the caretaker" (387). From there, it is only a matter of time until Jack—initially a flawed, but genuinely loving family man—is taken over entirely by the hotel. Although Wendy, Danny, and Dick manage to survive the onslaught and the hotel is destroyed, sinister forces still inhabit the site. As Dick puts it, "You'll never get me within a hundred miles of here again" (489). Furthermore, having realized that his own abilities helped power the monstrous evil that inhabited the hotel in the first place, young Danny believes "It was my fault. All my fault" (495).

To conclude, then, what we have in King's novel is a narrative that further illustrates Bergland's suggestion that all houses built on American soil are in some way haunted. As in *Hell House* and *Hill House*, however, this contention is combined with the implication that, stolen land aside, it is the uncanny interactions between the house/hotel and the people who willingly enter them that really cause the problems. Though two out of three of the novels discussed end with the triumph of good over evil, these victories come at great cost: two members of Matheson's investigative team (interestingly, the two most dog-matic characters, Lionel and Florence) are violently killed, while Jack Torrance perishes in the Overlook. There is not even the faintest hope of besting Hill House, and, as noted, Jackson's novel ends on an ambiguous but decidedly tragic note. While many of the same themes of colonial guilt and anxieties about possession and dispossession seen here also manifest themselves in the first category of haunted-house tales outlined by Bailey at the beginning of this article, what the psychics-entering-a-haunted-house plot does is bring the question of individual responsibility and vulnerability to the fore. Here, excessive sensitivity to the spaces around you makes you all the more vulnerable because it means that two different kind of "bad places"—the one that physically surrounds you and the one that lies within the darkest recesses of the psyche—may collide. As Emily Dickinson once put it,

> One need not be a Chamber—to be Haunted—
> . . . .
> The Brain has Corridors—surpassing
> Material Place—" (lines 1–4)

Combining these physical and mental corridors, as we have seen, always has dire consequences in American popular culture—and this is why you should never take a psychic to a "Bad Place."

Notes

1. In his study of the horror genre *Danse Macabre* (1981), King discusses his ideas about haunted houses and what he terms the "bad place" in some detail, referring to the Overlook hotel as "the apotheosis of the Bad Place" (298).

2. The term "paranormal" refers to happenings that are considered beyond the scope of the known laws of nature or present-day scientific understanding, which can therefore, one day, be rationalized and explained in these terms, whereas the term "supernatural" implies that the event or incident concerned is above or beyond nature, and thus can never be satisfactorily explained within a "rational" frame-work. Both *The Haunting of Hill House* and *Hell House* concern investigators

who believe the mysterious events they are investigating have rational causes, and solutions, and are therefore paranormal rather than supernatural.

3. It is worth mentioning here that the American horror/gothic genre began in New England with the publication of Puritan captivity narratives and jeremiads, and that the relationship between European settlers and the unfamiliar American landscape [and its soon to be dispossessed Native American inhabitants] would have a lasting impact upon the genre. Many of its most influential practitioners—including Hawthorne, H. P. Lovecraft, Jackson, and King—have either come from New England or set most of their fiction there.

Works Cited

Bachelard, Gaston. *The Poetics of Space*. Boston: Beacon, 1958.

Bailey, Dale. *American Nightmares: The Haunted House Formula in American Popular Fiction*. Bowling Green, OH: Bowling Green State UP, 1999.

Banta, Martha. *Henry James and the Occult: The Great Extension*. Bloomington: Indiana UP, 1972.

Bergland, Renée. *The National Uncanny: Indian Ghosts and American Subjects*. Hanover, NH: UP of New England, 2000.

Clute, John, and Peter Nicholls. *The Encyclopedia of Science Fiction*, London: Orbit, 1993.

Dickinson, Emily. "One Need Not be a Chamber—to be Haunted—." *The Complete Poems of Emily Dickinson*. Ed. Thomas H. Johnson. Boston: Little, Brown, 1998. 333.

Franks, Fred S. "The Early and Later Gothic Traditions." *Fantasy and Horror*. Neil Barron. Lanham, MD: Scarecrow, 1999.

Gauld, Alan. *The Founders of Psychical Research*. London: Routledge, 1968.

Goddu, Theresa. *Gothic America: Narrative, History, and Nation*. New York: Columbia UP, 1997.

Hines, Richard Davenport. *Gothic: 400 Years of Excess, Horror, Evil and Ruin*. London: Fourth Estate, 1998.

Jackson, Shirley. "Experience and Fiction." *Come Along With Me*. 1966. New York: Penguin, 1995.

_____. *The Haunting of Hill House*. 1959. New York: Penguin, 1987.

James, Henry. *The Turn of the Screw*. Ed. Stanley Appelbaum. New York: Dover, 1991.

Kafer, Peter. *Charles Brockden Brown's Revolution and the Birth of American Gothic*, Philadelphia: U of Pennsylvania P, 2004.

King, Stephen. *The Shining*. 1977. London: Hodder, 2007.

_____. *On Writing: A Memoir of the Craft*. London: Hodder, 2000.

Matheson, Richard. *Hell House*. 1971. New York: Tor, 1977.

Varma, Devendra. *The Gothic Flame: Being a History of the "Gothic" Novel in England*. 1957. Metuchen, NJ: Scarecrow, 1987.

CRITICAL
READINGS

Women Writers in the Haunted House of Fiction _____

Lucie Armitt

> If I were asked to name the chief benefit of the house, I should say: the
> house shelters day-dreaming, the house protects the dreamer, the house
> allows one to dream in peace. (Bachelard 6)

For Gaston Bachelard, there is a privileged relationship between the
home and the pleasurable discourses of fantasy. It is our originary
"paradise" (7), the primary source of our nostalgia, "the bosom" of
our beginnings (7). As he also admits, this fantasy is the by-product
of a removal in time and space. Only through memory is this resound-
ingly utopian dimension of home ensured and, through utopia, we are
brought closer to the literary: "we are never real historians, but always
near poets, and our emotion is perhaps nothing but an expression of a
poetry that was lost" (6). In fiction, however, the most frequent mode
of the fantastic to fasten upon the home is the gothic, in which the
house is far more often experienced as a place of mystery, tyranny,
even as a tomb. Particularly when written by female authors, the popular maxim that "a woman's place is in the home" renders the gothic or
haunted house an especially conflicted space, albeit one "naturally"
rooted in the fantastic. The same might be said of its iconic inhabitant—the ghost—for, as Julian Wolfreys observes, "the spectre, though
incorporeal, is incorporated into the very economy of dwelling" (7).

In "The 'Uncanny,'" Freud teases out his definition of the uncanny
(*unheimlich* in German), by taking it back to its etymological connection with *Heim* (home). The uncanny derives, he observes, from a
complex combination of the homely and unhomely and in part emerges from a paradox, namely that "among its different shades of meaning
the word 'heimlich' exhibits one which is identical with its opposite,
'unheimlich.' . . . On the one hand it means what is familiar and agree-
able, and on the other, what is concealed and kept out of sight" (345).
I would add that the uncanny can only emerge in a situation in which

one has formerly felt secure and comfortable—hence it creeps up on the modern-day teenager who, having looked forward to her parents leaving her alone at home overnight, finds every creaking floorboard or noise from the street invading her nighttime hours. It is when preparing for sleep that this becomes most acute: locking up becomes locking in, dousing lights reveals the certainty of strangers in wardrobes, and the monsters under the bed that have been banished for a decade rise again. Thus are we haunted, even today, and Freud is right to associate the uncanny so closely with the unconscious, for mere proximity to a lack of daylight consciousness is sufficient to render the uncanny "at home." Focusing, then, on female-authored fiction of the last 150 years, this essay centers upon the role played by the house as the uncanny enabler of fantastic, monstrous, or pathological women, beginning with Emily Brontë's novel *Wuthering Heights* (1847).

It is one of the most famous scenes in narrative fiction: Brontë's narrator protagonist, Mr. Lockwood, has been ushered to his bedchamber by Zillah, the "stout housewife" (Brontë 14), having been stranded at Wuthering Heights by a snowstorm. He picks up some old volumes he finds and, on perusal, discovers them annotated by diary entries inscribed in a female hand. Falling asleep he dreams strange, disturbing dreams, the shift between which is punctuated by the intrusive tapping of a branch at his window. Looking to remove the source of interference, he finds the clasp of the window soldered shut. In what is surely an intemperate response, he breaks the glass with his fist, reaches out and, in his horror, finds it "closed on the fingers of a little, ice-cold hand!" Struggling with the ghostly appendage, it begs him to permit entry: "I'm come home: I'd lost my way on the moor" (20).

What we have in this well-known snippet is a simple summary of the role played by houses in the gothic text, especially as explored by the female author. The house is both sanctuary from the unknown and conduit for the unknown. In a snowstorm, departure from the house might prove a simple prelude to death. Heathcliff warns, "People familiar with these moors often miss their road on such evenings" (9) and, in so doing, even before this ghostly encounter, shows the potential for the uncanny to take up external dwelling-sites. However, it is in the inhabitants' shared reluctance to guide Lockwood back to his own house that Cathy's living alter-ego, Catherine Linton Heathcliff, first raises the subject of spectres: "Then I hope his ghost will haunt you . . ." (13).

Even before we meet Cathy's ghost, however, the furniture of the room enables the "wood" suffix of Lockwood's name to join with its "lock" prefix to create more entrapments. Lockwood tells us, "I fastened my door" and then examines the wood in the room, comprising "a chair, a clothes-press, and a large oak case, with squares cut out near the top resembling coach windows. . . . In fact it formed a little closet, and the ledge of a window, which it enclosed, served as a table" (15). Having secluded himself inside, he discovers a specifically literary flavor to his entrapment. The ledge of the closet houses "a few mildewed books" and is "covered with writing scratched on the paint" (15). As Lockwood reaches down each volume for inspection, he discovers "scarcely one chapter had escaped a pen-and-ink commentary. . . . Some were detached sentences; other parts took the form of a regular diary, scrawled in an unformed, childish hand" (16). It is important to notice that these editorial intrusions are pushed into the margins and end-papers, for this ghost-writing inhabits those shadowy spaces that are visible yet invisible, absent yet present. The literary talent of this ghost presciently critiques the scolding retort launched by the then poet laureate, Robert Southey, at Emily's sister Charlotte in 1837: "Literature is not the business of a woman's life, and it cannot be . . ." (Gilbert and Gubar, 16). Cathy's place in this scene—again, at the margins of the home, neither fully inside nor outside—reflects a very common usage of the haunted house as a motif in the female gothic, namely that society of the time entrapped women in a form of domestic enslavement and only through transgressive modes of writing did it become possible to challenge the horror of those restrictions.

One of the features of Cathy's ghost that further renders her presence ambiguous is her slippery status in relation to age. In this ghost scene, she is depicted as a malicious or manipulative child, and yet she dies a married woman, albeit one whose wish is to be "a girl again, half savage and hardy, and free . . . among the heather on those hills" (Brontë 107). That freedom is equated with life on the moors is crucial, again, to her resistance to domestic confinement. Also significant is the fact that Catherine dies in "confinement" (childbirth), for home and hearth lead almost seamlessly to motherhood during this period.

This brings us to "The Old Nurse's Story" (1852), a gothic tale written by Elizabeth Gaskell five years after *Wuthering Heights*. Gaskell's text follows a traditional ghost-story format, being an oral narrative told to a group of assembled listeners, all of whom are removed by time and place from events, yet whose proximity is assured via the direct involvement of the first-person narrator (the closest form of narrative fiction to gossip). This combination ensures the authenticity of the tale is established while securing its larger-than-life characteristics. Our narrator is Hester, the eponymous nurse, who addresses the children of her own central character, Rosamond, telling them an uncanny story of what befell their mother after she was orphaned as a young child. Hester, then only eighteen, is charged with Rosamond's care and relocated to the home of Rosamond's maiden great-aunt, a building described as "large, and vast, and grand" (Gaskell 14). Its architectural interior reinforces a storytelling approach that will leave some things unexplained:

> At one end of the hall, was a great fireplace. . . . At the opposite end . . . was an organ built into the wall, and so large that it filled up the best part of that end. Beyond it, on the same side, was a door; and opposite, on each side of the fire-place, were also doors leading to the east front; but those I never went through as long as I stayed in the house, so I can't tell you what lay beyond. (14)

Particularly interesting to compare with *Wuthering Heights* is the exterior description of this house in relation to its grounds. It is "great and stately . . . with many trees close around it, so close that in some places their branches dragged against the walls when the wind blew. . . . Behind it rose the Fells . . ." (14). Again, then, we have a sense of such gothic structures being not only of lesser magnificence than formerly, but also of becoming embattled in a conflict with the natural environment. Though unspoilt, the wildness and isolated expanses of the Yorkshire moors and the Cumbrian fells lend themselves much more easily to the awe-inspiring aspects of the gothic than to the gentler pastoral woodlands and rolling countryside of the more southerly English Shire Counties. As such, their existence is as an environment in which tales of fantastic monstrosity are easily spawned and the border territories with dwellings and hamlets become especially susceptible to rumors of uncanny intrusion. Like Brontë's phantom, the ghost of "The Old Nurse's Story" is a child who "beat[s] against the window-panes, as if she want[s] to be let in" (24). Alike, too, in its affinity with wildness, this child seeks to lure Rosamond outside to an icy death. Hester ensures all doors and windows are bolted, keeping Rosamond inside and the ghost child outside, for the two become conjoined as fixedly as Cathy and Heathcliff. As the story progresses the compulsive passion of adoration merges increasingly with the demonic passion of violence as the door "[gives] way with a thundering crash" (30) and Hester clutches at her charge "tighter and tighter, till I feared I should do her a hurt; but rather that than let her go . . ." (31). This forms the narrative crescendo of the story, the house only withstanding the tumultuous invasion at the expense of Rosamond's aunt's life.

When one comes to Mary Elizabeth Braddon's novel *Lady Audley's Secret* (1862), one finds the opposite dynamic: a fiend who lurks within doors in the form of a vibrant, beautiful bride. The close connection Freud makes between the uncanny and secrets (he cites Schelling's belief that "everything is unheimlich that ought to have remained secret and hidden but has come to light" [Freud 345]) manifests itself, from the start, in the description of the main house, Audley Court:

It lay low down in a hollow, rich with fine old timber and luxuriant pastures; and you came upon it through an avenue of limes, bordered on either side by meadows, over the high hedges of which the cattle looked inquisitively at you as you passed, wondering, perhaps, what you wanted; for there was no thoroughfare, and unless you were going to the Court you had no business there at all. (Braddon 1)

This opening paragraph of the novel establishes the key plot device of the narrative, namely the problem of not being able to see the wood (the "fine old timber") for the trees (the "avenue of limes"), a self-willed blindness that befalls not only Sir Michael Audley, the owner of the house, but the reader, whose attraction to "our heroine" is established early on. Notice how the full view the text grants us is repeatedly compromised for its characters by this low-lying house being bordered (blinkered, perhaps) by "high hedges." That there is no way back for Sir Michael is also implied in the detail of this avenue being a dead end.

Such initial hints of concealment (in themselves impossible to gauge instantly as sure signs of duplicity) begin to build in the opening pages. As we reach the house we find a "gravelled walk . . . shadowed on one side by goodly oaks, which shut out the flat landscape, and circled in the house and gardens with a darkening shelter" (1). Even the door to the house "was squeezed into the corner of a turret at one angle of the building, as if it was hiding from dangerous visitors, and wished to keep itself a secret . . ." (2). At the same time, these suggestions are combined with several much more open and reassuring details; it is "a glorious old place—a place that visitors fell into raptures with" (2). This combination ensures that hesitancy is the key response in the reader, a dynamic Tzvetan Todorov associates directly with the fantastic. For Todorov, most fantastic narratives establish their impact on the borderlines between the uncanny and what he defines as the "marvellous." It is in the process of ongoing hesitancy on the reader's part as to whether what s/he is reading is a tale of the supernatural or of the psychological (a narrative based upon dreams, hallucination, or mental disturbance) that the thrill of the fantastic emerges. The moment one firmly decides that the plot falls into one category rather than another, the fantastic loses its impact. It is precisely this hesitancy that characterizes *Lady Audley's Secret*.

"Lucy" (Lady Audley's assumed name) gives the title to the opening chapter, which therefore frames the architectural approach to the house outlined above, despite her not being its named proprietor. She is the "new wife" of the widowed Sir Michael, twenty years old to his fifty-six. Doubts accrue, even in Sir Michael's mind, at the moment of his proposal, again conveyed through the use of the blinkered gaze. Lucy sits in profile to him, looking out of the window, preventing him access to the nature of her gaze, but, as in the opening pages, the reader is given a privileged view, sufficient to ascertain that this gaze "seemed as if it would have pierced the far obscurity" not only of the surrounds, but "into another world" (10). In this period, "another world" must evoke suggestions of death, and it is with death that the marriage proposal leaves us. Despite her acceptance, Sir Michael is left with "some stifled and unsatisfied longing which lay heavy and dull at his heart, as if he had carried a corpse in his bosom" (11).

This is, then, a marriage haunted by a buried (indeed a burial) plot, containing a replacement body, bigamy, attempted murder, and an abandoned child for, as Robert, Sir Michael's nephew gradually reveals, "Lucy Audley" is actually Helen Talboys, a woman who fakes her own death in order to be "free" to accept Sir Michael. Already married to George Talboys, a man who has gone to Australia to try and secure his fortune, she deceives George into believing she is dead by persuading her father to publish the death notice in the newspaper. By now she has also abandoned her infant son, whom she acknowledges she does not love. In what is believed to be Helen's grave lies the body of Matilda, a young woman who dies of consumption and whose mother is bribed by Helen to add to the pretense. However, as the plot starts to unravel due to Robert's investigations, Lucy/Helen throws George to the bottom of the well when he confronts her in the grounds of Audley Court and commits arson in an attempt to kill Robert, her accuser. Though both attempts fail, her designs upon the lives of each are clear.

Lady Audley is a painter, but it is only through Robert's eyes, a man described by Lady Audley's stepdaughter as a "ghost-haunted hero in a German story" (262), that we discover her to be as much artful as artistic. As she talks with Robert about her former employment as a governess, she speaks of spending her small salary on paints from Winsor and Newton's. She is painting as she converses, "copying a water-coloured sketch of an impossibly beautiful Italian peasant, in an impossibly Turneresque atmosphere" (117). Here, the repetition of the adjective "impossibly" reinforces the belief in the limitations of realism as a form. Turner is celebrated for his representation of "the play of light through smoke, fog, or mist" (Reynolds 12), a phenomenon that draws from "the real" but, like the literary fantastic, gives realization to the point at which realism fails and is replaced by that which is commonly rendered invisible (here, light and its disconcerting effects).

Akin to the marriage proposal scene, though Lucy looks "sideways at the painting," Robert is "fixed intently on her pretty face" (Braddon 117). There is a slippage in the wording of the narrative, here, sufficient to provoke another moment of hesitancy in the reader's mind as to whether the pretty face belongs to the peasant or to Lucy. It is Lucy's and, via the slippage, we see how Robert allows Lucy to reveal herself as a work of artifice: "The winter sunlight, gleaming full upon her face from a side window, lit up the azure of those beautiful eyes, till their colour seemed to flicker and tremble betwixt blue and green" (117). As Lucy senses herself revealed in her true colors, she retreats to "the deep recess of another window at a considerable distance from Robert Audley" and takes up some embroidery (118), weaving herself back into a story of her own creation. Nonetheless, she has been illuminated and, in being so, what is made visible is the veil of duplicity by which her beauty is cloaked, a duplicity for which she ultimately pays the price of incarceration within an asylum.

As the net gradually closes in and Lady Audley is conveyed to the asylum in deference to the shame that would greet Sir Michael should she be subjected to criminal justice, the surrounding architecture and "street furniture" take on a gothic hue:

> They . . . had emerged out of the great gaunt square, in which there appeared to be about half a dozen cathedrals, into a smooth boulevard, a broad lamp-lit road, on which the shadows of the leafless branches went and came tremblingly, like the shadows of paralytic skeletons. (386)

On final approach, she looks at an upstairs window, seeing it

> shrouded by a scanty curtain of faded red; and upon this curtain there went and came a dark shadow, the shadow of a woman with a fantastic head-dress, the shadow of a restless creature, who paced perpetually backwards and forwards before the window. (386)

Both of these passages demonstrate the limitations of a realist form for conveying the realities of middle-class female existence during this period. Though a criminal, Lady Audley is also the victim of a society that castigates women as "bold, brazen, abominable creatures" (207) and that ultimately reduces them to such restricted and impoverished social roles that villainy and monstrosity prove imaginative alternatives to a living death. Just as the winter branches simultaneously diminish and enhance the trees (though leafless, this renders them semihuman, as the personification in the passage suggests), so the woman inside the window is both reduced and magnified in her status. As a "creature" she is less than a woman, but as projected—indeed magnified—onto canvas she becomes a theatrical spectacle, complete with "fantastic head-dress," like a queen. As we oscillate between literal grandeur and diminution, we note how the shadow-play impinges directly on how we view the unseen body beyond the silhouette. As Susan Stewart observes, "Under a use-value economy, exaggeration takes place in relation to the scale of proportion offered by the body. . . . Exaggeration must be seen in relation to the scale of measurement, and thereby the scale of values, offered by a more abstract domain of social convention . . ." (Stewart xiii). It is through the play of light and dark upon the curtain, itself magnifying and distorting the unconventional form behind it, that we witness the distortions imposed on women by a patriarchal society that insists insanity, criminality, and illegitimacy are "natural" extensions of feminine wiles.

Attending to this shadow-play, equal attention falls on the strategic use of the adjective "fantastic" in this second passage. Here, "fantastic" can be interpreted in several ways: as large, as theatrical, as impressive, as ridiculous. None is firmly selected and, as such, all become subsumed under the literary heading "fantastic," a mode of writing erupting from within the real, but distorting, challenging and irrevocably disrupting it. By such means is the shadow on the curtain revealed as both a gothic doppelganger of the "monstrous other" (indeterminate and of unclear definition) and Lucy's own shadow, impossibly cast adrift from her body and floating free, unlike the entrapped "paralytic skeletons" of the branches. What haunts the reader is our awareness of the "dead-alive" women put to waste behind closed doors.

This brings us into the twentieth century and Daphne Du Maurier's *My Cousin Rachel* (1951), which, despite its publication date, bears a strong resemblance to the nineteenth-century novels previously discussed; it is the gothic preoccupation with familial inheritance in relation to property that conveys this similarity. Ambrose Ashley is a confirmed bachelor who, like Sir Michael Audley, suddenly marries a woman much younger than himself. Immediately this poses a threat to his nephew Philip's inheritance of the estate and possible continued residency there. Unusually, however, the house is far more of a home than an asset to Philip, which directly affects the extent to which it is displayed to our readerly eyes: in essence we learn far more of its interior than its facade. Affectionately recalling Ambrose's teasing of the vicar and Philip's godfather, Philip quotes him as saying: "And now sit back in your chairs and be comfortable, gentlemen. As there is no woman in the house we can put our boots on the table and spit on the carpet." Philip is quick to add, "Naturally we did no such thing" (Du Maurier 9). Only when Philip goes to Italy in fear of Ambrose's failing health do we receive an impression of how he might begin to view the house as an object, and in this case it conveys itself as a mausoleum. The house in question is Villa Sangalletti, belonging to Ambrose's wife Rachel, a home he first espies as "shuttered and lifeless" (33) and, on entering it, its tomb-like properties abound:

> The air was heavy with a medieval musty smell. In some of the rooms the walls were plain, in others tapestried, and, in one, darker and more oppressive than the rest, there was a long refectory table flanked with carved monastic chairs, and great wrought iron candlesticks stood on either end. (35)

Despite the gothic ornamentation and furnishings, however, and despite the fact that Ambrose dies what Philip fears is a lonely and victimizing death, this is a deathly but not a haunted space: "I could not see Ambrose in this house, or in this room. He could never have walked here with familiar tread . . ." (35). As with the uncanny, haunting requires the presence of former attachment. Leaving behind the alienation of the villa, a simple sight of his own home restores a sense of well-being, and we gain a glimpse of its architecture, as if reflected back at us in "the sun [shining] on the windows of the west wing, and on the grey walls, as the carriage passed through the second gate up the slope to the house" (52). It is here, by contrast, that Ambrose's presence is felt.

What most clearly differentiates *My Cousin Rachel* from *Lady Audley's Secret,* however, is the limited extent to which Philip, our central point-of-view male protagonist, illuminates his female antagonist for the reader. Indeed, rather than bringing to light Rachel's character (as one might say Robert Audley does with "Lucy"), the more involved Philip becomes with Rachel, the more opaque her character seems. Even when she falls to her death at the end and we are left with her staring directly into Philip's eyes, we are left wholly in doubt as to whether she is a villain or the victim of the paranoid ramblings of a seriously ill man. Either way, it is Philip who ends the novel believing himself the murderer: he knowingly allows Rachel to wander unawares onto the incomplete and unsafe bridge structure being built over the sunken garden, despite having been warned by the foreman: "The planking looks firm enough to the eye, but it doesn't bear no weight upon it. Anyone stepping on it . . . could fall and break their neck" (323). The reference to broken necks is especially apposite. The final words of the novel echo its opening: "They used to hang men at Four Turnings in the old days. Not any more, though" (335).

This is, then, a haunted narrative, a categorization ensured by the novel opening with a scene in which seven-year-old Philip comes face-to-face with death in the grisly form of a hanged corpse: "His face and body were blackened with tar for preservation. He hung there for five weeks before they cut him down, and it was the fourth week that I saw him" (Du Maurier 1). Though Ambrose has taken him to view the corpse as a warning to live "the sober life" (2), what Philip leaves with is a sense of shame, linked to a sense of being haunted by the image: "It would come into my dreams, lifeless and horrible." Furthermore, on the corpse being given a "real" name, Philip realizes: "Now it would have connection with reality . . ." (2). Philip's relationship with Ambrose is one of both admiration and similarity: "I have become so like him that I might be his ghost. My eyes are his eyes, my features his features. . . . Well, it was what I always wanted" (4). To resemble, then, becomes to haunt; to admire becomes realized most astutely in the act of replacing. Again, the final page of the novel reasserts this uncanny connection as Philip takes the hand of the dying Rachel:

> She opened her eyes, and looked at me. At first, I think in pain. Then in bewilderment. Then finally, so I thought, in recognition. Yet I was in error, even then. She called me Ambrose. I went on holding her hand until she died. (335)

One of the many ways in which Philip identifies himself as resembling Ambrose is in their relationship to the world of fantasy: "We were dreamers, both of us . . . and, like all dreamers, asleep to the waking world" (5). In the context of this novel, such "dreaming" can be said to contribute to the same type of blinkered awareness of reality we saw color Sir Michael's ability to "see" his wife properly. However, in the case of Robert Audley in Braddon's novel, dreaming works differently. Like Philip and Ambrose Ashley, Robert Audley is a dreamer, but in his case this immerses him further into the world of the uncanny. In two different chapters of Braddon's text he falls asleep and dreams unsettling dreams. In the first he dreams that somebody has removed the headstone from Helen/Lucy's grave (a dream later realized in the knowledge that it contains another corpse entirely). In the second dream, much later on, after Robert has satisfied himself that Lucy is "a designing and infamous woman" (Braddon 239), he travels to the seaside to investigate her past more fully. As he falls asleep to the sounds of the sea he dreams of

> Audley Court, rooted up from amidst the green pastures and the shady hedgerows . . . standing bare and unprotected upon that desolate northern shore, threatened by the rapid rising of a boisterous sea . . . As the hurrying waves rolled nearer and nearer to the stately mansion, the sleeper saw a pale and starry face looking out of the silvery foam, and knew that it was my lady, transformed into a mermaid, beckoning his uncle to destruction. (246)

Though manifesting themselves as nightmares, both dreams operate in the manner of the medieval dream vision, in which dreams operate as guiding messengers for characters, reencoding in narrative form fabular versions of realist events that, in disrupting the limitations of realism, enable the pieces to fall anew, revealing a hitherto unperceived solution to a riddle. Here the dream continues as a Turneresque storm at sea, with the emphasis, once again, upon painterly color:

Beyond that rising sea great masses of cloud, blacker than the blackest ink, more dense than the darkest night, lowered upon the dreamer's eye; but as he looked at the dismal horizon the storm clouds slowly parted, and from a narrow rent in the darkness a ray of light streamed out upon the hideous waves, which slowly, very slowly, receded, leaving the old mansion safe and firmly rooted on the shore. (246)

In *Wuthering Heights* the house takes its name from its surroundings, "'Wuthering' being a significant provincial adjective, descriptive of the atmospheric tumult to which its station is exposed in stormy weather" (2). As a result, "the architect had foresight to build it strong: the narrow windows are deeply set in the wall, and the corners defended with large jutting stones" (2). Audley Court, as we have seen, hides itself away from the elements and, though Robert's dream suggests that all will be well, Sir Michael eventually abandons it for another house, haunted as it is by "a brief dream of impossible happiness": pure fantasy, in other words (446). Though the houses of gothic novels do outlive their inhabitants, they typically do so at the expense of becoming haunted:

> There are those who speak to having met [Heathcliff] near the church, and on the moor, and even in this house. . . . Yet that old man by the kitchen fire affirms he has seen two on 'em, looking out of his chamber window, on every rainy night since his death. . . . I don't like being out in the dark now; and I don't like being left by myself in this grim house. . . . (288)

Such is also the case for Hundreds Hall, the house at the center of Sarah Waters's gothic novel *The Little Stranger* (2009). Hundreds belongs to the Ayres family, a family already scarred by two deaths: the Colonel and the firstborn and best-loved daughter, Susan, who died of diphtheria at the age of seven. The house has fallen into a state of disrepair and, in an attempt to reenliven it and restore it to former glory, the family hosts a party and invites a number of local friends and acquaintances, among them the Baker-Hydes, a wealthy couple who have just moved into the area with their young daughter, Gillian. At the party Gillian begins to tease the family dog, Gyp, a "game" that culminates in him savagely biting her face. What is most intriguing about this scene is the fact that it is understood, at least by Roderick, the grown-up son and heir, to have been caused by supernatural malice rather than the naive insensitivity of the child. While the party begins downstairs, Roderick is in his room, his entry having been delayed by the disappearance of his collar and cufflinks. What begins as the everyday occurrence of mislaid personal items quickly shifts into an encounter with a poltergeist, as first his collar and then his cufflinks drop from the ceiling into the soapy water, leaving behind a smudge on the ceiling. At this point the assault becomes more violent, and Roderick watches in horror as "the shaving-glass gave a sort of shudder . . . then rocked, then began to inch its way across the washing-stand towards him" (Waters 161). As Roderick watches, transfixed, the glass continues its progress to the edge: "He actually started to put out his hand, in an automatic response to keep it from tumbling. But as he did it, the glass suddenly seemed to "gather itself for a spring"—and the next moment it had launched itself at his head" (162).

It is at the boundaries between discrete entities (dog versus child, the inanimate versus the animate, the house versus the surroundings) that ghosts make their presence felt and here it tears at the fissures in Roderick's identity, split between "Master of the House" and youngest child: "His own first impulse on seeing his mother was . . . to clutch at her hand; but he'd also gathered his wits enough, he said, to know that he mustn't in any way involve her. . . . Once he almost broke down in tears—and then, he said, it was only the look of dismay and anxiety on his mother's face that gave him the strength to pull himself together" (163). Finally he demands the uncanny presence to "leave [me] alone, for God's sake!" and, as he does so, "felt at once that something had shifted—that the dreadful thing had passed away. He looked at the objects around him and . . . knew they were ordinary and lifeless again"

(164). Equally conflictual, however, what seems empowering one moment metamorphoses into self-loathing the next, as he realizes "the little girl must have been bitten at just about the time he had been calling out at that vicious presence . . . to leave him alone" (165).

In truth, children and their misbehavior haunt Hundreds Hall, be it in the form of a youthful Dr. Faraday who, at the age of ten, prizes a decorative acorn from a plaster border; the children of the council houses built on land sold from part of the Hundreds Hall estate, whom the adult Dr. Faraday fears will trespass onto the estate; or the mysterious appearance of childish writing in the alcove where Gyp bit Gillian. This latter is discovered by Betty, the maid, and the washerwoman, Mrs. Bazeley, as they try and restore order to the house after the party. Discovering "a jumble of *Ss*, done apparently in pencil" on the woodwork of the window alcove, Gillian is the obvious target for blame (298). As Mrs. Bazeley scrubs at it with a cloth, however, she considers, "I could almost fancy it's come up from *under* the paint" (299, original emphasis). As the week progresses, Roderick's sister Caroline detects a dripping noise coming from the salon when she passes it; the following day it is knocking from the room next to it, which both she and her mother hear. Later the same day Betty "stand[s] bewildered . . . while a soft, crisp drumming sound[s] from the panels of the wall high up above her head" (301). At this point we are returned to Bachelard's reassuring reading of the house, for momentarily the three women treat it as a game: "The sound was queer, but not menacing; it seemed to lead them almost playfully . . . from one spot to another, until the pursuing of it along the passage began to feel like 'a bit of a lark'" (302). Finally emanating from a cabinet on the stairs, the women reposition it to reveal that "the wall was marked with more of that childish scribbling: *SSS SSSS S SU S*" (303). Though Caroline persists in blaming Gillian, Mrs. Ayres identifies the writing as an attempt on her dead daughter's part to communicate. Caroline's response is instantaneous, full of rivalry and aimed directly at the house itself, as she abrasively declares: "The house is playing parlour games with us. . . . We shan't pay it any mind if it starts up again" (304). Despite her insistence, Mrs. Ayres remains gripped: as is true in all these texts, the ghost is never more powerfully present than when yearned for by those who mourn.

Our relationship with ghosts has shifted significantly since *Wuthering Heights* was published in 1847, and we live in less superstitious times. Consequently, our readerly relationship to gothic texts might be expected to have become less satisfactory and rely, instead, on more figurative interpretations of their presence—despite the fact that several of my students come to seminars on *The Little Stranger* frightened. In fact, reading these texts alongside each other we realize there remains plenty to be frightened about. Although Waters's novel was written 162 years after Brontë's and set precisely 100 years later, the gender politics of the two narrative settings have changed comparatively little. The year in which *The Little Stranger* is set, 1947, forms a landmark moment in the history of women's relationship to work and home. During World War II women had, for the first time, experienced the very real liberating vocational opportunities afforded them by wartime work on "the Home Front." Now they were now being propelled back into the home, and the writing was on the wall for a happy hearth and home life. In this context, Susan's ghost gives voice to the importance of asserting the rights of those who, like her, will be "cut off in their prime," returned to the domestic margins and end-papers of society. In this respect Robert Audley's words, in Braddon's novel, also echo in our minds:

> Women are *never lazy*. They don't know what it is to be quiet . . . they want freedom of opinion, variety of occupation, do they? Let them have it. Let them be lawyers, doctors, preachers, teachers, soldiers, legislators—anything they like—but let them be quiet. . . . (Braddon 207, emphasis original)

In none of these novels, however, do women "have it," and thus they most certainly will not be quiet. Lacking employment in the conventional sense, instead they take up occupation within haunted houses whose walls and edifices creak and moan at the resentments encoded in lives half-lived. Hence, though Bachelard may read the house as a space of peaceful dreaming, this is not the vision of domestic inhabitation afforded to these female-authored gothic texts. Whether the house be literally haunted (as in *Wuthering Heights*, "The Old Nurse's Story," or *The Little Stranger*), or metaphorically haunted by the clandestine, paranoia, or criminal activity (as in *My Cousin Rachel* or *Lady Audley's Secret*), these unquiet spirits give rise to a battle that is unseen, because privately fought and muffled by an apparently comfortable existence (none of these characters is poor or destitute). Like those ghosts who knock at the window demanding entry, the female-authored gothic continues to provide us with unquiet spirits who refuse to be consoled, shut out, or shut up—they are unsettling, baffling, and impossible to contain, but they tell the stories of women who refuse to play dead and will continue to do so into the twenty-first century

Works Cited

Bachelard, Gaston. *The Poetics of Space*. Trans. Maria Jolas. Boston: Beacon, 1994.

Braddon, Mary Elizabeth. *Lady Audley's Secret*. 1862. Oxford: Oxford UP, 1998.

Brontë, Emily. *Wuthering Heights*. 1847. London: J. M. Dent, 1978.

du Maurier, Daphne. *My Cousin Rachel*. 1951. London: Virago, 2003.

Freud, Sigmund. «The 'Uncanny.'» *Penguin Freud Library*. Ed. Albert Dickson. Harmondsworth, England: Penguin, 1990. 335–76.

Gaskell, Elizabeth. "The Old Nurse's Story." *Gothic Tales*. Ed. Laura Kranzler. Harmondsworth, Eng.: Penguin, 2000.

Gilbert, Sandra, and Susan Gubar. *The Madwoman in the Attic: The Woman Writer and the Nineteenth-Century Literary Imagination*. 1979. New Haven: Yale UP, 1984.

Reynolds, Graham. *Turner*. London: Thames and Hudson, 1969.

Stewart, Susan. *On Longing: Narratives of the Miniature, the Gigantic, the Souvenir, the Collection*. 1993. Durham, NC: Duke UP, 2007.

Tzvetan, Todorov. *The Fantastic: A Structural Approach to a Literary Genre*. Trans. Richard Howard. Ithaca: Cornell UP, 1975.

Waters, Sarah. *The Little Stranger*. London: Virago, 2009.

Wolfreys, Julian. *Victorian Hauntings: Spectrality, Gothic, and the Uncanny in Literature*. Basingstoke, Eng.: Palgrave, 2002.

E. T. A. Hoffmann and the Fantastic _____

Birgit Röder

It is almost impossible to overstate the importance of E. T. A. Hoffmann's contribution to the development of fantastic literature; this is because almost all of the genre's defining features appear in some form or other in his works. Although Hoffmann's *œuvre* (life work) is now regarded as an integral part of the canon of German romantic literature, during the nineteenth century critical opinion was much more divided. Johann Wolfgang von Goethe was just one of the writer's contemporaries who took a rather disparaging view of his work. Writing in 1827, and echoing Walter Scott's critique of the role of the supernatural in Hoffmann's work, Goethe noted that "those of us genuinely concerned about the development of a national culture can only look on in dismay at the way in which the ghastly works of that pathological writer [Hoffmann] have held sway over the past few years in Germany" (*Goethes Werke* 88, my translation). Such views were instrumental in shaping the perception of Hoffmann as an essentially trivial author whose talents did not extend beyond the production of ghost stories. At the same time, the suggestion that the elements of the supernatural and the fantastic in Hoffmann's work should be rejected as the products of a diseased creative imagination also hints at some of the reasons why the fantastic struggled to establish itself as a serious literary genre in the first half of the nineteenth century. Despite such damning criticism, Hoffmann's fiction did attract a devoted readership and, over time, exerted a profound influence on subsequent writers and intellectuals, including the likes of novelist Franz Kafka and Sigmund Freud, the founder of psychoanalysis.

Hoffmann's enduring interest in the fantastic can be traced back to the turbulence of his private life and to the radical upheaval of the social and political structures in Europe following the French Revolution of 1789. For the philosophers of the eighteenth-century Enlightenment, such as Immanuel Kant and Voltaire, what differentiated human beings from other objects in the natural world was a capacity for rational thought; and this faith in reason as the driving force in the advance of civilization is a common theme in the works of almost all the eighteenth-century philosophers. Reason was seen not only as a weapon in the struggle against superstition but was also regarded as a means of combating the blind acceptance of authority. Just as the philosophy of the Enlightenment had been responsible for enormous advances in the natural sciences, so too, it was widely believed, a rational critique of the prevailing social and political structures would inevitably bring about a better and more just organization of society. Seen in this light, the Enlightenment was not simply a philosophical idea, but a political movement that, by undermining the basis of feudal absolutism through its insistence on the natural rights of the individual, aimed at a radical transformation of society. Moreover, the French Revolution, with its ideals of liberty, equality, and fraternity, seemed to some at least to be the instantiation of these philosophical ideas at the level of practical politics.

But as the revolution unfolded, it was not long before the ideals that initially prompted the overthrow of the monarchy seemed to have disappeared from view amid the violent chaos of the Reign of Terror (1793–94). Within a relatively short space of time, the enlightened radicalism of the early revolutionaries appeared to have been replaced by the reactionary politics of figures such as Napoleon Bonaparte in France and Louis Ferdinand Metternich in Austria. For those intellectuals who had initially supported the revolution, the apparent collapse of the ideals that had originally set events in motion was a devastating blow; not only did it appear that human reason was incapable of bringing about a better society, but the violent course of the revolution seemed to offer incontrovertible evidence that human beings were not simply rational creatures.

The notion that explanations of human behavior could not be reduced to straightforward questions of rationality, but rather involved taking a diverse range of other apparently inexplicable forces into account, lies at the very heart of Hoffmann's *œuvre*. In addition, his understanding of the complexities of human behavior was reinforced by his professional experience as a judge in the Prussian civil service. Although Hoffmann always regarded himself first and foremost as an artist devoted to the sphere of the imagination—during his lifetime he worked as a writer, composer, conductor, theater director, and caricaturist—in order to secure a regular income he also worked as a legal counsel and judge. Historical accounts suggest that Hoffmann always took his role as a judge very seriously and discharged the duties of his office with great impartiality, setting aside the promptings of emotion and arriving at a judgment on the basis of a rational assessment of the facts. Yet confronted as he was throughout his career with instances of deviant behavior, he can hardly have avoided reflecting on the often complex psychological forces that had led those standing before him to resort to crime. Moreover, his interest in criminal psychology and the pathological workings of the human mind was not untypical of the age in which he lived. For the investigation of supposedly abnormal, irrational behavior is not only a recurring motif in his work, but one that was becoming an increasingly important issue in contemporary legal and medical discourses in early nineteenth-century Germany.

Time and again we are confronted with figures in Hoffmann's fiction who, while acting from a variety of motives, behave in a manner that, at least on the surface, seems strange and inexplicable. Very often these individuals are shown to be marionette-like figures no longer wholly in control of their actions and seemingly at the mercy of sinister supernatural forces. At the same time, in many of Hoffmann's works we encounter the juxtaposition of what early nineteenth-century bourgeois society regarded as "normal," morally acceptable, behavior, and that seen as "abnormal," morally reprehensible and even "insane." This tension—that we as readers experience no less than the characters themselves—is often conveyed through the evocation of the fantastic and the associated elements of terror and the uncanny. Indeed, a key aspect of Hoffmann's literary technique consists in subjecting us as readers to the same experience of threatening, sinister forces—whether real or imaginary—as the fictional characters themselves, with the result that we share their disorientation and confusion. Yet nothing is ever quite that straightforward with Hoffmann; and, as we shall see, in a number of his works—among them *The Golden Pot* (1814)—the supernatural forces at play appear to exert a benign influence on the characters, guiding them, in an almost fairy-tale-like manner, to a better understanding of themselves and, on occasion, to a state of paradise regained.

The Devil's Elixirs (1815/16)

Hoffmann's novel, *The Devil's Elixirs*, has certain affinities with the tradition of the English gothic novel insofar as its plot is loosely based on Matthew Lewis's 1796 novel *The Monk*. As in Lewis's novel, the reader is presented with the story of a Capuchin monk who abandons his order and becomes caught up in a range of sexual and criminal activities (including murder) that drive him insane. Nonetheless Hoffmann's version of the story ends on a more positive note; unlike Lewis's protagonist, Ambrosio, Hoffmann's Medardus regrets his actions and, following his repentance, experiences a state of catharsis. From a psychological perspective, *The Devil's Elixirs* is also a much more nuanced work than *The Monk*, and its complexity is a reflection of Hoffmann's handling of the supernatural and fantastic elements in the novel. As with many of Hoffmann's works, however, scholarly opinion on how this novel should be interpreted remains extremely divided. Horst Daemmrich cites the novel's treatment of existential questions, crises of identity, and the psychological analysis of the main protagonist as evidence that its author should be seen as a precursor of modernity. By contrast, James McGlathery regards the story as a projection of the central figure's sexual fantasies, an interpretation that, while not wholly implausible, fails to do sufficient justice to the sheer complexity and range of issues raised in the novel as a whole. Elizabeth Wright offers an illuminating account of the rhetorical devices through which *The Devil's Elixirs* evokes sensations of fear and terror, while Andrew

Webber explores the epistemological, aesthetic, and psychosexual aspects of the motif of the doppelganger.

In *The Devil's Elixirs* the reader is invited to accompany Medardus on what turns out to be as much a voyage of self-discovery as a physical journey through time and space. Yet as the novel unfolds, its true purpose becomes unclear to both protagonist and reader alike, as both are plunged into a state of chaos and disorientation caused by the exposure to mysterious uncanny forces that are both threatening and irrational. In part, the sense of confusion and uncertainty the reader experiences is a deliberate effect of the novel's narrative structure, based as it is (so the narrator claims) on a manuscript left behind by Medardus to atone for his crimes. However, it is soon obvious that this first-person narrator is fundamentally unreliable, and as readers we are left with a series of disturbing questions: Are Medardus's experiences merely hallucinations as a result of having drunk the devil's elixirs? Is Medardus simply insane? Have the criminal and sexual activities in which he has become involved prompted such extreme feelings of guilt that he has lost touch altogether with reality? Is he a tragic victim of devilish intrigue and other supernatural forces that he is powerless to resist? Is it simply fate that he bears the burden of his forefathers' guilt—a burden for which he, inexplicably, must atone? Despite the presence of a seemingly rational "editor" who introduces Medardus's manuscript, explains the complex story-within-a-story structure, and links the events in the story to Medardus's convoluted web of family relationships, the reader never receives an adequate answer to any of these questions. Indeed, far from clarifying the relationships within the novel, the editor's well-intentioned interventions often obscure matters further. But it is not simply the opacity of the novel's narrative structure that fills the reader with a sense of anxiety and helplessness; as we follow Medardus on his dramatic journey, we too are exposed to the full force of the dire messages of foreboding, the gruesome nightmarish visions of an often hostile nature, and the total collapse of any coherent sense of direction and purpose.

As the novel unfolds, Medardus is inexorably drawn down deeper and deeper into the vortex of his own guilt until, in a moment as ecstatic as it is traumatic, he finds himself face to face with his doppelganger: "suddenly a naked figure thrust itself waist-high out of the hole and stared at me like a gruesome spectre, leering and cackling like a madman. The full light of the lamp fell on his face and I recognized—*myself*" (Hoffmann, *Elixirs* 187). Medardus's confrontation with his devilish Other is a terrifying, though by no means isolated, experience. Although Medardus resumes his enigmatic journey, his doppelganger repeatedly reappears without warning, clinging to the unfortunate monk who, now on the brink of madness, tries in vain to shake him off. Eventually Medardus screams: "You are not me, you are the Devil!" (111); and yet even here it remains unclear whether the figure on his back is real or merely a projection of his paranoid imagination. Medardus's inability to rid himself of his demonic doppelganger plunges him further and further into a state of insanity, the full force of which is shared by the reader. Ultimately, the monk's capacity to do evil is shown to be an inherent part of his psychological make up and not the result of an external agency. For, as the novel demonstrates with horrifying clarity, the real power of the devil consists not in doing evil himself, but rather in exploiting the weaknesses of others and thereby persuading them to do evil on his behalf. Put another way, *The Devil's Elixirs* serves as a reminder that Satan is not, in any straightforward sense, an adversary to be overcome; rather the task for human beings is to overcome the potential to succumb to the temptation to do evil, a potentiality that lies latent within each and every individual.

The Sandman (1816)

Hoffmann's novella *The Sandman* has been the subject of extensive scholarly discussion, and while it is impossible to offer anything approaching a comprehensive overview of the secondary literature on this novella, a number of key trends can be identified. The most famous—though perhaps also the most idiosyncratic—interpretation of the novel is to be found in Freud's 1919 essay "The Uncanny," in which he famously refers to Hoffmann as the unrivaled master of the uncanny in literature. However, Freud reads the novella not as a conventional work of literature but interprets it as a pathological case study using the categories of psychoanalysis. For Freud, Nathanael's symbolic blinding and his subsequent obsession with the eye is to be seen as a form of castration anxiety that in turn is responsible for the protagonist's paranoid tendencies. By contrast, Siegbert Prawer takes a very different view, arguing that the elements of the uncanny in *The Sandman* are an integral part of a narrative technique in which psychological processes are constantly exposed and concealed. Finally, while Samuel Weber also focuses on the uncanny in the novella, John Ellis offers a more sociological approach to the story and sees Nathanael as the victim of a society dominated by a crude mechanistic concept of rationalism.

At the start of the novella we are presented with three letters (two from Nathanael and one from Clara) before the editor finally intervenes, requesting the reader's indulgence in a traditional gesture of *captatio benevolentiae*.[1] However, as is so often the case in Hoffmann's work, the narrator proves to be an unreliable point of reference as he offers a range of—sometimes contradictory—perspectives on both the character and appearance of Clara. This sense of uncertainty is compounded by the fact that the two interpretations of the events referred to in the letters of Nathanael and Clara are almost diametrically opposed to one another. As a result the reader is forced to consider whether Nathanael is increasingly drifting toward a state of mental instability or whether Clara, Lothar, and the other characters in the story are themselves, either wittingly or unwittingly, partly to blame for the predicament in which Nathanael finds himself.

Right from the start, Clara is presented as a wholly rational figure who continually appeals to Nathanael's reason in an attempt to shake him out of his paranoid state: "In my opinion all the terrors and horrors you describe took only place inside your head, and had very little to do with the real world outside you" (Hoffmann, *Sandman* 93–94). She refuses point-blank to make any concessions to his imagination— an imagination that is stoked by deep anxieties that themselves have their roots in his traumatic childhood experiences. Like Clara, we only learn about Nathanael's childhood gradually; and initially, our sympathies lie with her as she resorts to commonsense rationality in an attempt to stem her beloved's paranoid moods. As the novella develops, however, Clara's lack of imagination is increasingly exposed and, when confronted by Nathanael's wild fantasizing, her reaction is to retreat into the safe haven of the petty-bourgeois values of her philistine society. But while she can hardly be blamed for her failure to indulge Nathanael's grotesque fantasies, her inability to take seriously his deepest anxieties—together with her ill-considered advice that he throw his "crazy, senseless, insane story into the fire" (103)—are instrumental in bringing about the tragedy at the end of the story. The more Nathanael feels rejected by the rational Clara, the more fanatically he embraces the realm of the imagination, insisting that he possesses a unique ability to look beyond the surface of everyday reality and grasp a more fundamental truth. As he and Clara assume increasingly polarized positions, Nathanael can no longer find a niche for himself in society and instead seeks solace in the arms of the automaton, Olimpia. Overcome by a sense of solipsistic despair, he is driven mad and, having first attempted to destroy Clara by throwing her off the tower, commits suicide.

In the course of the story the motif of the eye (and sight generally) is of crucial importance. In the text the eye assumes a dual symbolic function as both an organ of perception and expression. On one level, the eye is the source of the recognition (or nonrecognition) of objects and states in the external world; but on another, the eye serves as a reminder that there is something there to be recognized. For Clara, the eye is a means through which the individual gathers data relating to the external world; for Nathanael, the eye is a surface onto which inner psychological states are projected. In this context it is striking to note that the novella begins with what can be termed a prohibition of the gaze. For Nathanael is strictly forbidden from setting eyes on the uncanny figure of the Sandman whenever he visits the family home. As a result, Nathanael is left with no alternative but to construct a fantasy image of the Sandman—a task that helps him to develop his imaginative faculties but one that also proves to have, quite literally, fatal consequences.

It is important to note, however, that Hoffmann's story does not only focus on the mechanisms of individual psychology, but also on the phenomenon of the uncanny and the feelings of alienation and fear it evokes in both in Nathanael and the reader. Ultimately there may well be a perfectly rational explanation for the strange and (in Nathanael's view) threatening behavior of Coppelius and the tragic death of his father; but the relationship between Coppelius the lawyer and Coppola, the dubious barometer salesman who visits Nathanael at the start of the story and in whom the young man seems to recognize his old adversary, is never really resolved. Is Coppola to be regarded as a unique individual in his own right? Or is he merely a projection of Nathanael's fevered imagination? For whenever the figure of Coppelius/Coppola appears in the narrative, the very name appears to trigger a crisis of increasing proportions within Nathanael. And what is the reader to make of the fact that, at the end of the novella, the elderly Coppola disappears as mysteriously as he had reappeared?

Although for rationally inclined readers there is something almost comic about Nathanael's infatuation with the mechanical doll, Olimpia, the episode is also not devoid of tragedy either; for the fact remains that the young man falls hopelessly in love with her, abandons his loyal fiancée, and is quite unable (or perhaps unwilling) to recognize that she is a lifeless automaton. But while the reader, like some of the other characters in the novella, harbors suspicions that Olimpia is not quite what she seems, it is impossible not to share Nathanael's agony and horror when he sees Spalanzani and Coppelius tearing their creation apart until all that is left is a pair of lifeless eyes: "Thereupon

Nathanael noticed a pair of bloody eyes lying on the floor and staring at him. Spalanzani picked them up with his unscathed hand and threw them at Nathanael, so that they struck him on the chest" (*Sandman* 114). It may appear that Nathanael recovers from this terrible experience; but as the story shows, it is only a matter of time until he descends into madness and attempts, unsuccessfully, to kill Clara before hurling himself to his death from the tower. And while the story ends with the suggestion that Clara has got over Nathanael and found domestic bliss with a husband and two children, even here we are left with a deep-seated feeling of unease. For Clara's dream of bourgeois happiness stands in the sharpest possible contrast to the contents of Nathanael's nightmarish imagination. However, this dream is called into question through the subjunctive modality of the novella's closing sentence: "This *would seem to suggest* that Clara succeeded in finding the quiet domestic happiness which suited her cheerful, sunny disposition . . ." (*Sandman* 118, my italics).

Don Juan (1813)

The source for Hoffmann's novella *Don Juan* is Wolfgang Amadeus Mozart's opera *Don Giovanni*, a work that itself draws on a long tradition of literary representations of the arch-seducer. However, for the most part, Hoffmann ignores the historical background of the legend, offering instead a literary reworking of the relationship between art and life embedded in the genre of the fantastic. Through the juxtaposition of the actress playing the role of Donna Anna and the fictional character herself, the novella explores the discrepancy between the desire to experience the absolute on the one hand, and a state of self-realization within the realm of the absolute on the other. The interrelationship of different levels of reality—discussed at length in Klaus Deterding's analysis of the story—is a key theme in the critical literature on the story. Other critics have approached the story as a model of literary communication. Accordingly, for David Wellbery, Hoffmann's story is to be read as a semiotic model in which the following roles are assigned: Mozart (sender)—Don Giovanni (message)—narrator (receiver/ sender)—*Don Juan* (message)—Theodor (receiver).[2]

Hoffmann's novella is presented in the form of a letter from the narrator (the "travelling enthusiast") to his friend Theodor. In it the narrator recounts how the room at the inn at which he is staying has (quite inexplicably!) direct access to a box in the local theater. From the outset the reader is disoriented by the logical gaps in the text and forced to abandon conventional concepts of time and space as he accompanies the narrator on his fantastic voyage. For, while the narrator is describing the first act of Mozart's *Don Giovanni* unfolding on stage, a female figure—Donna Anna as it turns out—mysteriously joins him in the box. However, it remains unclear whether it is the singer playing the part of Donna Anna or the fictional character herself. But while the reader is confronted with a situation that is both unsettling and which defies rational explanation, the narrator views the twilight realm of the theater as an idyllic *locus amoenus*[3] in which all his romantic yearning and desires will be fulfilled. For as he, caught up in the fantasies of his imagination, declares: "Only the poet understands the poet; only a Romantic spirit can fathom the Romantic" (*Don Juan* 512). This observation amounts to a direct invitation to the reader to turn his back on the prosaic world of everyday reality and to embrace the poetic world of the imagination instead. For the narrator, it is music that, of all the arts, speaks most directly to the poetic spirit and which inspires human beings to seek out a higher, transcendent realm. In this context we might note that there is more than just an echo here of Hoffmann's essay, on "[Ludwig van] Beethoven's Instrumental Music" (1813), in which music is referred to as "the most romantic of all arts, one might almost say the only one that is genuinely romantic, since its only subject-matter is infinity" ("Beethoven's Instrumental Music" 97).

After Donna Anna has departed the narrator watches the second act, a spectacle that causes him to experience "the most unspeakable joy" ("Don Juan" 515) for it is "as though a long-promised fulfilment of a most beautiful vision from another world were come to life" (509). In short, he experiences a synthesis of imagination and reality; through art he has been afforded direct experience of a realm of transcendence. But hardly has the reader had the opportunity to reflect on the narrator's words than, as is so often the case in Hoffmann's work, he is mercilessly catapulted back in the world of everyday reality and confronted with the prosaic comments of the members of an audience (whose failure to appreciate the music stands in stark contrast to the narrator's ecstatic response). Fascinated by the performance he has just witnessed and still in a state of intense excitement, the narrator returns to the theater at midnight in the hope of meeting Donna Anna again. Under her guidance he outlines a theory of the relationship between art and life, and between the realms of aesthetic and rational truth. But while the narrator, following the glimpse of a transcendent world brought about by the intense musical experience, returns to reality, the actress playing Donna Anna identifies so completely with her role that, for her, such a return proves impossible. We learn that she died during the night at exactly 2:00 a.m., that is to say at precisely the moment at which the narrator was granted access to the "celestial plains" (515)—a realm of experience that defies representation in rational discourse. For the female artist, there is no way back and, like the moth drawn inexorably toward a burning flame, her death is the price she pays for her total commitment to the pursuit of the absolute.

The narrative structure of this novella also invites us to view a set of concepts that, although at first sight seem to be diametrically opposed to one another, are on closer analysis intimately bound up with each other. Not only do different levels of reality merge into each other during the narrative, but the reader is confronted with a variety of apparent contradictions that, in the realm of the fantastic, seem to be resolved. For example, the narrator abandons his role as an explanatory agent and becomes himself a figure in need of an explanation; the female performer merges with the figure of Donna Anna and dies at the same moment; the banality of the inn setting is transformed into a stage on which the most miraculous events take place; and the boundary between the world of everyday reality and the transcendent realm of the romantic imagination becomes so blurred that each seems to flow into the other. Indeed the fantastic dimension of the novella is, to a large extent, an effect of the tensions between the call of everyday reality and the demands of the romantic imagination. As a result, we as readers are left with a sense of being suspended between two extremes: at one level, the story is an exhortation to create a space in the real world in which the products of the imagination might be indulged; at another level, it serves as a warning of the fatal consequences that lie in store for those who attempt to embrace the transcendent realm of the ideal too intensely. Seen from these perspectives, Hoffmann's novella represents an attempt to reconcile the apparently opposed worlds of art and life, and of ideal and reality, even if the resulting synthesis is, at best, a fleeting glimpse of a utopian realm.

The Golden Pot (1814)

Hoffmann's fairy tale *The Golden Pot* is regarded by almost all critics as a masterpiece of its kind, and Paul-Wolfgang Wührl speaks for many when he refers to it as one of Hoffmann's "finest works" (3). Even Hoffmann himself was convinced of the story's quality, and, in a letter written to his friend Hippel two years after its publication, he lamented the fact that he would probably never again write a work of such quality. Despite its fairy-tale structure, however, not all critics have accepted that the story is altogether devoid of irony. John Reddick, for instance, stresses that the relation between myth and reality remains ambiguous throughout the novella. For her part, Maria M. Tatar seeks to relate the fantastical elements of the story to developments in romantic science.

In stark contrast to the other works discussed above, here the fantastic is not something terrifying and threatening, but rather a benign, therapeutic power that is instrumental in bringing about the story's happy ending. In keeping with the tradition of the romantic fairy tale (cf. Novalis's *The Apprentices of Sais* and the collection assembled by the Grimm brothers), the central protagonist, Anselmus, has to complete a set of tasks in order to prove himself worthy of the hand of his beloved. The "hostile principle" that obstructs the benign supernatural elements in the story manifests itself in the mundane petty bourgeois philistinism of the inhabitants of contemporary Dresden and, above all, the Paulmann family who conspire to put a stop to Anselmus's excursions into the realm of fantasy by dismissing them as "fits" (*Golden Pot* 9) and attempting to turn him into a respectable member of society (and, by the same token, a viable husband for Veronika). But the student Anselmus has other ideas. His mind is opened up to the power of the romantic imagination following his magical encounter with the three little snakes; and he is consumed by a passion for Serpentina, the youngest. However, he can only win her hand if he allows himself to be controlled by her father, the magus-like archivist Lindhorst, and embraces in its totality the fantastical realm inhabited by Lindhorst's daughter. Although willing in principle, Anselmus suffers from doubts originating in his rational self that prompt him to reject the path of romantic fantasy and turn his back on the transcendent realm of the imagination. For this he is punished by being imprisoned in a crystal bottle until, having finally seen the error of his ways, he is reunited with his beloved, and we learn of "the sublime happiness of the student Anselmus, once he was wedded to the lovely Serpentina and had departed for the wondrous and mysterious realm which he acknowledged as his home and for which his heart, filled with strange premonitions, had so long been yearning" (*Golden Pot* 79).

Beneath the surface of this dramatic narrative that oscillates between the extremes of an unbridled romantic imagination on the one hand and a crudely conceived rationalism on the other, there is also a complex story-within-a-story in which we are invited to reflect on the philosophical ideas underpinning the main narrative. This consists of a mythological account of an originary utopian state of nature in which the intellect and the imagination coexisted in perfect harmony. Like Anselmus, the reader of *The Golden Pot* is always at risk of being overcome by the sheer wealth of magical and fantastic elements in the story. But if the reader suspends his rational, critical faculties, and allows himself to accompany Anselmus on this magical journey into the world of the imagination then, like the protagonist, he finds himself confronted with a world in which anything seems possible. And it is precisely this opening up of the imagination that Hoffmann's fairy tale is at pains to promote. Nonetheless, even in this work, the possibility of a flight into a realm of fantasy that is so detached from everyday reality is subtly undermined through the use of irony. Friedrich Schlegel maintains that "irony is a form of paradox" (153). It is precisely this type of irony that Hoffmann deploys, for he is only too well aware that is impossible for either the narrator or the reader to follow Anselmus into the magical realm of Atlantis. Through a series of observations that emphasize the impossibility of immersing the self in a transcendent realm in the way that Anselmus envisions, Hoffmann adopts an ironic perspective on this dilemma:

I may be permitted, kind reader, to doubt whether you have ever been enclosed in a glass bottle, unless some vivid dream has teased you with such magical mishaps. If that has been the case, then you will sympathise warmly with poor Anselmus's misery; but if you have never had such dreams, then you will do me and Anselmus a favour by letting your active imagination enclose you in the crystal for a few minutes. (*Golden Pot* 67)

While it is made absolutely clear that, because of the limitations of the temporal world, the narrator and the reader will never be able to succeed in setting foot within such an absolute realm of romantic mythology, at the same time, it is equally clear that, as far as the realization of his fantastic journey and discovery of his true self is concerned, even Anselmus is dependent upon both Hoffmann and the reader. Neither Atlantis nor Anselmus can be regarded as part of the contingent world of empirical reality and both owe their very existence to the workings of the creative imagination. Accordingly the fantastic tale is only created through the cooperative efforts of both author/narrator and the reader at the level of the imagination. For ironically, the text reveals how, far from being diametrically opposed to each other, the worlds of the imagination and the worlds of reality are in fact inextricably linked; for the one cannot exist without the other. It is in this sense that *The Golden Pot* moves beyond the parameters of the conventional fairy tale and can be seen as an idealized version of the romantic *Kunstmärchen* (literary fairy tale); at the end of the story we witness the yearning of the narrator finding its consolation in poetry. Moreover, during a concluding dialogue between the narrator and Anselmus about the possibility—or indeed impossibility—of a life lived wholly within the realm of art and poetry, the contradiction between the desire for total immersion of the self in an aesthetic realm, and the impossibility of ever realizing such an ideal is never resolved (even though it is precisely this that Anselmus has succeeded in doing, albeit within the fairy-tale setting). For both narrator and reader the transcendent realm of the imagination is a discursive space that can only be accessed via dreams and fantasy; but it is in this very realm that the narrator and reader, trapped as they are within the parameters of temporal reality, find solace. For there are no limits to the world of the imagination, provided that the reader embraces it in its entirety—in stark contrast to Veronika and her petty-bourgeois family: "Weren't you in Atlantis yourself a moment ago," the archivist Lindhorst asks, "and haven't you at least got a pretty farm there, as the poetic property of your mind?" (*Golden Pot* 83).

Conclusion

The disruptive impact of the fantastic on the crudely rationalistic world of bourgeois reality is a key theme in a number of Hoffmann's other works, including *Mademoiselle de Scudery, Councillor Krespel, The Mines at Falun,* and *Princess Brambilla.* When Hoffmann confronts his readers with literary representations of the fantastic, more often than not, this is accompanied by a stinging critique of a philistine bourgeois society that cannot look beyond the parameters of its mundane existence. Seen in this context, Hoffmann's presentation of miraculous, fantastic, and irrational events is both threatening and provocative. Although many of his characters may appear to be the victims of mysterious powers, as readers we must always consider the extent to which the prevailing social structures—and their associated psychological mechanisms—also have a profound effect on the behavior of the characters. How far are the dominant social conventions to blame for the labeling of Hoffmann's protagonists as "abnormal" and "insane"? Indeed, on closer analysis it often appears that it is precisely these conventions that are irrational and "abnormal." Accordingly the basic premise underpinning so many of Hoffmann's stories—that the dividing line between the world of reality and the world of imagination is much less clear-cut than we may wish to believe—amounts to an appeal for a more tolerant attitude toward those aspects of human behavior that we are inclined to dismiss as pathological simply because they fail to conform to the conventional categories of bourgeois society.

While in a number of Hoffmann's stories the experience of the fantastic provokes reactions of fear and terror in the protagonists and plunges them into a tragic state of solipsistic despair, in other works we see quite the opposite as the experience of magical, fantastic events liberates the creative imagination of the protagonists and transports them to a higher state of self-understanding. However, it is important not to mistake Hoffmann's emphasis on the imagination and the fantastic for an outright rejection of rationality and the intellect. Rather it should be seen as a reminder of the essentially romantic notion that a productive synthesis of the real and the imaginary is vital if human beings are ever to realize their true potential. Reason and the imagination are two sides of the same coin; and to pursue one at the expense of the other leads either to the cultivation of a bourgeois philistine existence, or to a detachment from reality that, in extreme cases, borders on insanity. Hoffmann's works continually remind us of the productive tension between the real and the fantastic, between reason and the imagination; and it is this that explains the lasting appeal of his work even today.

Notes

1. Latin for "catching the goodwill," *captatio benevolentiae* is a common term that refers to any literary or oral device that seeks to secure the goodwill of the recipient or audience.

2. Semiotics is the study of signs and sign processes (as founded by the Swiss linguist Ferdinand de Saussure, 1857–1913). Semiotic approaches are often used in the analysis of texts; however, a "text" as defined by semiotics can exist in any medium and may be verbal, nonverbal, or both. The term "text" usually refers to a message that has been recorded in some way (e.g., writing, audio- and video recording) so that it is physically independent of its sender or receiver. A "text" (a summary of signs, e.g., words, images, sounds, or gestures) consists of a "message" which is on the one hand constructed (by the "sender") and on the other interpreted (by the "receiver").

3. Literally "pleasant place" in Latin, *locus amoenus* is a literary term referring to a safe and comfortable haven.

Works Cited

Daemmrich, Horst. *The Shattered Self. Hoffmann's Tragic Vision*. Detroit: Wayne State UP, 1973.

Deterding, Klaus. *Die Poetik der inneren und äußeren Welt bei E. T. A. Hoffmann*. Frankfurt am Main, Germ.: Lang, 1991.

Ellis, John M. "Clara, Nathanael and the Narrator: Interpreting Hoffmann's *Der Sandmann*." *German Quarterly* 54 (1981): 1–18.

Falkenberg, Marc. *Rethinking the Uncanny in Hoffmann and Tieck*. Bern: Lang, 2005.

Freud, Sigmund. "The Uncanny." *The Standard Edition of the Complete Psychological Works of Sigmund Freud*. Vol. 17. Ed. and trans. James Strachey. London: Hogarth, 1953. 219–52.

Goethe, Johann Wolfgang von. *Goethes Werke, hrsg. im Auftrage der Großherzogin Sophie von Sachsen. Abt. 1*. Vol. 42, 1. Weimar, Germ.: Böhlau, 1904.

Hoffmann, E. T. A. *The Devil's Elixirs*. Trans. Ronald Taylor. London: Calder, 1963.

_____. "Beethoven's Instrumental Music." *E. T. A. Hoffmann's Musical Writings*. Ed. David Charlton. Cambridge, Eng.: Cambridge UP, 1989. 96–97.

_____. "*Don Juan*." Trans. Abram Loft. *Musical Quarterly* 31.4 (1945): 504–16.

_____. "*The Golden Pot*" and "*The Sandman*." *The Golden Pot and other Tales*. Trans. Ritchie Robertson. Oxford: Oxford UP, 1992. 1–83 and 85–118.

McGlathery, James. "Demon Love. E. T. A. Hoffmann's *Elixiere des Teufels*." *Colloquia Germanica* 12 (1979): 61–76.

Prawer, Siegbert Salomon. "Hoffmann's Uncanny Guest: A Reading of *Der Sandmann*." *German Life and Letters* 18.4 (1965): 297–308.

Preuß, Karin. *The Question of Madness in the Works of E. T. A. Hoffmann and Mary Shelley*. Frankfurt am Main, Germ.: Lang, 2003.

Reddick, John. "E.T.A. Hoffmann's *Der goldne Topf* and its 'durchgehaltene Ironie.'" *Modern Language Review* 71 (1976): 577–94.

Röder, Birgit. *A Study of the Major Novellas of E.T.A. Hoffmann*. Rochester, NY: Camden House, 2003.

Schlegel, Friedrich. *Kritische Ausgabe*. Ed. Ernst Behler, Jean-Jacques Anstett, Hans Eichner, et al. Vol. 2. Paderborn: Schöningh, 1958.

Scott, Walter. "On the Supernatural in Fictitious Composition; and Particularly on the Works of Ernest Theodore William Hoffman." *Foreign Quarterly Review* 1.1 (1827): 60–98.

Tatar, Maria M. "Mesmerism, Madness and Death in E. T. A. Hoffmann's *Der goldne Topf.*" *Studies in Romanticism* 14 (1975): 365–89.

Webber, Andrew. *The Doppelgänger: Double Visions in German Literature*. Oxford: Clarendon, 1996.

Weber, Samuel. "The Sideshow; Or, Remarks on a Canny Moment." *Modern Language Notes* 88.6 (Dec. 1973): 1102–33.

Wellbery, David, E. "E. T. A. Hoffmann and the Romantic Hermeneutics: An Interpretation of Hoffmann's *Don Juan.*" *SiR* 19 (1980): 455–73.

Wright, Elizabeth. *E. T. A. Hoffmann and the Rhetoric of Terror: Aspects of Language Used for the Evocation of Fear*. London: University of London, Institute of Germanic Studies, 1978.

Wührl, Paul-Wolfgang, ed. "Erläuterungen und Dokumente: E. T. A. Hoffmann, *Der goldne Topf.*" Stuttgart: Reclam, 1982.

Prosper Mérimée's Playful Fantastic_____

Peter Cogman

The greater part of the contributions of Prosper Mérimée (1803–70) to imaginative literature were published in the period running from 1825 to 1831, when he started a career as a civil servant. They included plays, a novel, and "translations" of folk ballads (of his own invention). Most notable is his short fiction, however, prompted in part by the co-incidence of a crisis in publishing in Paris—the result of the spread of *cabinets de lecture* where subscribers could read books and periodicals, an influx of translated foreign works, and overproduction—with the appearance of reviews offering a new outlet for short works. Mérimée's "Mateo Falcone," arguably the first recognizably modern short story in French, appeared in 1829. Although his later production consisted mainly of historical and archaeological works and translations from Russian (including Aleksandr Sergeyevich Pushkin's short story "Queen of Spades"), he returned intermittently to short fiction; among the eleven short fictions written after 1831, which included "Carmen" and "Colomba," five are in some way fantastic.

Mérimée referred in an 1851 article to the fantastic tale as if it had a set formula:

> The recipe for a good fantastic tale is well-known: begin with the firmly delineated portraits of strange but possible characters, and give their features the most minutely observed reality. The transition from what is strange to what is marvellous is imperceptible, and the reader will find himself surrounded by the fantastic before he realises that the real world has been left far behind. (Raitt 185; Mérimée "La littérature en Russie")

What is interesting here for analyzing Mérimée's practice is not the habitual emphasis on creating an illusion of reality, but the reference to oddity in characterization. This reference is reminiscent of Ludwig Tieck's argument that "comical, individualized features" confuse the reader's judgment (Mücke 5). Additionally, it is a reminder that the bizarre gradually takes us from our familiar world to the fantastic.

In spite of the dismissive term "recipe," and his own reference to his short fictions as "amusements" ("drôleries"; *Correspondance* 248), Mérimée's fantastic works show him skillfully exploring the possibilities of the fantastic, while insistently returning to his own underlying preoccupations: the fragility of civilization and of the control of reason, a fascination with the primitive that is linked to violence and sexuality. This can be seen in three stories taken from across his career: "The Vision of Charles XI" (1829), "Il Viccolo di Madama Lucrezia" (written in 1846 but unpublished), and "Lokis" (1869). The three titles all contain a foreign element: a king, a street name, a strange word. All three stories conform to the accepted pattern of the fantastic as defined by French critics. In a realistically portrayed but remote setting (seventeenth-century Sweden, a decrepit house in Rome, a country chateau in Lithuania), events occur that seem inexplicable in that world and represent a "scandalous" (Caillois 15) or "sudden" ("brutal," Castex 8) intrusion, a "rupture in the constancies of the real world" (Vax 169). In the first a vision predicts future events; in "Il Viccolo" a long-dead notorious figure reappears; in "Lokis" a bride's mutilated body is discovered the day after her wedding.

The three tales can be mapped on Tzvetan Todorov's tripartite division of the spectrum of the fantastic. The king's vision, duly recorded in a document, remains inexplicable, and the tale closes by outlining the fulfillment in 1792 of a prophecy made a century earlier: this is Todorov's *merveilleux* ("supernatural," usually translated as "marvellous"; 25). In "Il Viccolo di Madama Lucrezia" the mysterious events are explained as a case of mistaken identity (Todorov's *étrange* or "uncanny").[1] And in the purely fantastic "Lokis," the reader is left with an unresolved alternative between an unconvincing rational explanation and one that is biologically impossible: that the groom's "father" was a bear. As Todorov argues, since the fantastic is based on a particular perception of a strange event, the characterization of its witness is crucial

(83). In all three of these works the main witness is clearly distinct from Mérimée the author and crucial to the effect produced.

"The Vision of Charles XI" appeared shortly after the first French translations of works by E. T. A. Hoffmann (1828), the catalyst author who combined the popularity of the gothic novel with a reaction against the post-Enlightenment dominance of reason, triggering the French fashion for the fantastic. The work's title and its epigraph from *Hamlet* ("There are more things in heav'n and earth, Horatio . . .") announce the inexplicable events that are to follow, in which a late seventeenth-century Swedish king witnesses a vision that foretells the fate of his dynasty. A modern narrator introduces the tale not as a fiction but as an occurrence recorded in a document: he is thus external to the situation and events to be narrated. In the terms of Gérard Genette, he is a heterodiegetic narrator (245). Although external to the story's events, the narrator is able to comment on them: he notes that the report of the prediction is "duly drawn up" (Mérimée, *Ille* 47) and that its existence was known before its accomplishment; additionally, his summary of the historical significance of Charles XI shows he is well informed. So we trust him as a journalist or historian reporting on an authentic document; this in turn is the source of the account the narrator gives of the vision of the king (characterized by the narrator as devoid of imagination); the report is further corroborated by three other witnesses.

But the unsettling effect of the tale comes not simply from the fact that the record of the vision is said to be authentic, nor from its subsequent fulfillment. In fact the "report" is spurious. Documents recording such a vision first circulated in the mid-eighteenth century, when it was said to have occurred either in December 1676 or April 1697; Mérimée's source was the translation of an article by E. M. Arndt published pseudonymously in a German periodical in 1810, which included a more recent version of the "document," which was in fact a forgery circulated to influence opinion over the succession to the Swedish throne (Wilpert 183–5). The effect is created in large part by Mérimée's literary reworking of his material. He changes the emphasis of his source (which simply transcribes the king's account of the vision) to create an equal emphasis on the vision and its four witnesses, creating a human event full of tension, doubt, and anxiety. His main witness is the king, inflexible but unsettled by the recent death of his wife; the three other witnesses provide differing responses: the chamberlain, a figure of authority, is concerned for the king's physical safety; the doctor, a skeptic, is rational but reluctant to remain alone; the practical concierge is surprised, baffled, and then superstitiously fearful. Such conflicting responses provide fertile ground for the hesitation necessary to the genre of the fantastic.

The initial scene-setting evokes a domestic interior: on an autumn evening, the king sits before a fire in dressing-gown and slippers, chamberlain and doctor in attendance. The banal becomes unsettling: the king is reluctant to be alone "without knowing why" (*Ille* 48), and things occur that seem "strange" (49) to the witnesses: the king sees a light through a window, and then the chamberlain sees it as well. Successive attempts to explain the event are dismissed: the light could be a servant's torch—but why is he there? Or it could be a fire—but there is no smoke. Black hangings could have been ordered to hide the light—but were not.

As the four witnesses progress around the horseshoe-shaped palace from the king's private apartment to the assembly hall, the king is driven forward by curiosity and determination. He takes the initiative by seizing the key to the hall himself, challenging the apparition, but this is accompanied by fear: "his expression revealed a sort of superstitious fear" (49). Tension is heightened as the doctor's candle blows out; the characters' emotions have escalated from curiosity and vague apprehension to the chamberlain's fear of hell and the king's invocation of God's help (62). Until this moment, events, though odd, could be explained (albeit with increasing difficulty) in rational terms, providing the "loophole," "so narrow as not to be quite practicable," that M. R. James saw as desirable in a fantastic tale (359). When the door is opened, however, ambiguity is dispelled. From the king's apartment and the gallery there is an abrupt transition to a scene totally different in scale: the great hall, the "innumerable" torches, the "immense assembly," all dressed in black (*Ille* 51), and a tableau of a royal corpse on the throne, as well as a crowned child, an older figure, and judges. This static confrontation of vision and witnesses frozen in their tracks gives way in the following paragraph to action (the execution of a young noble). This prompts the king to challenge the older figure: the latter utters his solemn prophecy, and the vision abruptly disappears. The vision is now undeniably supernatural for the narrator: the older figure is a "phantom" (52), the torches "ghostly" (53) ("fantastiques" in the original French). The vision's authenticity is confirmed by the witnesses but also by one small but undeniable physical detail—a characteristic feature of the inexplicable fantastic (Whitehead 118) in that it cannot be dismissed as a dream or a hallucination—the bloodstain left on the king's slipper. An everyday object in the initial scene-setting thus authenticates the supernatural vision.

In the main body of the story, the narrator has effaced himself to present the characters' actions, perceptions, and emotions. In the concise conclusion he reverts to his initial role as journalist/historian, summarizing subsequent events: the drawing-up of the written account of the vision, its suppression, a brief quotation as further authentification, and an outline of the prophecy's fulfillment. The changing role of the narrator, shifting from presence to self-effacement to reappearance, the balancing of witnesses and their responses against the vision, the pacing of the narrative as it progresses from domesticity to horror, are thus crucial in persuading the reader of the vision's authenticity. Its unsettling quality lies not simply in the intrusion of the inexplicable into everyday reality, but in the general implications of such a prophecy and its fulfillment. These implications call into question the autonomy of the individual: we are confronted with a world in which the future is already decided, in which the individual (even a king) is helpless to change fate. Mérimée challenges the notion of human free will and responsibility; this questioning is also present, in different forms, in the other two stories to be discussed.

"Il Viccolo di Madama Lucrezia" represents a more extended, more playful use of the fantastic. The opening paragraph again implies a specific narrator: here a character who participates in the situations and events recounted (homodiegetic) and is apparently the main one (what Genette would label autodiegetic; 245), giving a retrospective account of his stay in Rome at the age of twenty-three. There are hints of some amorous secret in the past: of the dozen letters of recommendation the narrator's father has given him, one, addressed to the Marchesa Aldobrandi, is sealed; his father mentions her beauty, and she seems linked to a portrait of a Bacchante (a female votary of the Roman god of wine) in his study.

In Rome the narrator's first visit is to the Marchesa (who owns a portrait of Lucrezia Borgia in the costume portrayed in his father's miniature); she introduces him to her younger son Don Ottavio, destined for the priesthood. The narrator's stay in Rome consists of sightseeing with Ottavio (who is covertly scornful of priests and preoccupied with liberal politics) and Abbé Negroni (a constant companion of the now devout Marchesa), evenings at the Aldobrandi palace, and visits to a French painter he knows. Storytelling is selective: here the narrator omits many details (sightseeing, cuisine); the reader assumes that the occurrences that he does record (encounters, conversations) will offer some coherence and point, but although they seem interconnected, they offer no immediate explanation.

One series of occurrences builds up a sense of disquiet, as if the narrator is being singled out by someone or something. The first occurs after a storytelling evening at the palace involving a friend of the Marchesa and Negroni. The narrator, returning to his lodgings alone, unsettled by their Hoffmannesque tales (Decottignies 592–6), is thrown a rose by a woman in white at a window in a deserted street; she disappears. His initial self-flattering explanation—that he has attracted her attentions as a Frenchman—is undercut when he finds, the next day, that the alley is named (like the portrait) after "Madama Lucrezia"; the old woman who holds the key to the empty house tells how the murderous Lucrezia Borgia used it for her amorous assignations. The painter jokingly formulates possible explanations for events, posing an alternative between the supernatural (Lucrezia's ghost resuming her past activities) and the flippantly realistic (the old woman is letting the house for prostitution)—alternatives that leave the narrator, like the reader, dissatisfied. Subsequent detours down the alley yield nothing apart from a woman's laugh once heard coming from the house. Events then take a more dramatic turn. As the narrator leaves the Marchesa's, he is passed a note from "your Lucrezia" warning him not to come that night; a shot is fired from the window when he nevertheless returns to the alley.

The narrator cannot doubt that these events are occurring: petals (in the street, inside the house) provide physical confirmation in the same way that the slipper did in the "Vision." The only imprecision surrounds the figures seen at the window in the night: the narrator only glimpses a woman in white, he only "thought he saw" (*Ille* 201) a figure silhouetted against the room behind. The narrator is driven toward the supernatural (linking the woman in white and Lucrezia Borgia) as the only possible explanation.

Narrator and reader thus slide into increasingly unnerving events; then, just when the narrator prepares to leave Rome (accompanied by Ottavio, who is seeking to flee the priesthood), Mérimée introduces the climax. The narrator resists a final temptation to his curiosity (a knotted rope hanging from the window) and returns to his lodgings to be told that "Madama Lucrezia" is waiting in his room. Conventional elements again increase the narrator's "superstitious terror and curiosity" (206) (the combination of the desire to know and fear of what he could discover echoes the contradictory impulses generated by the two figures glimpsed at the window, and also the king's emotions as he enters the hall in the "Vision"): the servant's candle blows out, a literary horror tale (from Lewis's *The Monk*) comes to his mind, and the narrator enters his room unaccompanied. A veiled woman dressed in white greets him as her "beloved" (207), and a cold hand seizes his, echoing the fate of Don Giovanni in Wolfgang Amadeus Mozart's opera, dragged down to hell by the icy hand of the statue of the commander he had killed in the opening scene. Then the extraordinary abruptly becomes commonplace: the woman realizes that the narrator is merely Ottavio's friend, and the narrator realizes that she is Ottavio's pregnant mistress who is trying to escape Rome, and that he has been mistaken for Ottavio by both Ottavio's friends and his enemies.

One sequence of events in the course of the tale arouses disquiet, intensified by coincidental factors that seem so clichéd that the reader is not sure how seriously to take them: the old woman has (like a witch) both black cat and cauldron, and a procession carrying a body to burial interrupts him as he lingers by the window. A second series of occurrences, overlooked by the narrator, at the same time points to possible explanations. One set of such clues prepares the solution (hinted at but never explicitly stated)—that Ottavio is the narrator's half brother, a result of his father's affair with the Marchesa. Resemblances can point to a truth: those between the woman in his father's miniature and the Marchesa, and between the costumes in the miniature and the Marchesa's picture, indicate that the miniature depicts the Marchesa when young; the Marchesa sees that the narrator resembles his father when young, and urges him to see her as his mother (she knows that he and her son share a father).

But such "clues" are ambiguous. In the course of the narrative identities are not recognized: the old woman tells how Lucrezia Borgia fatally failed to recognize her brother at night, and she quotes the proverb: "In the dark all cats look grey" (197). Fortuitous resemblances can mislead. It is coincidence that Ottavio's mistress has the same name as the alley; coincidence that the subject of the Marchesa's picture is Lucrezia Borgia and that both she (supposedly) and Ottavio and his mistress used the house for their assignations. The narrator makes fun of the old woman's garbled tale of "Madama Lucrezia" (which confuses Lucrezia Borgia, lover of her brother Cesare, with Lucretia, the noblewoman raped by the Roman ruler's son Sextus Tarquinius), but he creates a similarly garbled tale, based on coincidence of names, to account for what is happening to him.

What is crucial in the tale is the distinction often noted in autodiegetic story-telling between "narrator" and "hero" (Genette 252), between the older narrating self who is now in full possession of the facts, and the younger experiencing self who is still encountering events. In the "Vision," the journalist/historian writing in 1829 is potentially omniscient (he knows the thoughts of all the characters as well as the subsequent course of history) but restricts himself in the main narrative to what the characters then knew, felt and experienced, to maintain suspense and uncertainty. In "Viccolo," the narrator and the protagonist are one, but although the narration is retrospective, focalization (the narrator's point of view) is restricted to his perceptions as events occurred. But if we witness and attempt to interpret events through the eyes of his younger self, there are a series of pointers from the narrating self, aware now both of the facts and of the inexperience of his younger self. What we read initially as amused condescension toward this younger self in fact points to why he misinterpreted things. He distances himself from his earlier complacent assumptions: "at that time I was very much a Frenchman" (*Ille* 193).

Mérimée is not so much deceiving the reader as (deliberately) misleading him, just as the younger narrator (together with those who took him for Ottavio) was (accidentally) misled. In misleading, no lie is told; the misled person participates in the error. The narrator is misled by resemblances and coincidences because of his self-centeredness; the reader is misled because of his expectations of fiction—here that the protagonist will be the central figure, and that key events will relate to him. The narrator's blindness is a product of his vanity. Confident of his understanding of "the ways of this world" (185), he deduces a liaison between his father and the Marchesa, but not its consequences; when the flower is thrown at him, he ascribes this to the attractiveness of Frenchmen to foreign women; Ottavio, he judges, is "too much taken up with politics to give any useful advice in a love affair" (198).[2] A Parisian, he is condescending toward foreigners and provincials: Ottavio's political attitudes remind him of "one of our liberals from the provinces" (189). But he is in another country and loses his bearings. Impatience and incaution lead him into error and discomfiture: proud of his fashionable gloves, he tears one opening the padlock of the deserted house; hearing that "Madama Lucrezia" is waiting in his room, he goes straight there without reading the long (and probably explanatory) letter that Ottavio has left him.

This misleading of narrator and reader is not inappropriate in a story of deception and secrets. With hindsight we realize the hidden secrets on which the story hinges: the narrator's father hides from his son his affair with the Marchesa; the Marchesa hides from Ottavio and the narrator their relationship (she hopes they will become friends "as you ought to" [187]). The true nature of things is concealed in the course of the story. It opens with a sealed letter; the now pious Marchesa conceals her flighty youth; Ottavio hides from Negroni his political ideas by conversing with the narrator in French, and he receives foreign newspapers from him concealed in religious books; Ottavio and Lucrezia plan to leave Rome in disguise (as the narrator's servant and his *amica*).

The reader is led into two readings of the story: we first accept the perceptions of the young narrator, share his curiosity, then bafflement, then apprehensions; subsequently we see the significance of the clues we had overlooked and of the pointers to the smug vanity of his younger self. The suspense of an initial reading is replaced by the pleasure of seeing how the trick was played; we can now integrate all the elements of the tale to form a very different jigsaw than the one that the narrator anticipated.

"Viccolo," like the "Vision," shows an escalation of emotional tension: the latter moves from a domestic interior to a shocking vision; "Viccolo" moves from the young narrator's flippancy and hedonism to a moment of terror. But again the story is concluded abruptly after the shock revelation. An intervention by the narrator ("To tell you the truth . . ." [208]) and a summary of the consequences round the story off with a briskness and neatness (including the convenient death of Ottavio's older brother) that seem perfunctory. It has been suggested that this reduces the story to the level of a "comedy of errors" (Chabot 231) with no serious point, "a bare-faced hoax" written simply for "the unworthy pleasure of hoodwinking us" (Raitt 196). In general it has been plausibly argued that to explain fantastic experiences in terms of the psychology of the individual narrator (here, his juvenile self-centeredness) removes any general challenge to commonly accepted assumptions that these experiences had posed (Düring 174). But in "Viccolo" the narrator's error does raise two related wider issues. On one level it points to how easily we can deceive ourselves, especially in a disorienting environment. More importantly, the initial events experienced by the narrator provoke positive, then negative emotions because they suggest that he is being singled out—enticed by a woman, targeted by a man. He finally realizes that he has been mistaken for someone else (someone he had treated with a certain disdain), that he is not the center of events but peripheral: "the role of confidant was the only one entrusted to me in this adventure" (*Ille* 207). Albeit on a humorous level, the story poses a challenge to the individual's perception of himself: the narrator (he is young) thinks himself the center, not just of his world, but of the world; he discovers that he is part of a larger web of relationships than he realized, and no longer the organizing consciousness in his own world.

The two introductory paragraphs of "Lokis," like those of the "Vision," establish a frame for the presentation of past events; but here the frame introduces a character, Professor Wittembach, who proceeds to read, or improvise from notes (Bellemin-Noël 163), to a small group his account of events he witnessed in 1866. His trustworthiness as a narrator is established: he is a protestant minister traveling to Lithuania for linguistic research to translate the Gospel of St. Matthew into the Jmoude dialect,[3] and thus someone with whom we can identify as a civilized (Prussian) traveler to an alien world; but Wittembach is also eccentric and obsessive: he has postponed his marriage for linguistic research, and his preoccupations—a "lively" (*Ille* 153) dinner conversation turns on comparative linguistics—could lead him (as in "Viccolo") to overlook things that the attentive reader might note. The core of his narrative is his stay with Count Szémioth, owner of a rare catechism and a collection of Jmoude folk poetry.

Again the leisurely but selective account is composed of a series of incidents, narrated from the point of view of the experiencing witness/narrator in which interlocking themes and motifs gradually build up. Wittembach's ten or so days of research in Szémioth's library (of which he says little) is punctuated by meal-time conversations with the count and Dr. Froeber, who is caring for the count's disturbed mother. His research is also interrupted by an excursion to an ancient tumulus in the forest and by two visits to Dowghielly, the residence of Ioulka, a young noblewoman the professor had met earlier in Wilno (Vilnius) and her aunt. Wittembach is later invited back to the chateau to celebrate the marriage of Szémioth and Ioulka, and in the final chapter his account of the wedding is followed by the horrific climax when Ioulka is discovered the next morning with her throat torn open; Szémioth has vanished.

Wittembach is warned before his visit that Szémioth is "somewhat eccentric" (127), and a series of pointers reinforce this: his physique (hairy arms, eyes that are too close together) seems at odds with his courteous manners; he suffers from migraines (etymologically "half cranium," suggesting a divided self), which become worse when he visits Ioulka; he spies on the professor from a tree outside his window before their first meeting; most animals fear him, but a she-bear acts protectively toward him; he talks in his sleep as if obsessed with Ioulka's white skin and blood, after the professor has told of being forced by thirst to drink horse's blood in Uruguay like the locals.

The anecdotal conversations between Wittembach, the count, and the doctor raise inconclusively a series of issues. As in "Viccolo," the narrator is selective. On the principle of narrative economy seen in that story, the reader assumes that there is a key that will integrate the disparate elements (the signs of the count's oddness, the discussions between the characters) to the two violent but unexplained events that open and close the narrative: the doctor's account, on Wittembach's first night, of how, shortly after the marriage of the count's father, a bear carried off his young bride during a hunt, and of the countess's subsequent madness, exacerbated by the birth of her son; and the death of Ioulka after her marriage. The three voices offer contrasting views of mankind. The doctor and Wittembach are both reassuring, according to their respective professions: Froeber, a crude materialist for whom humans can be seen as a "mechanism" (134), sees the count's migraines as the result of sexual abstinence, and inexplicable impulses as caused by a rush of blood to the head. Wittembach, a minister, stresses the ability of the rational mind to resist temptation. Szémioth, however, is troubled by the "duality" in mankind (159), the tension between his duties and responsibilities, and irrational impulses that can be suicidal and homicidal, strikingly close, as Castex notes (274), to Edgar Allan Poe's idea of the "Imp of the Perverse" (exemplified in "The Black Cat"), a "primitive impulse," the "perverseness . . . through [whose] promptings we act, for the reason that we should *not*" (Poe 1: 476, 2: 191; Mücke 99–102.).

The reader, who is unlikely to question the veracity of Wittembach's account,[4] is left, as in the early stages of the "Vision" and "Viccolo," with an unsatisfactory alternative, here never articulated by any of the characters. A rational explanation is possible but difficult to fill in: an intrusion by an animal (a bear?), killing Ioulka and abducting the count—but leaving no trace? An inexplicable madness of the count, fleeing after murdering his bride—but with a bite? Such rational explanations provide M. R. James's "loophole" but fail to account for many of the components of the narrative, leaving it as a random series of incidents with little meaning. The other explanation is unacceptable in terms of the world the reader has been placed in (here biologically impossible rather than supernatural): that the bear that carried off

Szémioth's mother impregnated her, and that the count has reverted to his "bestial" nature. This explanation both integrates all the incidents and is implied in the linguistic exposition in Wittembach's final paragraph: in Lithuanian, "Michael" or "Miszka"[5] (the count's first name) commonly replaces the generic name for bear, *lokis*, just as in French the name of one fox in the medieval *Roman de Renart* (as *renard*) supplanted the generic name of Latin origin, *goupil*. Mérimée in his correspondence implies that this is the "true" answer, but the effectiveness of the story comes from the issue being left open (*Correspondance* 223; *Théâtre* 1625). As in "The Venus of Ille" (1837), Mérimée's other story of the unresolved fantastic, the only person who knows what happened is now mad.

Although it could be seen as a variant on the theme of the werewolf (transformation of human into animal) or the minotaur (human/animal offspring), "Lokis" is clearly a pessimistic reversal of the fable of Beauty and the Beast (where love overcomes fears of "bestial" male sexuality and transforms the Beast into a handsome man) (MacKenzie 196). Nevertheless its point remains elusive. Indeed, too precise an interpretation risks making it a straightforward allegory, which, for Todorov, would disqualify it as fantastic (62–74). Sexuality is clearly linked to violence, but is the "bearishness" of Szémioth an individual aberration, or is his ursine paternity a cover for something common to all men? After all, the discussions throughout the tale are phrased in general terms: the count talks of the duality of "our nature" (*Ille* 159). Is Ioulka's power of sexual attraction dangerous (MacKenzie 203)? Is her "civilized" side (her vanity, her flirtatiousness, the tricks she plays on men) inappropriate in this primitive world, and responsible for unleashing something in the count? As the doctor warns, she is "a real flirt, and will drive him off his head" (*Ille* 130).

A recurrent theme of the tale is the survival, alongside the cosmopolitan and civilized (Wittembach's learning, the count's manners, Ioulka's fashionable dress), of the primal: Jmoude is said to be closely related to Sanskrit, the oldest of the known Indo-European languages;

the tumulus visited by Wittembach was the site of primitive rituals, perhaps human sacrifice; within the forest, in which live species long extinct elsewhere, lies the *matecznik*, the "womb" that, in local tradition, is the origin of life and where animals live together; Ioulka performs a prettified version of a traditional dance, the *russalka*, in which a water nymph carries a man to his death beneath the waters. To see the survival of the primitive and the primal as central to the possible meanings of "Lokis" situates it in a nineteenth-century context, whether one sees this in terms of an awareness of the unconscious (MacKenzie relates it to Schelling and Schopenhauer [196]), attributes to it a Darwinian sense of man's animal origins, or links it to the "erosion of ideas of psychic unity" in the nineteenth century (Jackson 86).

Roger Caillois has argued that the fantastic is "a game with fear" ("un jeu avec la peur" [26]); we know we are in the world, not only of literature, but literature of a certain genre whose conventions we know, just as Mérimée know his "recipe," and that offers a certain escapist pleasure (Castex 398). Mérimée knows that literature, unlike the history to which he devoted much of his efforts in later life (Raitt 197), is an amusement, a process of deceit knowingly entered into by the reader. His stories play tricks on the reader. The narrative perspective of "Viccolo" misleads the reader just as the young narrator was misled. Mérimée plays with ambiguous words in "Viccolo," where apparently innocent expressions seem to point to the supernatural: the narrator refers to "that accursed house" (*Ille* 199), the old woman attributes the difficulty of opening the padlock to "more devilry" (195). In "Lokis," Ioulka accuses the count's hug of crushing her "like the bear that he was" (152). Mérimée is teasing the reader, used (especially in fantastic fiction) to finding a possible hidden meaning in a set phrase, a figurative expression being realized literally (Todorov 79). He plays with ambiguous objects that both tempt the reader to interpret them as sexual symbols but at the same time seem too obvious to be taken seriously: the key that will not turn the lock in "Viccolo" (Chabot 246); the forest that protects the "womb" of nature guarded by a slimy swamp (MacKenzie

204). Mérimée plays with local color, using it to create the illusion of reality, to highlight the otherness of his worlds, but he makes fun of its proliferation in "Lokis": Szémioth jokes at the "local colour" offered by a snake-charmer at the foot of a *kapas* in the presence of a German professor and a Lithuanian nobleman (*Ille* 146), and the story contains elements that Mérimée had lifted from non-Lithuanian sources (the *russalka* is Russian and the subject of a poem by Pushkin) or invented (there is no *russalka* "dance"). Mérimée began his literary career with a supposed translation of a nonexistent Spanish dramatist (*The Plays of Clara Gazul*, 1825) and translations of largely invented Illyrian folk poetry (*The Guzla*, 1827), and the tales abound in deliberate deceptions of various types: the "Vision" presents as authentic a reworked version of a forged document; "Lokis" abounds in deceptions by Ioulka, who passes off her translation of a ballad by the Polish author Miçkiewicz as an authentic *daïna* in Jmoude, dances the *russalka* that lures men to their deaths, and plays a humiliating prank on the male guests after dinner that leads them into putting, blindfolded, an index finger into "something cold and sticky" (154), which turned out to be a pot of honey (both the link with bears and the sexual symbolism are obvious). These two instances show that deception is not innocent fun (Carpenter 34); playful ambiguity can also disorient and increase the reader's uncertainty. "Lokis" is carefully constructed to frustrate the reader seeking a satisfactory solution, like Mérimée's earlier story "The Venus of Ille," with which it shares a scholarly narrator from outside the region and a parallel climax: the murder of a spouse on his or her wedding night.

For Mérimée the move to the fantastic is gradual and insidious, leading up to a moment of shock. Fantastic stories frequently show a preoccupation with means of vision or indirect vision that defamiliarizes the known world: mirrors, reflections, portraits (Jackson 43), and it is windows in all three stories that provide at nighttime, when darkness sustains uncertainty, the first glimpse into a strange world, raising questions for the characters about what they are seeing: the lit windows in "Vision" (seen through the king's window), the window at which the two figures appear in "Viccolo," the bedroom windows through which Wittembach sees Szémioth for the first and last times: the first time his impression is of an animal, the second of a man. Which is "true"?

At the same time the world of the fantastic stories remains that of Mérimée's realistic fiction, showing the same view of humanity as "constantly shaken by feelings and appetites which it cannot control and which defy rational analysis" (Raitt 130). Just as much as the Saint Bartholomew's Day Massacre in *Chronicle of the Reign of Charles IX* or the unpredictable passion of the heroine and Don José's inner violence in *Carmen*, the contrast between rational present and the archaic and primitive points to the fragility of civilization, the threat of the irrational, of violence (most clearly associated with sexuality in "Lokis"), the survival of the primitive on the margins of modern civilization. Jackson has noted how fantastic works "subvert and interrogate nominal unities of time, space and character" (175). The experience of reading is destabilizing: Mérimée breaks down reassuring distinctions between past and present, man and animal. A powerful autocrat sees human autonomy called into question as the future is revealed to him; a smug young traveler learns that the confident individual may not be at the center of things; the linguistic and anthropological order that the German professor seeks to impose on the world is disrupted by primitive violence.

Notes

1. The English translation as "uncanny" is unfortunate, borrowing a term from the translation of Freud's *unheimlich*, where Freud discusses a story that is in Todorov's terms fantastic: see, for example, Cornwell 37.
2. On this blindness, see Mortimer 90–91.
3. Mérimée's transliteration of *Żmudź*, the Polish term for the dialect (Jasenas 157).
4. Siebers's argument that Wittembach's frustrated desire could have led him to murder Ioulka and imply Szémioth's guilt (92) seems implausible.
5. In Lithuanian, "Meška" (Jasenas 161).

Works Cited

Bellemin-Noël, Jean. *Vers l'inconscient du texte*. Paris: P. U. F., 1979.

Caillois, Roger. «De la féerie à la science-fiction (l'image fantastique).» *Images, images: Essais sur le rôle et les pouvoirs de l'imagination*. Paris: Corti, 1966.

Carpenter, Scott. *Aesthetics of Fraudulence in Nineteenth-Century France: Frauds, Hoaxes and Counterfeits*. Farnham, Eng.: Ashgate, 2009.

Castex, Pierre-Georges. *Le conte fantastique en France de Nodier à Maupassant*. Paris: Corti, 1951.

Chabot, Jacques. *L'Autre Moi: Fantasmes et fantastique dans les nouvelles de Mérimée*. Aix-en-Provence, Fr.: Edisud, 1983.

Cornwell, Neil. *The Literary Fantastic: From Gothic to Postmodernism*. London: Harvester Wheatsheaf, 1990.

Decottignies, Jean. "Il Viccolo di Madama Lucrezia. L'élaboration d'une nouvelle de Mérimée.» *Revue d'Histoire Littéraire de la France* 64 (1964): 589–604.

Düring, Ulrich. «À la recherche de la raison perdue: la critique et la littérature fantastique.» *Œuvres et critiques* 9 (1984): 167–84.

Jackson, Rosemary. *Fantasy: The Literature of Subversion*. New York: Methuen, 1981.

Genette, Gérard. *Narrative Discourse*. Trans. Jane E. Lewin. Oxford, Eng.: Blackwell, 1987.

James, M. R. *Casting the Runes and Other Ghost Stories*. Oxford, Eng.: Oxford UP, 1987.

Jasenas, Eliane. "Prosper Mérimée and Lithuania." *Journal of Baltic Studies*, 8.2 (1977): 150–61.

MacKenzie, Robin. "Space, Self and the Role of the Matecznik in Mérimée's *Lokis*." *Forum for Modern Language Studies* 36.2 (2000): 196–208.

Mérimée, Prosper. *Correspondance générale*. Ed. Maurice Parturier. Vol. 14. Toulouse: Privat, 1961.

_____. «La littérature en Russie.» *Revue des Deux Mondes* 15 Nov. 1851.

_____. *The Venus of Ille and Other Stories*. Trans. Jean Kimber, London: Oxford UP, 1966.

_____. *Théâtre de Clara Gazul: Romans et nouvelles*. Ed. Jean Mallion and Pierre Salomon. Paris: Gallimard, 1978.

Mortimer, Armine Kotin. «Mérimée palimpseste dans Il Viccolo di Madama Lucrezia.» *Poétique: Revue de Théorie et d'Analyse Littéraires* 20.77 (1977): 77–92.

Mücke, Dorothea von. *The Seduction of the Occult and the Rise of the Fantastic Tale*. Stanford: Stanford UP, 2003.

Poe, Edgar Allan. *The Complete Poems and Stories of Edgar Allan Poe*. Ed. Arthur Hobson Quinn. New York: Knopf, 1964. 3 vols.

Raitt, A. W. *Prosper Mérimée*. London: Eyre, 1970.

Siebers, Tobin. "Fantastic Lies: Lokis and the Victim of Coincidence." *Kentucky Romance Quarterly* 28.1 (1981): 87–93.

Todorov, Tzvetan. *The Fantastic. A Structural Approach to a Literary Genre*. Ithaca: Cornell UP, 1975.

Vax, Louis. *La Séduction de l'étrange*. Paris, Fr.: P. U. F., 1965.

Whitehead, Claire. *The Fantastic in France and Russia in the Nineteenth Century: In Pursuit of Hesitation*. Oxford, Eng.: Legenda, 2006.

Wilpert, Gero von. «Die Vision Karls XI. bei Arndt, Alexis, Mérimée und Fontane: Ein Plädoyer für etwas mehr Komparatistik.» *Arcadia* 27 (1992) 182–89.

The Pedagogical Fantastic in Edgar Allan Poe and Vladimir Odoevsky

Slobodan Sucur

In studies of the fantastic[1] in literature, it is usually a given that some of Edgar Allan Poe's classic tales of terror will be mentioned. In the broader context of world literature, particularly if Poe is the focus, names such as Dostoevsky, Kafka, and Borges often appear comparatively, but no mention is usually made of Vladimir Odoevsky, Poe's contemporary in Russia in the first half of the nineteenth century and a striking example of literary confluence.[2] Odoevsky was late in discovering Poe, after most of the former's major works in the gothic vein had already been written, while Poe had never known of Odoevsky. Odoevsky eventually preferred to think of his fiction as written in a style closer to Poe's than that of the German romantic writer E. T. A. Hoffmann (Terras 314). These reasons alone already justify a comparative look at Poe and Odoevsky, while the writers' similar use of the fantastic further strengthens the need for such an analysis.

Tzvetan Todorov's sandwiching of the idea of the fantastic between the uncanny and marvelous (41), while an effective starting point for discussion, does not allow for a full grasp of Odoevsky's and Poe's often complicated uses of the fantastic. Claire Whitehead's recent study of the fantastic already points out some of the weaknesses in the Todorovian definition, particularly in relation to Todorov's separation of third-person voice and irony from the realm of the true fantastic (Whitehead 22, 120), but a close look at Poe's only novel, *The Narrative of Arthur Gordon Pym* (1837–38), and a significant novella by Odoevsky, *The Salamander* (1841), will make evident the need for more tinkering with the definition, and categorization, of the fantastic. Poe's and Odoevsky's use of uncanny and occult elements and motifs can be read, in contrast to Todorov's definition, as a legitimate form of the fantastic that emphasizes its pedagogical pleasures (e.g., the discovery of occult knowledge within a gothic text), whereas their selective use of more sensational examples of the fantastic, often alongside romantic irony (a metafictional irony that upsets genre conventions or expectations),[3] is lightened in weight and in this way approximates Todorov's understanding of the marvelous.

Before proceeding to a survey of some of the polemics of literary criticism, as applied to Poe and Odoevsky and to a circumscription of their treatment of the fantastic, brief commentary on the idea of the fantastic is called for. The fantastic, observed generally, takes readers beyond the expected boundaries of literature that deals with the world's functioning according to laws of physics and biology, as exemplified by the realist tradition of later nineteenth-century literature. Because of the nature of the fantastic, it is most often found within genres such as the gothic or science fiction. Foundational definitions of the fantastic that permeate across various genres, such as Todorov's definition (c. 1970), focus on the reader-text relationship in order to determine whether or not a particular work of fiction can be read as fantastic. Todorov defines reader hesitation as being essential to an experience with the fantastic, hesitation both in terms of a reader's own (rational) expectations of a text and in terms of the characters' worlds in such fiction (i.e., whether or not things obey the rules of these worlds as they are presented). At some point, because of the rather psychological experience Todorov sees in the fantastic, readers will identify to an extent with a main character in the text, usually with someone already experiencing hesitation within the narrative (25, 33).

It is not difficult to see how Todorov's definition of the fantastic, because of its emphasis on a text's psychological richness, overlaps with Freud's explanation of the uncanny in a 1919 article of that name. Freud interprets E. T. A. Hoffmann as the "unrivalled master" of the uncanny (386), suggesting that the uncanny is produced through "intellectual uncertainty" and dread of the "castration-complex" (385), reminders of "repetition-compulsion" (391), and effects of "repression" (396). While Freud's emphasis on castration and repression steer his definition of the uncanny in the direction of psychoanalysis (368), the mention of uncertainty as one of the requirements for the uncanny to emerge brings the Freudian definition halfway between Todorov's own understanding of the fantastic and uncanny, thereby creating further confusion in relation to the idea of the fantastic and what it means.

The main evidence for the existence of the Todorovian fantastic in a text is when the reader's hesitation is presented within the text itself, preferably by means of the depiction of a specific character, whom the reader has previously identified with, himself experiencing hesitation in the face of certain events (33). Beyond this, contradictions begin to emerge in Todorov's categorization itself, such as his suggestion that the fantastic is not "an autonomous genre," since it is "located on the frontier" of the marvelous and uncanny (41), even though "the uncanny is not a clearly delimited genre, unlike the fantastic . . ." (46). This contradiction serves as the basis for Todorov's now well-known comment on Poe, that "we do not find the fantastic in Poe's works" but various, uncanny, and sometimes marvelous effects that combine into "an experience of limits" (47–49). Especially ambiguous is Todorov's treatment of the marvelous, an element he sees in some of Poe's works but that is considered as separate from the fantastic, since the marvelous does not "provoke" specific reactions in characters in a text or in readers, it being more an "anthropological" (e.g., fabulous transformations in fairy tales) than psychological phenomenon (53–7).

Owing to such weaknesses in the Todorovian classification of the fantastic, more recent studies have attempted to bridge the gap between certain points in Todorov's system. Whitehead's work, for example, has shifted attention away from Todorov's largely thematic interpretation of hesitation and the reader-text connection and focuses more on the reader's experience (7) of story events that are of course linguistically represented (154). This has allowed Whitehead to argue that Todorov's reader-identification with a narrator is not an objective test of the fantastic's presence, and that comparison between a first-person narrator's personality and the textual "nature of events" will yield more concrete results (48). Greater emphasis on linguistic (syntactical) evidence of the fantastic in a text has also resulted in other possibilities according to Whitehead: that third-person voice does not contaminate the fantastic (22), that a character's madness may contribute to (rather than resolve) supernatural events (78), and that a fourth possible category, of "ironic fantastic" texts (131), may also be read as fantastic if readers are well versed in the "conventions of the fantastic" (121). This last category goes well beyond Todorov's understanding of the fantastic but may allow for more effective readings of Odoevsky's and Poe's works as representative not only of the fantastic in literature but also of late romanticism, a period in which many authors were consciously parodying their own styles and those of other popular texts (e.g., penny dreadfuls).[4]

Limitations in understandings of the fantastic, as well as nuanced ways in which the idea can be approached within fiction, have perhaps best left their mark on the oftentimes polemical literary criticism that defined Poe and Odoevsky scholarship until at least the 1950s. While the body of work on Odoevsky is not nearly as extensive as Poe criticism, the similarities are worth noting. Tension is already seen in Odoevsky scholarship as early as the 1840s when the critic Vissarion Belinsky, to some extent an admirer of Odoevsky's society tales with their didacticism (e.g., "Princess Mimi"), refers to the second part of *The Salamander* as "pseudo-fantastic trash," gives a lukewarm reception to the publication of Odoevsky's collected works in 1844, and prefers to draw attention to Odoevsky's pioneering activities in Russian philosophy in the 1820s (qtd. in Cornwell, *Romantic Poetics* 104). For most of the nineteenth century, Odoevsky criticism separates romantic from realist elements in his work (e.g., Belinsky, Pavel Sakulin) or begins with the premise that nothing is wrong with romanticism anyway (e.g., Ivan Kotliarevsky, Zinaida Gippius). The former attitude would continue well into the Soviet period, with Odoevsky's realist works being praised and his fantastic ones condemned (*Romantic Poetics* 39). More objective attempts to treat what Gippius calls Odoevsky's "pessimistic dualism" (qtd. in *Romantic Poetics* 38) would take place in post-1960 scholarship, with critics devoting more attention to the influence of German romantic philosophy (e.g., Friedrich Schelling)[5] on Odoevsky (E. A. Maimin, qtd. in *Romantic Poetics* 43) and his "progressive" relationship with romanticism (V. Feierkherd, qtd. in *Romantic Poetics* 44). Cornwell implies that the polemics found in Odoevsky criticism are in part a result of the many influences operating in his work, particularly in his more fantastic texts: Schelling's *Naturphilosophie*, Neoplatonism, themes of madness and obsession, the inadequacy of language to express clear thoughts, the idea of inherited memory, Oken's understanding of natural philosophy as a mixture of "empiricism and speculation," the dissolving or broaching of space and time, and romantic irony with its "ironic distance" and self-parody (*Romantic Poetics* 46–53).

Similar critical tensions are also seen in Poe criticism, where they have been voiced more extensively. Poe's reception as an author was at best lukewarm until the publication of his famous poem "The Raven" in January of 1845, followed later that year by the collection *The Raven and Other Poems*. His earlier work in poetry, simply entitled *Poems* (1831), received mixed reviews, while his first attempt at a collection of short stories, *Tales of the Folio Club* (c. 1832), that was to be a frame-tale collection (a popular literary device in the romantic period because of its exotic tribute to such earlier collections as the *Arabian Nights*) was never published. Many of the tales that were to comprise that collection were later published individually, and Poe's next story collection, *Tales of the Grotesque and Arabesque* (1839), did not follow a frame-tale organization. In fact, already by the mid-1830s many of Poe's tales were paradoxically considered either too grotesque (e.g., "Berenice") or too obscure (e.g., his comic tales) by publishers for a middle-class readership, and this may have convinced Poe to experiment with the novel. His only result in that area was *The Narrative of Arthur Gordon Pym*, a work that has generated its own critical industry of polemical debate and at times some rather ingenious interpretations. A survey of *Pym* criticism of the last several decades finds to some extent a reduplication of the same polemics applied to many of Poe's tales until well into the 1940s, namely that the tales are either great exemplars of late romantic aesthetics or works devoid of didactic value.

With *Pym's* replacing of "The Fall of the House of Usher" (1839) as the central text in Poe scholarship by the 1990s, much of the tension of previous criticism has been carried over, creating a situation in which *Pym* is now seen either as Poe's great and successful experiment in the longer narrative form or as a bad novel that hardly lives up to Poe's theory of how a literary work should carry a preconceived and unified effect (c. 1842). Critics such as G. R. Thompson suggest that much of the disagreement found in Poe scholarship, be it in terms of his tales or *Pym,* is the result of German romantic influence (qtd. in Lamb 3), particularly of romantic irony (i.e., structural irony) that, as Cornwell indicates of Odoevsky, allows for an ambiguous type of self-parody to emerge.

Critical tensions evident in both Odoevsky and Poe scholarship, while not always effective at acknowledging the various ways in which the two authors approach the fantastic and its relationship to readers, are in some way products of the multifarious endeavors of Poe and Odoevsky themselves. Odoevsky began his intellectual journey as a student in the early 1820s philosophical circle of Professor S. Raich in Moscow, edited the short-lived philosophical almanac *Mnemozina,* and played a major role in the other important society of the age, *Lovers of Wisdom,* which met secretly in his study and focused on German philosophy (Cornwell, *Life* 7–11). After the failed Decembrist coup of December 26, 1825, Odoevsky entered government service in St. Petersburg and focused more on literature than pure philosophy, this being the period in which his mystical novellas, tales, and frame-tale novel *Russian Nights* (1844) were written. Beyond his philosophical and literary endeavors, Odoevsky is perhaps best known today as a music critic who resurrected interest in J. S. Bach in the romantic period and supported some of Russia's earliest composers (e.g., Mikhail Glinka). Such variety of interest also characterizes Poe's life, which in the 1820s is marked largely by his idealistic wish to be known as a poet more than anything else.

After being expelled for disobedience from West Point in 1831 and to some extent disillusioned with the myth of the Southern gentleman and its corresponding, leisured lifestyle, Poe turned his attention to the slightly more profitable genre of the short story and particularly to literary criticism, with his work for the *Southern Literary Messenger* in Richmond of the mid-1830s already displaying the critical sharpness that would later earn him the label of "Tomahawk man." Poe would continue to juggle roles as critic, editor, short story writer, and poet well into the 1840s, and would finally turn his attention to greater philosophy itself, best represented in his cosmological prose-poem about how the universe was created, *Eureka* (1848). Looked at more broadly, Poe's and Odoevsky's careers read often like mirror images, with Odoevsky transforming from philosopher to litterateur and finally critic, and Poe transforming from poet to critic and finally philosopher.

Turning to Poe's and Odoevsky's applications of the fantastic in two of their central works, what becomes evident is that the promise of pedagogical pleasure (e.g., the pleasure found in learning or discovering something new, perhaps occult information) is fundamental to how their interpretations of the fantastic unfold. In contrast to this, their selective use of a more sensational (pulp) version of the fantastic is often counterbalanced not with the typical Todorovian uncertainty expected in such cases, but with a more cosmic, ironic indecision that deflates such extremes in their works, thereby rendering those episodes knowable and graspable.

Poe's *Narrative of Arthur Gordon Pym,* a nautical-exploratory novel that takes the first-person narrator Pym on a strange journey into the South Polar regions (and that inspired later works in the exploratory sub-genre such as Melville's *Moby-Dick*), presents a scene late in Chapter 7, wherein Pym masquerades as a recently deceased crew member, Hartman Rogers, in order to attempt to take control of a whaling ship from a piratical clique that has been organized by several mutineers. Pym first gives a lengthy description of the loathsomeness of the corpse and of its "chalky whiteness" (Poe 62) against the backdrop of a raging storm, with the body "floundering about" through the rolling of the ship. The body is then stripped of its clothing, thrown overboard, and Pym's impersonation of Rogers's corpse proves to be a faithful reproduction of its "horrible deformity" once he sees his reflection in a mirror, the impression being one of "vague awe" (63). Pym's reasoning behind this impersonation is that the chief mate (and leader of the piratical clique) had poisoned Rogers and that the horror of such revivification will work on the mate's "guilty conscience" (61), buying Pym and company much-needed time, a factor often either literally lacking in the narrative or treated in disorienting terms in the narrative (Weinstein 82, 88).[6]

The masquerade is successful, with Pym descending into the mate's cabin on the signal of his companion Dirk Peters and paralyzing the mutineers with fear long enough that they are eventually overpowered. The episode is significant because, alongside the increasing storm, the superstitions the sailors have been discussing previously in the cabin (Poe 66), and the hesitation the mutineers experience briefly while witnessing Pym's impersonation of Rogers, it becomes a perfect example of the sensational fantastic typical of horror. The episode recycles various gothic clichés, appearing fantastic to the mutineers but looking somewhat contrived and cheap to readers. The fact that the chief mate is first to drop dead from fright, not uttering a syllable and being rolled "like a log" to a corner of the cabin by the lurching ship (67), undercuts the psychological tension of what would otherwise be a seriously fantastic moment (since it makes the mutineers hesitate) and an example of the Burkean sublime.[7] The chief mate's rolling back and forth doubles Rogers's bloated "floundering" above deck, this duplication being made possible through Pym's mannequin-like impersonation of the corpse and Peters's somewhat odd comment to the mate before Pym arrives: that it might be better to throw Rogers overboard, since he is "floundering about in the scuppers" (66). The real Rogers's corpse is already absent by this point, since Pym and company dumped it overboard earlier (63), and the episode thus acquires a chronological clumsiness that ironically begins to draw more attention to its practical aspects (i.e., that it required that someone dress up as the deceased Rogers) than to its fantastic possibilities and the psychological hesitancy that the mutineers, however briefly, experienced. Earlier, the fact that Pym is below deck when Rogers dies but somehow manages to see the body "a few minutes after death" (62) already "raises serious questions . . ." about the whole spectacle (Kennedy 169). In other words, the improbability that Pym saw the corpse soon after Rogers's death, and Peters's inaccurate suggestion to the chief mate that they throw the body overboard (even though it has already been thrown away), frame this entire episode within questionable circumstances that undercut its success as an example of the fantastic, wherein the mutineers were psychologically paralyzed and then disarmed.

In contrast to the fantastic sensationalism of the Hartman Rogers episode that, when stripped of its psychological tension, reads more like the unemotional transformations (e.g., Pym-as-corpse) of the Todorovian marvelous (with its whimsicality), Pym's encounter with islanders near the South Pole and the novel's abrupt ending signal the emergence of a more abstract mode in which the fantastic is seen to operate. This pedagogical fantastic functions more like Todorov's understanding of the term in that it requires some degree of reader identification with the narrative. Unlike Todorov's classification, however, Poe's metaphysical application of the fantastic operates more so through occult and uncanny channels, tantalizing the audience with the promise of great intellectual discovery, cryptographic deciphering (Rosenheim 59–60), the sharing of occult knowledge, or some broader form of information overload that in turn makes it pedagogically friendly, elevating it beyond a mere fantastic sensationalism.

In the later chapters of the novel, Pym, Peters, and other crew members of the schooner *Jane Guy* land on the inhabited island of Tsalal, a region described as different and possibly dangerous to them, where both rocks and water are "utterly incredible . . ." (Poe 135). A survey of the island's interior takes place, and a primitive trading post in *bêche de mer* (sea cucumbers) is then set up before the islanders orchestrate a man-made cave-in in one of the ravines that leaves Pym and Peters the only survivors of the South Polar expedition (142, 147). Pym and Peters's final investigation on the island, of several strange chasms (160–3), is soon followed by their escape by canoe, together with a hostage, toward the South Pole: a region of flickering vapor and milky ocean interrupted by the emergence of a "shrouded human figure," whereupon the narrative ends (175). The only purely fantastic item in the Tsalalian episode is this human figure that terminates the text, but the general uncanniness of these sections of the novel, such as the search for the missing Aurora islands that precedes discovery of Tsalal (119–20), when coupled with Pym and Peters's exploratory fervor, translates most of the journey into a fantastic endeavor that culminates in contact with this shrouded figure and promises, via a final note added by a fictional editor who is neither Poe nor Pym, the opening of a new phase of "speculation and exciting conjecture" (177–78).

The excitement of being on the brink of something knowable, tactile, larger than the supposedly scientific information that has already been recorded by Pym and retold to his audience, is interwoven into the text through Poe's often unorthodox layering of what on the surface appear to be disjointed fragments of information. It is such disparity that frequently makes no sense to critics beyond being uncanny or odd, but that may hold the promise of metaphysical knowledge and a more delicate, pedagogical fantastic if, as Kotliarevsky suggested of Odoevsky, Poe is read "between the lines" (qtd. in *Romantic Poetics* 36). The variety of interpretations of the shrouded figure alone is enormous. Edward Davidson suggests that Pym has traveled back to the primordial universe, John T. Irwin reads the shrouded figure as Pym's shadow, Walter Bezanson reads it as Pym's return to his archetypal mother via a "cosmic milk bath," Tod Lieber interprets it as the symbol of Pym's overactive imagination, Charles O'Donnell comments that it is merely an illusion, and so on (qtd. in Harvey 13). More broadly, the Tsalal episode has been read as an allegory of slavery in *antebellum* America (Harvey 144) through contrast between the blackness of the island (and its inhabitants) and white items brought by the *Jane Guy* that are considered taboo by the islanders (Poe 157).

Satisfying though such interpretations are, they still do not unlock the pedagogical potential of the later chapters. Pym's singular digression on the trading of sea cucumbers, considered by Chinese custom as having power to replenish "the exhausted system of the immoderate voluptuary" (144), and his comment that the women of the island "were most obliging in every respect" (145) draws attention to a neglected (if not entirely ignored) aspect of the text: namely the coming of age and sexual awakening of an adolescent narrator whose great discovery at first leads to gothic disaster (the orchestrated cave-in on the island) and then to measured, quasiscientific exploration of several chasms that are made up largely of "scoria" (166; volcanic rock) that is "granulated" with "metal" (160, 167). The chasms, being rich with the same metal (vanadium) that constitutes 10 percent of the *bêche de mer*'s blood cell pigment, read as references back to the trading post in aphrodisiacs, several pages after that business was extinguished. The "immense scorpions" (Poe 167; *Eurypterids*) that threaten Pym and Peters with their virility as the two make their final escape, together with the ocean's milky texture and pervading whiteness as they are carried toward the South Pole, only serve to strengthen such a (sexual) reading of the closing chapters.

Most importantly, the promise of still more knowledge is maintained both by the novel's final note and by Pym's hesitation while exploring the chasms. His disagreement with Peters as to how certain indentations that appear on one of the walls should be read (163) indicates not only Pym's uncertainty about the intellectual value of his journey but also leaves readers unsure as to what is being presented as truth (or fiction) by the narrator. This indecision regarding knowledge and its presentation in *Pym,* no matter its nature (e.g., philosophical, temporal,

occult), marks the emergence of the pedagogical fantastic near its dé-
nouement, a subtle form of the fantastic that suggests how intellectual
pursuit, more than the psychological effects found in sensational examples of the fantastic (e.g., Pym's masquerading as a corpse), allows
for certain texts to transcend some of the expectations and limitations
of the gothic genre.

The questionable bi-part structure of Odoevsky's *The Salamander,*
termed by him a "dilogy," suggests, according to Cornwell, a "radical
break" in the work in terms of narration and emphasis (Odoevsky 6).
In this sense it already bears (structural) resemblance to Poe's *Pym,*
wherein the voyage on the *Jane Guy* in the second half mirrors developments on board the whaling ship *Grampus* in the first half of the
novel, and where the question of genre has been applied creatively,
Pym being read as satire, hoax, allegory, mythic quest, tale of terror,
bildungsroman,[8] and so on (Farrell 215). Similar to Poe, Odoevsky
treats the fantastic in two ways in his novella: selectively applying a
more sensational fantastic that is often ironically undercut, and allowing for a more transcendental fantastic to emerge through occult and
mystical patterns that are given emphasis within the narrative. *The Salamander* outlines in the first part, in third-person voice, the journey of
Yakko the Finn from his position as adopted son in a Finnish hut to his
more elaborate role as purveyor of Russian Enlightenment in the St.
Petersburg of Peter the Great. In its second part the novella recounts a
scene in Moscow of the 1830s, wherein it is learned eventually, through
a story the uncle of the first-person narrator tells, that Yakko, falling on
hard times, became involved in alchemy and the occult, finally to disappear mysteriously when his laboratory burned down, although the
conclusion suggests multiple interpretations (Odoevsky 212).

Tying together both halves of the novella is Elsa, grandchild of
the elderly couple that adopted Yakko, and gifted with a second sight
variously described as "falling sickness," "witchcraft," and "for-
tune-telling" (153, 165, 168). It is primarily around Elsa's role that
Odoevsky presents a pulp version of the fantastic typical of gothic fic-

tion. While visiting Yakko in St. Petersburg (in the first half of the novella), Elsa is caught laying a strange packet under the mattress of the protagonist's love interest. Questioned about the incident near a fireplace, she lapses into one of her visions, telling Yakko in cryptic language that she is searching for her "little sister" in the fire and that she now knows and sees "everything" (166). With the rest of the household not knowing how to react to this shocking scene, Yakko replies indecisively that "something strange [is] happening" and sends for a German doctor (167). The doctor's tobacco-chewing presence, rather than countering the previously frightening scene of possession with serious, rational explanation, and thereby maintaining the hesitation expected of the fantastic, reduces the event to a grotesquely comedic exchange when Elsa responds in German to the doctor's questions (having never known the language) and is prescribed opium and plenty of coffee, an ineffectual treatment that not only keeps her bedridden for several days but also induces recitation of Finnish epic songs (168–72).

In the second part of *The Salamander*, the narrator's uncle tells a strange story that may explain supernatural phenomena sometimes taking place in a dwelling he used to visit. The story relates how Yakko, moving to Moscow from St. Petersburg after Peter the Great's death, took up the study of alchemy and set up a laboratory in his house. Collaborating with a mysterious old count,[9] Yakko proceeds to toil through various alchemical distillations, when Elsa once again arrives, first as a salamander-like vision in the flame he keeps watch over, and then as the real Elsa soon after (who has come to visit him, bringing much-needed money). There is a "mysterious connection" between Elsa's vision in the novella's first half and here in the uncle's tale (Cornwell, *Romantic Poetics* 152), particularly so because both moments of the fantastic are undercut by other events. In much the same way as the doctor's arrival reduced the impact of Elsa's earlier vision, her physical return in the second part of the novella, after her double has already appeared in the alchemist's fire, brings a cosmic tension into the text. Yakko is dumbfounded when he sees Elsa materializing in the fire as a "stream of white flame" (Odoevsky 197), as a protector of his alchemical project, and "the Salamander" itself that will reveal great secrets to him (196). During one of the distillations Elsa-as-Salamander, anticipating Lovecraftian mythology,[10] tells Yakko that such experiments may eventually "awaken . . . the supreme ruler over all elements" (199). This double Elsa serves as tutor and helps Yakko discover both a blue dye valuable in the textile industry (200) and the philosopher's purple stone (206). The real Elsa's presence, in contrast, destabilizes the centrality (and depth) of these visions with contamination by everyday problems. Her money drives Yakko's wife further into alcoholism (200), she appears ignorant of her double that appears in the alchemical fire (198), and she proceeds to commit adultery with Yakko (203–4). Yakko's wife's eventual death from spontaneous combustion (attributed to drinking) leaves on her bed "an indescribable black mass" (204) that reads like a moral stain on the household, reducing what initially appeared as a tale of the fantastic to an allegory of neglect and callousness. Ironically, these are qualities, or failings, that the alchemist possesses in abundance, since nothing will "distract" him from his experiments (205). The entire sequence of events, as Whitehead suggests of Gogol's *The Nose* (1836), thereby vulgarizes the supernatural (141).

Odoevsky employs a more subtle form of the fantastic when focusing on Yakko's own development that, while to some extent tied to Elsa's double in the second part of the novella, holds the promise of greater occult discovery and in this sense overlaps with Poe's conclusion to *Pym*. While ironic undercutting of more robust examples of the fantastic in *The Salamander,* as with Elsa, reduces those episodes to something approximating the Todorovian marvelous with its whimsicality and anthropological detachment, or more appropriately the marvelously grotesque (e.g., trance, spontaneous combustion), the changes Yakko undergoes suggest more mystical possibilities. Yakko's transformation in the first part of the novella is from Finnish peasant to civilized representative of Russian Enlightenment. His change of name to Ivan Ivanovich (147) and his new occupation as translator and typographer to the Tsar (149) are not supernatural alterations, but their potential to become a part of fantastic projects within the novella is where their uncanniness is to be found. The first image of this is a juxtaposition of Yakko, now as cultural outsider (Ivan Ivanovich in his "rich German kaftan"), against the Finnish wilderness to which he has returned in order to find Elsa. Soon follows Elsa's trip to St. Petersburg that ends in disaster because of her visions. The conclusion to the first part of the text returns Elsa to her Finnish hut but also has Ivan Ivanovich arrive a second (and final) time to leave a gift of money. This financial gesture will be duplicated toward the end of part two of the novella but is here expanded into a legend that tells of how a wealthy lord wanted to take a girl to St. Petersburg; she instead "ran away from riches out of love for her native hut" (176).

The chronology of events (outsider, journey, return, money) allows for uncanny possibilities that will, in the second part of the novella, connect together to establish the pedagogical fantastic: exemplified through the narrator's journey not only to piece together Yakko's own, esoteric life, but also to suggest the occult way in which knowledge functions in this text. Parallels are already established by this point in the narrative between Ivanovich's new role as translator/typographer (someone who channels information and manipulates type) and what is happening within the (fictional) reality of the text, in this case the "translation" of a rather mechanical clash of cultures into a more organic mythology that swallows historical fact. Ivanovich-as-typographer thus becomes the pragmatic, enlightened counterpart to Yakko-the-alchemist (i.e., the darker metaphysician) of the second part of the novella. Both versions of Ivanovich distill things, be it language or chemical compounds.

Yakko's second transformation, from Ivanovich to the nameless old count he works for as apprentice, is not only sinister but one of the most purely fantastic moments in the text. Wishing to become the count who oppresses him with constant alchemical experiments, he looks into a mirror to see that his "desire" (as Elsa tells him) has been fulfilled;

he has become the old count himself and leaves for his dwelling in the evening, carrying with him the philosopher's stone (209). Several years then pass, filled with carousing and lavishness, and Yakko-as-count prepares to marry a young princess who cannot stand him (210). Yakko's life as the count suggests that the previous uncanniness of his role as translator and legend-maker in the first part of the novella has here been surpassed by mystical knowledge gained from alchemy, a type of knowledge that allows for direct manipulation of reality (words now being supplanted by deeds). Also significant is the fact that, as count, Ivanovich wears a "kaftan" (209) resembling his dress from the conclusion to part one, suggesting the possibility of a more transcendental fantastic: namely, that Ivanovich's return to Finland, with a gift of money for Elsa, was not as Ivanovich but as the old count he has transformed into in part two of the text, the same episode appearing as two moments in time because of the narrative's bi-part structure.

This more overarching fantastic is made possible through the occult significance of Yakko's becoming the count, especially so because Yakko's body now disappears from the narrative. Elsa's visit to the count's chambers, whereupon she reminds him that they should return to Finland, is condescendingly given "a purse filled with gold," and she proceeds literally to burn the house down with a phantasmagorical "guffaw" (211), strengthening the connection between Ivanovich's uncanny presence in Finland at the end of part one and the shape-shifting that has taken place near the novella's conclusion. The Schellingian *Naturphilosophie* that Limon sees operating in Poe's *Pym,* where there is an appropriation of "scientific findings into . . . metaphysical model[s]" (qtd. in Harvey 156), also characterizes Ivanovich's magical transformation into the count in *The Salamander.* Odoevsky's metaphysical use of the fantastic here invites much speculation, especially in that the fantastic may be a vehicle for Schellingian thought that indicts Yakko as the real gothic villain in the text. Schelling's idea that nature is "visible spirit" (qtd. in Harvey 157) is imparted when Ivanovich's human nature breaks through as deformed spirit, via his transformation into the old count. Similarly, Odoevsky's own theory of instinctual balance as being necessary for the maintenance of historical significance and what Walicki terms "social cohesion" (qtd. in Cornwell, *Life* 82) is at the center of his use of the fantastic in this novella; the real story is that Ivanovich, a figure of pure reason near the conclusion to part one, was then just as flawed as during his revelry in pure instinct while being the old count. Both extremes allow for uncanny and occult manifestations and may be a repudiation of "the [same] Newtonian/Cartesian mechanistic model of nature . . ." (Harvey 156) that Poe attempts to overturn in the Tsalal episode in *Pym*.

Surveyed broadly, Poe's and Odoevsky's treatments of the fantastic appear to develop in two directions. A more typical, sensational-fantastic is selectively used to locate texts like *Pym* and *The Salamander* within a particular genre (i.e., the gothic), thereby making these narratives familiar both to readers and the authors themselves since common manifestations of the fantastic are often undercut via a general, structural irony (of plot limitations) akin to romantic irony, generating light parody of genre conventions (e.g., that readers are indeed reading horror and anticipate certain episodes or motifs when they access such texts). By familiarizing the fantastic, the Hartman Rogers episode in *Pym* and Elsa's visions in *The Salamander* suggest that pulp renderings of the supernatural evoke mixed feelings from audiences or leave them apathetically amused, similar to the whimsical effects brought on by the Todorovian marvelous. On the other hand, Poe's and Odoevsky's experimentations with a more subtle, metaphysical fantastic that offers the promise of pedagogical/informational discovery (e.g., occult pathways to knowledge) and the synthesis of contradictions and binaries (e.g., chronological advancement/regression) are seen in the Tsalal episode in *Pym* and through Yakko's transformations in *The Salamander*. Truth be told, these more delicate occurrences of the fantastic are usually described as being no more than occult or uncanny patterns in fiction, and this is one of the reasons why Todorov sees no examples of the fantastic in Poe, but the structural (and narrative) ambiguity found in both texts (e.g., doublings, multiplicities of voice) makes it impossible for readers "to resolve . . . uncertainty" (Whitehead 65).

Tension within the pedagogical fantastic maintains this interpretive indecision as well, since these episodes simultaneously pull in a mystical direction and a "civic, instructional" one that Feierkherd finds characteristic of much of Odoevsky's prose (qtd. in Cornwell, *Romantic Poetics* 44) and that Nemoianu suggests is endemic to the late romantic or *Biedermeier*[11] epoch with its oscillation between "uneasy empiricism" and "organic vitality" (Nemoianu 8). Simply put, it is as if Poe and Odoevsky are, as late romantic writers, uncertain of the applicability of purely fantastic episodes within gothic fiction. They suggest through the pages of *Pym* and *The Salamander* that what would eventually come to be known as the Todorovian fantastic is brief, unsustainable for any duration, and often collapses owing to surrounding plot devices such as irony, characters who contradict one another, and various motifs. Through experimentation with the fantastic, Poe and Odoevsky suggest that it best endures in the metaphysical, often esoteric pathways wherein knowledge circulates in the gothic genre, and it is thus never fully observable. Only through smaller, uncanny manifestations can the fantastic be glimpsed within the worlds that characters inhabit.

Notes

1. Literature that, according to Todorov, makes readers hesitate in terms of rational or supernatural explanations of events; the uncanny is thus closer to the rational realm since it can often be explained in scientific terms, whereas the marvelous is clearly beyond rational explanation; the marvelous however, in contrast to the fantastic, is understood in more emotionally detached, anthropological terms (e.g., physical transformations in fairy tales).

2. A similarity among texts by authors who were not aware of one another's works.

3. A concept proposed by the Schlegel brothers around 1800; it differs from standard irony in that it is more metafictional in implication (e.g., playing with genre conventions).

4. Cheap, mass-produced imitations of more famous gothic novels during the later eighteenth and early nineteenth centuries; other synonyms are "gothic blue-books," "shilling shockers," and "half-penny marvels."

5. Friedrich Schelling's philosophical career spanned several decades during the romantic period and can be subdivided into three general phases: (a) the establishing of connections between nature and the mind *(Naturphilosophie)*; (b) the search into what constitutes identity, free will, and the question of good/evil; (c) and the juxtaposition of questions of free will and identity against the backdrop (and meaning) of history.

6. Particularly significant in Weinstein's reading of *Pym* is that the chronometer stolen from Captain Barnard's person by the chief mate during the mutiny is not mentioned by Poe after the successful countermutiny, suggesting the disappearance of temporal orientation from the text.

7. Edmund Burke's definition of the sublime (c. 1756) is a heavily psychological one, suggesting that an exhilarating emotional experience is best attained if one is in close proximity to danger; such a concept would soon find expression in the gothic fiction of the later eighteenth century.

8. A novel dealing with a character's formative years; also known as a novel of apprenticeship.

9. Most likely inspired by the historical Jacob Bruce, scientist and military leader in the Russia of Peter the Great; also perhaps inspired by the Count of St. Germain, a famous adventurer and alchemist of the eighteenth century.

10. Author H. P. Lovecraft developed a pantheon of ancient, alien gods that he used as a plot device; the pantheon was expanded after his death and renamed the Cthulhu Mythos.

11. Refers to romanticism between the time of the Congress of Vienna in 1815 and the revolutions of 1848; the period is characterized as an ironic, fragmented, morbid, oftentimes comic reduction of grand, synthesizing projects of an earlier generation of romantics.

Works Cited

Cornwell, Neil. *The Life, Times and Milieu of V. F. Odoyevsky: 1804–69*. London: Athlone, 1986.

_____. *Vladimir Odoevsky and Romantic Poetics: Collected Essays*. Providence: Berghahn, 1998.

Farrell, Grace. "Dream Texts: *The Narrative of Arthur Gordon Pym* and *The Journal of Julius Rodman*." *A Companion to Poe Studies*. Ed. Eric W. Carlson. Westport: Greenwood, 1996. 209–35.

Freud, Sigmund. *Sigmund Freud: Collected Papers*. Vol. 4. Ed. Ernest Jones. New York: Basic, 1959.

Harvey, Ronald C. *The Critical History of Edgar Allan Poe's The Narrative of Arthur Gordon Pym: A Dialogue with Unreason*. New York: Garland, 1998.

Kennedy, J. Gerald. "*Pym* Pourri: Decomposing the Textual Body." *Poe's Pym: Critical Explorations*. Ed. Richard Kopley. Durham: Duke UP, 1992.

Lamb, Robert Paul. "Flight of the Raven: A Retrospective on the Scholarship of G. R. Thompson." *Poe Studies/Dark Romanticism: History, Theory, Interpretation* 39–40 (2006–7): 1–16.

Nemoianu, Virgil. *The Taming of Romanticism: European Literature and the Age of Biedermeier*. Cambridge: Harvard UP, 1984.

Odoevsky, V. F. *The Salamander and Other Gothic Tales*. Trans. Neil Cornwell. Evanston: Northwestern UP, 1992.

Poe, Edgar Allan. *The Narrative of Arthur Gordon Pym*. Ed. J. Gerald Kennedy. Oxford: Oxford UP, 1998.

Rosenheim, Shawn James. *The Cryptographic Imagination: Secret Writing from Edgar Poe to the Internet*. Baltimore: Johns Hopkins UP, 1997.

Terras, Victor. "Odóevsky, Prince Vladímir Fyódorovich (1803 or 1804–1869)." *Handbook of Russian Literature*. Ed. Victor Terras. New Haven: Yale UP, 1985. 314.

Todorov, Tzvetan. *The Fantastic: A Structural Approach to a Literary Genre*. Ithaca: Cornell UP, 1975.

Weinstein, Cindy. "When Is Now? Poe's Aesthetics of Temporality." *Poe Studies: History, Theory, Interpretation* 41.1 (2008): 81–107.

Whitehead, Claire. *The Fantastic in France and Russia in the Nineteenth Century: In Pursuit of Hesitation*. London: Legenda, 2006.

Borges and the Fantastic _____

Donald Shaw

It is a commonplace to remind ourselves that in "high" literature of the modern period especially, the function of fantasy has been to tell us something challenging about "reality," in contrast to "pop" writing, whose chief purpose is to entertain and usually to reinforce our comfortable presuppositions. But what might it be telling us? A familiar answer to that question suggests that the fantastic in literature tends to be subversive of established presuppositions and even of ideals and values. That is to say, if we look at some recent books on the topic, what we see is an extension of Todorov's notion of ambiguity as a prominent characteristic of the fantastic in a more negative direction, emphasizing an alleged collapse of certainty about the way things are.

A glance at works by Irène Bessière, Christine Brooke-Rose, Amaryll Chanady, Lucie Armitt, and especially Rosemary Jackson reveals a clear line of development during the 1970s and 1980s that, in relation to Spanish American fiction, has been cogently studied by Jesús Rodero. His conclusion, briefly stated, is that in this particular field, Jackson's postulate of the subversiveness of fantastic literature does not go far enough. We are all familiar with Jean-François Lyotard's famous assertion in *The Postmodern Condition* (1969) that one feature of postmodernism is the loss of confidence in the overarching patterns of belief (religious, rationalistic, or whichever), inherited from the past, on which older worldviews used to be based. Without referring directly to Lyotard, Rodero and other prominent Spanish American critics, including Jaime Alazraki (perhaps the most important critic of Jorge Luis Borges), appear to regard the alleged subversiveness of fantastic literature as existing in parallel to the failure of confidence that Lyotard believes himself to have identified. Criticizing Jackson, Rodero asserts, "Lo fantástico moderno manifiesta no tanto su propia imposibilidad como la imposibilidad de instaurar en la cultura relativizadora occidental valores estables . . ." ("The modern fantastic reveals not so much its own impossibility as the impossibility of establishing stable values in relativizing Western culture" [25]).[1] This is the context in which we need to situate Borges's use of the fantastic in his tales.

Before proceeding, however, we need to make a couple of distinctions. Not all Spanish American fiction is related to the fantastic. But where the term might apply in current critical terminology, we find three special categories of Spanish American writing that are relevant. All truly fantastic writing requires suspension of disbelief. This is what distinguishes the fantastic from the category of the "marvelous real" in Spanish America, as postulated by the Cuban novelist Alejo Carpentier in the famous prologue to his novel *El reino de este mundo* (*The Kingdom of this World*, 1949) and elsewhere in his work. In some of his fiction and nonfictional writing, he strove to suggest that there were aspects of observable historical and present-day reality in Latin America that were inherently marvelous. His later novel *Los pasos perdidos* (*The Lost Steps*, 1953) describes a journey through the interior of northern Spanish America in which "marvelously real" events, people, and discoveries figure prominently. They include, for example, individuals like the Adelantado and Friar Pedro, who seem to belong to the period of the European conquest of South America, and a native ceremony that, the narrator suggests, illustrates the remote origins of all music. But this is not what concerns us here.

A third category, magical realism, has to be taken into account, since Borges has sometimes been regarded as a magical realist. In his companion volume to the movement, Stephen Hart suggests that what we are confronted with in magical realism is "a sense of the world as containing a magical dimension" (4)—not, we notice, merely marvelous, but magical—to which we must add that this magical dimension is presented to the reader as a rule with a perfectly straight face, as if it were to be taken for granted. But where does this "magical" view of reality come from? It has been persuasively argued that in Latin America it comes from what Erik Camayd-Freixas calls "un modo de cosmovisión propio del pensamiento 'mágico primitivo' de las sociedades arcaicas" ("a kind of world-view belonging to the magical-primitive thinking of archaic societies" [3]), in other words, from the mentality of certain ethnic groups such as black Caribbean people, the Central American Indians, or extremely isolated rural *mestizo* (mixed racial) communities. By this standard, the most extreme examples of magical realism would be novels such as *Hombres de maiz* (*Men of Maize,* 1949) or *Mulata de Tal* (*Mulata*, 1963) by the Guatemalan Nobel Prize–winner Miguel Angel Asturias. In the former, the maize-growing land of a group of Central American Indians is desecrated by commercial growers and the community's chief is poisoned. But he is magically reborn and avenges the outrage with the help of others, ful-filling the curse laid on the commercial growers by the local witch doc-tors. In the latter novel, Celestino Yumí sells his wife to the devil out of greed and is severely punished by a series of magical events. Camayd-Freixas rightly points out that this is a long way from what he calls "Post-Vanguardist" fantastic writing that comes from developments in Western metropolitan culture. This is where Borges's fantastic writing, like that of his fellow Argentine, Julio Cortázar, belongs.

Borges (1899–1986) is beyond all doubt the most important Span-ish American writer of the twentieth century, even though he never received a Nobel Prize. Paradoxically, Gabriel García Márquez and Mario Vargas Llosa, two of the writers of the Latin American Boom movement in fiction, which in some ways grew out of Borges's writ-ings, were so honored. After contributing massively in the 1920s to a radical shift in Spanish American poetry, he almost single-handedly changed the course of Spanish American fiction during the 1940s, a critical decade for prose. Almost all the major novelists of the next generation have attested to his influence. Dozens of books and literally thousands of chapters in books and articles have been published about his work, so that keeping up with the criticism is an almost impossible (Borgesian) task.

His legacy to those younger novelists can be summed up in three postulates. The first of these is that the reality surrounding us, which we take for granted, is in fact mysterious (not magical!) and that we may not be programmed to understand it. The second is that our internal, psychological reality is also hard to understand: we are a mystery to ourselves. The third is that even if these two postulates did not apply, language would remain inadequate to the task of conveying anything meaningful about reality. Reality, Borges affirmed on several occasions, is not verbal. These three notions dominate Borges's thinking in the most important of his collections of essays, *Otras inquisiciones* (*Other Inquisitions*, 1952). Most of his best short stories in *Ficciones* (*Fictions*, 1944), *El Aleph* (*The Aleph*, 1949), *El informe de Brodie* (*Brodie's Report*, 1970), and *El libro de arena* (*The Book of Sand*, 1975) are superbly crafted allegories, parables, or fables that explore the first two postulates mentioned above and seek to subvert our confidence in our comfortable presuppositions about the world around us and about the predictability of our own behavior.

We can divide these stories roughly into three categories. First, there are the stories that are purely fantastic, such as "Las ruinas circulares" ("The Circular Ruins"), "La biblioteca de Babel" ("The Library of Babel"), "La casa de Asterión" ("The House of Asterion"), or "La lotería en Babilonia" ("The Lottery in Babylon"). Next, there are the stories that begin soothingly as apparently realistic stories but gradually or suddenly turn into fantastic ones, such as "El jardín de senderos que se bifurcan" ("The Garden of Forking Paths"), "Funes el memorioso" ("Funes, His Memory"), or "El otro" ("The Other"). Finally there are stories that are not fantastic at all but merely contain the unexpected, such as "Hombre de la esquina rosada" ("Man on Pink Corner"), "La muerte y la brújula" ("Death and the Compass"), or "La noche de los dones" ("The Night of the Gifts"). What almost all these stories have in common is that they reveal to the alert reader a deeper meaning than appears at first sight. More importantly, they illustrate the way in which so much modern "high" literature has moved from incorporating reassuring metaphors of the intelligibility of the universe and of human behavior to disturbing metaphors that radically question some of our assumptions about the real and about ourselves.

This has led a number of critics to assert that Borges was a total skeptic who at times doubted his own skepticism. This is true up to a point, in the sense that Borges seems to have believed that what we call reality in each of our own cases was no more than a selection of observable phenomena; a construct composed of what we can live with, while outside all is total chaos. This last is symbolized by the complete incomprehensibility of the contents of the books in the Library of Babel and the lack of any catalogue of the Library (reality) by which we could make some sense of it. This is why among Borges's favorite adjectives are *atroz* ("atrocious") and *vertiginoso* ("dizzying"): because reality is incomprehensible. But we also read that in the books on the Library's shelves there is not a single "disparate absoluto" ("absolute piece of nonsense" [*Collected Fiction* 117]). What does this mean? I take it to mean that nothing in the Library contradicts the law of causality: all effects have causes. If that were the case, the Library would contain a residue of order, even if we, its inhabitants, were unable to perceive it or any other hidden source of design and meaningfulness. What we perceive here is that Borges wavers. On the one hand he suggests that reality outside our comfortable constructs is atrocious because it is pure chaos. But on the other hand, the fact that it never contains effects without causes might imply that that there are hidden laws governing the apparent chaos of reality that our minds are not wired to recognize. Hence, in his poem "In Memoriam A. R." in *El hacedor* (*The Maker,* 1960), he was able to allude too:

> (El vago azar o las precisas leyes
> que rigen este sueño, el universo.)
> The vague happenstance or the precise laws
> which govern this dream, the universe. (1–2)

Borges's skepticism is thus not absolute. He does not make categorical affirmations. Many of his stories are "what if" stories: what if we had total recall, like Funes? What if we were immortal, not in heaven or in the afterlife, but here and now? What if time were not what we think it is? What if everything in life depended on pure chance or was created solely by our perceptions? These are some of the kind of questions Borges asks in his stories. We can see that they are designed to shake our faith in what we normally take for granted. Borges wants to poke holes in our comfortable self-protection and induce us to face up to the inclemency of the human condition.

Let us glance at some of the most famous stories. One of the most purely fantastic is "Las ruinas circulares" ("The Circular Ruins") from his anthology *Ficciones* (1944). We notice at once that it has no recognizably realistic setting: we are in the realm of created, reality, not the observable world. The story itself is quite fantastic. It takes place in a riverbank temple in a wholly imaginary Eastern country. Its central character is a wizard. It deals, like "Pierre Menard, autor del Quijote" ("Pierre Menard, Author of the *Quixote*") and "El acercamiento a Almotásim" ("The Approach to Al-Mutasim") with the Borgesian idea of the impossible task. In this case, the self-imposed task for the wizard is to create by dreaming a new being, and to impose him on the world. Such a being could not, by definition, be real; he is no more than a simulacrum, the apparent materialization of a dream in the mind of the wizard. After much effort, the latter appears to have succeeded in accomplishing his task. But then, the true nature of his "son" is revealed when he is seen to be impervious to fire. At the climax of the tale, the wizard himself is shown to be equally impervious and thus just as much a simulacrum as his creation.

The meaning of the tale is clear: if the "son" is a simulacrum, and if the wizard is also a simulacrum existing in the mind of a preexisting being, then quite possibly we the readers may also be no more than simulacra, mere dreams in the mind of God or apparently materialized individual expressions of some kind of all-embracing "Oversoul." This is surely why the first words of the story describe the night unexpectedly as "unanimous" (single-souled, i.e., already containing all things; Borges often toyed with the idea that "All is in All," everything is an outward manifestation of a single—possibly divine—mind) and why the prevailing symbolism at the opening of the tale is circularity. The adjective, for the alert reader, prefigures the ending; meanwhile, the whole thrust of the story is periodic futile repetition. Now, observe: if there is one thing about which we never allow ourselves to harbor doubts, it is about the real, indisputable existence of the self. But one of Borges's early essays was significantly called "La nadería de la personalidad" ("The Nothingness of the Personality," 1925). Here we have a typical example of Borges's technique of implicitly calling on us his readers to be ready to question even our most deeply rooted convictions.

What do we learn from a careful reading of "The Circular Ruins"? First, the story itself is, like Borges's best stories, fascinatingly original and can be read simply for its intrinsic interest. But second we learn that, having enjoyed the story, we are led to interpret its deep theme: that our sense of the reality of our own selves might be illusory. Then we recognize how superbly Borges crafts the story as a mechanism in which every element is functional. Finally we see that the story includes what Borges referred to as "inlaid" details such as the "unanimous" night and the fact that the wizard's wounds heal magically overnight, which prefigures his unreality (Irby 26). This is how to read a Borges story: for itself, for its meaning, for its craftsmanship, and sometimes for especially revealing, "inlaid" details.

Let us consider some other truly fantastic stories. For example, "The Lottery in Babylon." Once more we are instantly gripped by the extraordinary beginning—the opening paragraphs of Borges's short stories always have to be read and reread with extreme care. As in "The House of Asterion," we overhear a voice making a series of astonishing statements: "he yugulado ante una piedra negra toros sagrados" ("standing before a black altar, I have slit the throats of sacred bulls"; *Collected Fictions* 101) or "he sido declarado invisible" ("I was declared invisible" [101]). We are impelled to read on. The speaker is far from his country, Babylonia; he is about to embark on a sea voyage—where to? We do not know. To whom is he speaking? We have no idea. Why does his right hand lack the index finger? This we can guess at: he can point to no ultimate explanation of what he is about to describe, but only tell us how it came to be. As we read on, we see that Borges is creating a vast allegory: human life is presented as a lottery; all is pure chance. Borges's problem at this stage of the story is to create a pattern of development in terms of which an everyday sweepstake is gradually transformed until it corresponds to a particular vision of human experience in general. What Borges does is to postulate a series of modifications to the original sweepstake until it becomes a metaphor of human life. These are gradually intensified until the lottery is free, universal, and compulsory. It includes every kind of reward and punishment, and, moreover, its very organization is apparently governed by chance. At this point, the unwary reader is likely to conclude that he or she has figured out what Borges is driving at in this case and is inclined to move on to the next story. Wrong!

Going back (as we must) to the beginning and rereading the tale, we notice that alongside the theme of life as a lottery, there is another theme: that of the existence of "the Company" possibly running the lottery. What the alert reader now perceives is that, as Borges develops the original sweepstake into its final existential form through a set of carefully orchestrated changes, he subtly shifts the emphasis from the lottery theme to the theme of whether there is an all-powerful, mysterious "Company" (God) directing the Institution. Here we have to notice two things: first, it seems clear that the Babylonians want there to be a Company, however mysterious and secret its workings may be. Second, that in contradiction to this popular desire, there are "heresiarchs" and "despicable" individuals who either disbelieve in the existence of the Company or hold that its possible existence has no influence on the infinite interplay of chance events which appears to constitute our existence. It goes without saying that such individuals enjoy Borges's approval.

A third truly fantastic story is "La biblioteca de Babel" ("The Library of Babel"). Once more we are in the presence of an allegory of human existence: the Library stands for the universe. At the origin of the story is the supposed proof of God's existence known as "the Argument from Design." The world manifests some clearly recognizable and predictable patterns of order: the sun always rises in the East and sets in the West; two and two always make four, fill a kettle with water and light the gas under it and it will always boil, in the end. This implies that there are laws governing the universe that constitute evidence for design, and this in turn indicates the existence of a Designer. This is where "The Library of Babel" begins from. The opening paragraph heavily emphasizes the fact that the architecture of the Library is totally orderly and predictable: each gallery is identical in construction with all the others. The third paragraph reemphasizes the same point: all the shelves hold the same number of books that all share the same format. But, between the first and the third paragraphs, Borges cunningly interpolates a paragraph telling us that the narrator (the Librarian, Everyman), even before finishing his description of the regularity of the Library's structure, has gone off in search of the catalogue (without which, of course, no library could be regarded as functional). And the implication is that he has not found it! Worse still, however regular and predictable the bindings and the typefaces of the books on the shelves are, the contents of the books bear no relationship to anything printed on their covers and are in fact totally unintelligible. This is what the alert reader now has to figure out.

We notice at this point that the traditional pact between the writer and the reader has to some extent changed. Formerly the writer's task was to observe, describe, and confidently interpret the reality his work reflected while the reader was normally expected to accept passively what the writer told him or her. Nowadays, however, we are challenged to find out for ourselves as readers how to understand "The Library of Babel." We are faced with the need to interpret the text for ourselves, to "crack" it like a puzzle and implicitly, as we read, to get additional pleasure from doing so. After all, life is often puzzling. If literature is to reflect life meaningfully, it too can test our wits.

Probably, then, the regular architecture of the Library represents the laws of, say, (Newtonian) physics, while the incomprehensible contents of the books represent our daily experience, the fog of everyday life that is all too unpredictable. The Librarian now completes his description of the Library and its contents (as the totality of the universe) and proceeds to offer us, rather scornfully, a series of attempts to make sense of them or simply live with them. Some men seek their "Vindication" (Salvation or Life-Project), others despair of finding any meaning, others accept pure chance, and others (mystics, philosophers, theologians) employ more or less crazy methods based on absurd assumptions. Borges is clearly satirizing all attempts to reach a cosmic explanation. (Does this, by the way, align Borges with Lyotard's assertion that in the postmodern period all overarching cosmic explanations have collapsed? Is Borges a postmodern writer, or does the fact that he seems to accept that literature retains a residual truth-telling function make him, in Anglo-Saxon terms, a modernist?)

At this point, the Librarian does two things: first, like the wizard in "The Circular Ruins," he prays. When all else fails, Borges seems to be implying, people naturally turn to religion. Even the Babylonians, as we saw, want there to be a "Company." But second, he offers his own cosmic explanation. Let us be clear what it is: the Library is infinite but "periodic." I take this to mean that it contains endlessly recurring cycles in which time simply goes round and round instead of moving forward: the famous myth of eternal return. This might possibly represent Borges's own view; it is not completely at variance with some of his statements. But this is doubtful. More probably Borges is suggesting to the reader that men in general cannot do without some way, however implausible, of making sense of existence, even if, as he asserted in his essay "El espejo de los enigmas" ("The Mirror of Enigmas"): "es dudoso que el mundo tenga sentido" ("it is doubtful whether the world has any meaning"; *Otras inquisiciones* 150).

Plunging the reader directly into the realm of the fantastic is not Borges's only strategy. At other times he uses what looks like realism as a springboard into the fantastic, so that readers are initially lulled into believing that they are embarking on one kind of story, when in fact Borges is enticing them into another, more abstract kind. Perhaps the best example is "The Garden of Forking Paths," which appears to be a quite original spy-story of the First World War. In it, Yu Tsun, the spy in Britain, has to convey to his control in Berlin the word "Albert," which indicates the place of an Allied attack. To accomplish this he kills a man named Albert so that reports of the crime will reach Berlin and alert his spy-masters. The main function of this frame-story is to manipulate the readers so that they drop their guard and read on avidly.

Then Yu Tsun takes a train to visit Albert. Such journeys, as we see also in "El Sur" ("The South"), cause the central character to pass from one dimension of reality to another. Thus, when Yu Tsun arrives at his destination, the children at the station already know where he is bound. To get to Albert's house Yu Tsun has to make his way through a network of country lanes, a static labyrinth, reference to which begins to soften us up in preparation for the next labyrinth. In the meantime, we are offered five symbols of circularity: the full moon, a circular (drum-shaped) lamp, a gramophone record, a phoenix, and a round clock-face. Circularity in Borges implies futility; the function of the five examples is to foreshadow the futility of Yu Tsun's endeavor. The second labyrinth turns out to be a hugely complicated novel by an ancestor of Yu Tsun in which all possible combinations of activities by the characters are followed out and intersect with each other. Only Albert had figured this out, and now, ironically, he is the one man whom Yu Tsun must kill. Before he does so he is granted a vision of time, not just as one line of development from the past through the present to the future, but as a network or labyrinth of ever-changing lines of time, of which we are programmed only to perceive one. What if, the nub of the story asks us, time were really like this and not as we assume it to be? The story closes with Yu Tsun's arrest and condemnation to death. The reader who bothers to check up the background is rewarded with the knowledge that the Germans knew all along that the Allies would attack from Albert, which makes Yu Tsun's action doubly ironic. Hence the references to circularity/futility.

The labyrinth or maze is Borges's favorite symbol of human existence. It is to be thought of always as circular, and with neither an entrance nor an exit. We are born inside it and die in it after trying to figure out its deceitful combination of orderliness and confusing passageways. We may reach its center. But if we do, we find either who we really are or, more commonly, death. Juan Dahlman, in "The South," is an example of a man who reaches the center of his own personal labyrinth. As he convalesces from a near-fatal illness, we see him take a train to his ranch out on the pampa. Ironically—Borges is a master of irony—he believes he is going toward renewed health; actually he is going to his death. By one of the infinite interplay of chance events that Borges postulates in "The Lottery in Babylon," he has to get off the train at an earlier stop than he intended. At a village store-cum-bar he stops to eat and is insulted by a local redneck who challenges him to a knife fight. An old gaucho throws him a knife. Dahlman accepts the challenge. He has discovered who he is: a man of honor and a thorough-going Argentine. So far, so good; but a series of clues (among others: the barman looks like a male nurse at the clinic he has recently left and knows Dahlmann's name, and the old gaucho wears impossibly anachronistic clothes) suggests that the whole journey and incident may be a feverish hallucination and that Dahlman may never have left the clinic. If we are not programmed to understand reality, how can we tell? Not for nothing does Borges cast "Funes el memorioso" and "El acercamiento a Almotásim" as nonfiction, in the first case as a memoir and in the second as a book review. By presenting purely imaginary stories as if they were not fictional creations, Borges, with great originality, makes the way the stories are presented—the medium—underline the message: we are not programmed to know the difference between observed reality and created (fictitious) reality.

But what if we did? What if we could contemplate the whole of reality as it really is? This is the theme of "El Aleph" ("The Aleph"). "Borges," the tale's narrator, has been in love with Beatriz Viterbo, who is now dead. Now he visits her grotesque cousin, Carlos Argentino Daneri, who writes poetry about observable reality on this planet. Carlos, who writes about this Earth, is a kind of anti-Dante (who wrote in *The Divine Comedy* about purgatory, hell, and heaven, but not about the here-and-now). Similarly, Beatriz is an anti-Beatrice. In the *Divine Comedy*, Beatrice guides Dante in heaven toward the beatific vision. Through Beatriz Viterbo, however, as "Borges" goes down into Carlos's cellar (and moves from the reality of a Buenos Aires suburb into the realm of the purely fantastic) "Borges" is led to the antibeatific vision offered by the Aleph. It is the unbearably horrible vision of all things (including, dear reader, your face!). At the end of the story, all "Borges" wants to do is to forget what he has seen. But not so fast: we have just seen that one of the chief characteristics of "high" literature is irony. Another is ambiguity. Life, alas, tends to be rich in irony and am-biguity, and great literature needs to reflect as much. An unexplained ambiguity at the end of "The Aleph" suggests that the Aleph of the story may be a false Aleph. Perhaps this is because what "Borges" sees by means of it are only objects juxtaposed to one another in utterly chaotic disorder; there are no patterns, no system of causes and effects. A labyrinth, we recall, the true symbol of human existence, does not contain total disorder. It has a center that one can sometimes reach.

Perhaps the best, and most ambiguous, of Borges's late stories is "The Other." It takes place in Cambridge, a suburb of Boston, Massa-chusetts, in 1969. All is perfectly realistic and familiar until the young man who sits down beside "Borges" on a bench by the Charles River turns out to be "Borges's" younger self, living in Geneva at the end of the First World War. Which of them is real? Which of them is dreaming the other? Above all, why does the older "Borges" wish to forget the episode, so as not to lose his mind? The two figures engage in a sharp debate in which the younger one desperately tries to assert his reality in the face of the older one's ability to recall events that have intervened in the fifty-one-year gap since 1918. He makes some good points (e.g., that if the encounter were real and the older "Borges" equally real, the older "Borges" would remember the meeting as having taken place when he was nineteen, which he does not); nevertheless the younger "Borges" loses out. But that does not end the matter. In the course of the incident, the older "Borges" achieves some new realizations about his own selfhood. They are clearly worrying, since the older "Borges" refers to what is happening as "horrific" and as undermining his self-assurance. The worry is at least twofold. On the one hand, the younger "Borges" is condemned to follow out deterministically the life of the older one. What does that tell us about human existence and freedom of action? Secondly, the older "Borges" is constantly rendered aware that the identity through time of the human personality depends on memory of the individual's past, and human memory is fallible. Is this a sign of "The Nothingness [nonexistence] of the Personality"? If the younger "Borges" is simply an insubstantial figment of the older man's (fallible) imagination, what guarantees the substantiality of the older man's identity? Perhaps all is ever changing, like the water in the Charles River.

It is stories such as these, which question our understanding both of exterior reality and the reality of the self, that have been taken to imply that Borges was totally skeptical and that his fantastic tales are subversive of all certainties, including moral certainties. But this is not the case. Borges never questioned two certainties: the value of physical courage (as when Dahlman picks up the dagger) and, far more so, the value of ethical behavior. Correctly interpreted, some of his stories, beginning with "Man on Pink Corner," are really moral fables. I should include "The House of Asterion" and "Deutsches Requiem," both of which are about man-as-monster and about evil. Reina Roffé once asked Borges whether the vision of the world as complete chaos, as in the books of the Library of Babel, reflected his own view. Borges memorably replied:

Es lo que siento desgraciadamente, pero quizás sea secretamente un cosmos, quizás haya un orden que no podemos percibir; en todo caso debemos pensar eso para seguir viviendo. Yo preferiría pensar que, a pesar de tanto horror, hay un fin ético en el universo, que el universo propende al bien, en ese argumento pongo mis esperanzas. (11)

[It's what I feel unfortunately, but perhaps it is secretly a cosmos; perhaps there is an order which we cannot perceive; in any case we should believe that in order to go on living. I should prefer to think that, in spite of so much horror, there is an ethical objective in the universe, that the universe tends towards the good; I base my hopes on that argument.]

Near the end of his life in "El hilo de la fábula" ("The Thread in the Fable") in 1984, he wrote that we have a moral duty to seek the thread that will lead us to the center of the existential labyrinth, even if we can never find it. This is one of the keys to his writings.

Notes

1. All unattributed English translations in this discussion are my own.

Works Cited

Alazraki, Jaime, et al. *Teorías de lo fantástico*. Madrid: Arco, 2001.

Bessière, Irène. *Le Récit fantastique: La Poétique de l'incertain*. Paris: Larousse, 1974.

Borges, Jorge Luis. *Collected Fictions*. Trans. Andrew Hurley. New York: Viking, 1989.

———. "In Memoriam A. R." *Dreamtigers*. Austin: U of Texas P, 2004. 75–76.

———. *Obras completas*. Buenos Aires: Emecé, 1989.

———. *Otras inquisiciones: 1937–52*. Buenos Aires: Sur, 1952.

Brooke-Rose, Christine. *A Rhetoric of the Unreal*. Cambridge, Eng.: Cambridge UP, 1981.

Camayd-Freixas, Erik. *Realismo mágico y primitivismo*. Lanham, MD: UP of America, 1998.

Chanady, Amaryll B. *Magical Realism and the Fantastic: Resolved versus Unresolved Antinomy*. New York: Garland, 1985.

Hart, Stephen, and Wen-Chin Ouyang. *A Companion to Magical Realism.* Woodbridge, Eng.: Tamesis, 2005.

Irby, James E. *Encuentro con Borges.* Buenos Aires: Galerna, 1968.

Jackson, Rosemary. *Fantasy: The Literature of Subversion.* London: Methuen, 1981.

Lyotard, Jean-François. *The Postmodern Condition: A Report on Knowledge.* Minneapolis: Minnesota UP, 1989.

Rodero, Jesús. *La edad de la incertidumbre.* New York: Lang, 2006.

Roffé, Reina. *Espejo de escritores.* Hanover, NH: Norte, 1985.

Todorov, Tzvetan. *The Fantastic: A Structural Approach to a Literary Genre.* Cleveland, OH: Case Western Reserve UP, 1973.

Fictional World Polyphony and the Image of Modern Consciousness in Novels by Hermann Broch and Milan Kundera

Tomáš Kubíček

The intention of this essay is to pursue one particular aspect of modern fiction that forms a line of continuity between Hermann Broch's novel *The Sleepwalkers* (1932) and Milan Kundera's novel *The Farewell Party* (1976). This aspect can be labeled "fictional polyphony" and is a means of establishing a specific fictional world. Polyphony in fiction denotes a multiplicity and equality of voices in which no single one dominates and none is mere accompaniment. It can emerge as a consequence of the use of devices associated with the genre of the fantastic. This does not mean, however, that either of the works addressed here necessarily becomes "fantastic" as a result. In examining this aspect, this essay will concentrate on the tools that construct polyphony and its consequences for the construction of meaning in a novel. Last but not least, it will demonstrate how this aspect is related to what Broch has called "the depiction of reality," which he views as the ethical duty of the modern novel and which Kundera has referred to as the noetic function of a novel[1]—that is, the function by means of which a novel becomes a tool of knowledge.

In Chapter 2 of *The Sleepwalkers*,[2] Broch's hero Esch, an accountant, decides to go to Badenweiler to try to find a businessman named Bertrand. He wants to convince him to intervene in favor of his friend Martin's release from prison in Mannheim, where he has been detained on suspicion of organizing workers' rebellions. Martin tries to dissuade Esch from the visit, arguing that Bertrand will not be in Badenweiler because he is always traveling. But Esch is unnaturally sure: "No, he's in Badenweiler" (*Sleepwalkers* 290).

The decision has been made and Esch will not be diverted by Martin's objections that he is unlikely to be allowed in to see Bertrand. But why should a simple accountant living on the edge of poverty be allowed to see one of Germany's richest businessmen? Nor does Esch's decision seem to chime with the thoughts about the world he has expressed up to this point or his confidence in his place in this world. Esch is a rationalist: he is an accountant, not merely by trade. He is used to calculating human relations and evaluating them as he would a balance sheet. Esch's world must be precise and transparent. Then suddenly we witness this decision to visit Bertrand that resists any notion of rationality or transparency. Esch sets off for Badenweiler to see Bertrand, to whom he is about to declare that he intends to denounce him to the police for his (at that time criminal) homosexuality. What happens next surpasses all expectations, but not those of Esch.

Broch's novel is considered by many critics to be a crystal-clear example of a modern novel; not only due to its structure, its means of expression (the resignation of the narrator to an integrating point of view, the mixing of narration and essay, which thereby thematizes the act of writing and indicates the plot as a part of the novel's noetics), but also due to the accentuation of one of the most important issues of modern fiction. For Broch, the novel becomes a noetic deed that goes hand in hand with existential philosophy, from which it also derives its function.

In the essay he wrote to mark Irish writer James Joyce's fiftieth birthday, Broch defines the novel as a mirror of the spirit of the epoch with which it shares its fate. And it is his opinion that if the modern world's unity falls apart, the novel must follow this decomposition and become its testimony (*Román* 14). However, the result must not be a decomposed work but a work that rediscovers integrity. Broch calls such a work (the best example of which he considers to be Joyce's *Ulysses*) a total work of art characterizing the singularity of the epoch (*Román* 15). But let us not be misled: Broch does not want the novel to become a portrait of its era, an image of some sort of external reality. He wants it to be more: a portrait of this era's spirit. In his opinion, an artist has an undeniable duty to depict, by means of which act a "super-organic, generally true obligation of literature" is also generated (41).

Through this duty, literature passes into the sphere of knowledge—and this transition is an expression of its ethical objective. Broch chooses the key word "polyphony" to designate the means of expression and depiction that a novel uses to create this specific type of fictional world. In the impassioned finale of another of Broch's essays, "The Portrait of the World in a Novel," we read:

> As the task of literature always remains the same, it is an eternal and abiding expression of the human soul's desire, which has always belonged in its polyphony; but through the creation of a new novel literature reaches such orchestral broadness, and the new novel, through its rational-irrational polyphony, represents such an excellent symphonic instrument that for the one who wants to hear, a promise of the future resounds in each of its organ tones. (*Román* 236)

The key phrase for the purposes of this essay is "the novel as rational-irrational polyphony."

Until the moment of Esch's decision to set out to find Bertrand, the fictional world of *The Sleepwalkers* is transparent, despite its long cast list and various deviations from the main storyline. The heterodiegetic (third-person) narrator has his part to play in this structural feature and remains, paradoxically, simultaneously an observer situated above the depicted world and a character with the ability to penetrate all its mental areas—that is, the thoughts of the other characters. Still he remains restrained: the reader hears him narrate but does not take particular notice of his presence. This is the basic means by which classical realist narration creates the illusion of reality—the illusion that the narrated story forms part of our world. The moment of Esch's decision inspires not only a transformation in the plot (an element of the story) but also in the nature of the fictional world as a whole. The new tone in the novel's construction becomes an expression of its polyphony and at the same time an expression of its specific ontological nature.

The first significant transformation is that the narrator steps into the narration. Not into the story, but into the narration (the telling of the story/plot). The expression of this intervention is an essay titled "The Disintegration of Values," which is incorporated into the text of the novel and thematizes the concept of values and freedom. Consequently, a character from the novel—Esch—turns into a general principle, a phenomenon that undergoes a noetic examination through the world of fiction. This narrative gesture seems to indicate that the introduction and development of Esch's character is not intended to help construct a plausible story world but is rather informed by the desire to introduce concepts issuing from the domain of existential philosophy, such as freedom, responsibility, deed, decision making—and, of course, values—that underpin human existence. Esch is a product of these concepts, and, thanks to the intervention of the narrator, it becomes evident that he is an artificial construct employed for the purposes of this fiction. He thereby becomes the expression of a process of definition, within the scope of which the reader (guided by the narrator) finds out that "imperceptibly the words with which things are labeled have lapsed into uncertainty: it is as if all words were orphan strays" (*Sleepwalkers* 292). At the same time, the consequence of this manner of thematizing general concepts is that we are obliged to accept Esch, and along with him the whole fictional world, as a challenge to the consideration of basic concepts of human, and therefore also our own, existence. It constitutes a moment similar to the one of which Theodor Adorno speaks when he claims that the modern novel goes beyond the borders of the aesthetic.

The first part of the interpolated essay—about a deed that represents a leaving of the beaten track, causing things to lose their outlines and inducing a feeling akin to being on the verge of sleepwalking—ends, and Esch's story may then continue. Only now does the reader discover how profoundly Broch has decided to change the rules of the fictional world and what other various forms polyphony may take in this novel. For the narrative to follow Broch makes adjustments to the genre that deviate radically from the structural rules of the formation of a fictional world which are on display in the first part of Esch's story. Instead of a real space we appear now to be in some sort of dream-like space. Unexpectedly, Esch is not only introduced to Bertrand, but he does not have to explain anything, and Bertrand hears him out sympathetically as he explains his decision to denounce him to the police. The conversation between Esch and Bertrand resists the logic of narration that has been seen to be in operation up to this point. Broch depicts the whole scene using means of expression that create a situation in which the limits of probability are transgressed on multiple occasions. We are, in fact, entering an area of a myth that establishes its own rules for the construction of a reality within a fictional world. Here Bertrand's character becomes the representation of a natural order that stands above all other events in the novel. He becomes an "image of someone more essential and perhaps greater who remained in concealment, so simply and smoothly, so effortlessly did everything go" (298). The nature of the myth that is created inside the world of the novel should leave no one in any doubt; it is indicative of the sentences that reshape objects and events into parables.

Esch's entrance into this mythological space blurs the clear contours of reality as they are presented in the preceding narration. It would perhaps be most suitable to designate this new space as the space of an idyll:

> At the top of the sloping deep green lawn, which lay in the morning shadow, stood the house, a villa executed in severe and solid style, and as though the wayward and evanescent coolness of the morning, as though the symbolism of the scene wished once more to duplicate itself, at the end of the slope rose an almost soundless fountain, and its waters were like a crystalline draught which one longed to drink simply because they were so limpid. (297)

Esch, accompanied by the porter, enters Bertrand's house, which has a similarly soothing, almost dream-like nature:

They entered a cool and shadowy ante-room, and while the other vanished through one of the many white varnished doors, which softly opened before and softly closed behind him, Esch felt the soft yielding carpet under his feet and waited for the messenger, who presently returned and led him through several apartments. (298)

Bertrand reacts to Esch's decision to denounce him to the police in a surprisingly conciliatory manner, even urging Esch to do it, in so doing transferring this concrete deed onto the level of a necessary course of action—and therefore order. In this form, the denunciation therefore becomes Esch's duty.

The conversation between Bertrand and Esch does not lack features that would categorize it as characteristic discourse:

"Oh Esch, you make my heart heavy. You hope for too much. Time has never been reckoned yet from the day of death: it has always begun with the day of birth."

... "Many must die, many must be sacrificed, so that a path may be prepared for the loving redeemer and judge. And only through his sacrificial death can the world be redeemed to a new innocence." (301)

To avoid any misunderstanding as to which scene this refers, the narration continues:

Bertrand made a slight, somewhat contemptuous, hopeless gesture with his hand:

"No one can see another in the darkness, Esch, and that cloudless clarity of yours is only a dream. You know that I cannot keep you beside me, much as you fear your loneliness. We are a lost generation. I too can only go about my business."

It was only natural that Esch should feel deeply stricken, and he said:

"Nailed to the cross."

. . . "Yes, Esch,—nailed to the cross. And in the hour of final loneliness pierced by the spear and anointed with vinegar." (302)

The myth has been activated; there is no choice but to sit down to the Last Supper in the garden. The idyll culminates in the final scene, in which Esch and Bertrand sit at a table, as two old friends who know everything about each other, in absolute reconciliation. When they say goodbye, because the meeting is at an end, Esch feels:

> an overwhelming desire to bow over Bertrand's hand and kiss it. But the driver of the car sounded his horn loudly, so that the guest had hastily to climb in. Hardly was the car in motion before a powerful, yet warm wind arose, so that house and garden seemed to be whirled away. . . . It was Esch's first drive in a motor-car, and it was very beautiful. (302)

Did that encounter happen at all, or did Esch dream it? The narrator, who has appeared so far as a reliable guide through the fictional world of the novel, does not want to give us an unambiguous answer. We follow Esch home and learn how he writes the denunciation and takes it to police headquarters. In the evening he learns of Bertrand's suicide from the newspaper. Is the suicide a consequence of Esch's denunciation? No, because the denunciation was made after the suicide. Broch says this clearly enough: at noon, Esch enters a kiosk to buy the newspaper and an envelope. He puts the denunciation into the envelope and delivers it to police headquarters; he puts the newspaper into his pocket. Only in the evening does he open the newspaper and learn of Bertrand's death. Was his belated deed therefore in vain? But why then did Bertrand's suicide happen? If it was not motivated by Esch's denunciation, could it have been motivated by the meeting with him? Did that meeting even take place? But if not, did the fictional death occur for no reason? How then can an unmotivated death occur in such a causally linked world? Does Bertrand's suicide ironize Esch's deed? But even in the case that it does, it remains a deed of denunciation. Does Bertrand's suicide ironize the logical structure of the fictional reality's structure? Is Bertrand's death therefore accidental, desultory? But what function does chance have in the intentional world of a novel? Is chance but a result of a cause that escapes us? At any rate, the rules of the rational world in which one event is a transparent, logical consequence of another become muddled without the event losing its validity.

Nevertheless, the inability of the reader to decide the answers to these questions is not the result of some sort of failure in the narration, but it is evidently a result of its semantic construction. It is part of the meaning of the fictional world of Broch's novel. It is the result of a union of two different genres, within whose scope two different types of reality are constructed. The first type is that of a realistic narration which allows the reader to assess actions on the balance of probabilities derived from rules valid in the real world as we know it. The other type of reality, however, is based on different rules, and its result is the construction of a fictional world which establishes its own rules of probability. What will happen if both types of reality meet within one fictional world? And what rules of genre does the scene of Esch's meeting with Bertrand follow?

The hesitation thematized by Broch's novel is the hesitation that is inherent to all fantastic literature. It is one of its key conditions. Tzvetan Todorov says that in the case of fantastic literature, "the text must oblige the reader to consider the world of the characters as a world of living persons and to hesitate between a natural and supernatural explanation of the events described" (33). In the first case there is an explanation of an irrational phenomenon and its translation into the coordinates of rationality; while the other case aims at the acceptance of the supernatural. However, the pure fantastic, in Todorov's opinion, remains unexplained, unseized by human intellect. In such cases, neither the character nor the reader will ever be able to decide if the events depicted by the narration are a dream or reality. If uncertainty or doubt is present, then reality becomes ambiguous. The fantastic, according to Todorov, lasts for the time of uncertainty.

The passage in Broch's novel describing the meeting between Esch and Bertrand could quite easily be simply the expression of a parable; it could be a hypothetic possibility, or it could be a dream. Nevertheless, the narration does not choose unambiguously any of these options. Moreover, this event has a specific result in the form of Bertrand's suicide—a consequence of another form of the first type of fictional reality. Therefore, it leaves us, as described above, in a position where we find it impossible to decide and, as such, it becomes one of the key means by which the fantastic works. The person who has to decide is not Esch, but the reader. According to Todorov, after all, the fantastic presumes the integration of the reader into the world of the characters. So the fantastic serves Broch as an aesthetic category and takes part in the formation of a unifying meaning for Broch's text and the whole specific fictional world.

The result of Broch's writing, though, is not the production of fantastic fiction, but the use of the means of fantastic literature so that irrationality can enter the narration. The irrational that is part of this fictional world is simply not explicable. The fictional world does not have the ability to identify this irrationality as unequivocally unreal and thereby demarcate its own sphere of meaning that would be delineated by the firm border of critical rationality. A significant consequence of the genre of the fantastic is the fact that the rational world does not become nonsensical due to its clash with the irrational; its logic is not destroyed, but rather both alternatives of the world maintain an equal validity.

What, then, is the motive that lies behind this mixture of genres? The fantastic allows a connection between both domains of the world: the rational—that is, the cognizable and explicable by the intellect—and the irrational, which resists the critical rational approach but demands its respect. Here we are getting to another form of Broch's fictional polyphony, which is a consequence of the introduction of generic means associated with the fantastic into the novel, which ought to be an image of the world, a specific testimony to the possibility of knowing a reality containing both rationality and irrationality. "Working *well*," says Broch in his essay "Evil in the Value System," "must be related to the discovery of new knowledge and new forms of seeing and observing, which bestow the general cognitive character not only upon visual art and literature, but upon the whole area of artistic creation" (Román 155). In his opinion, though, literature that deals with the question of values and a value system heads off into the realms of irrationality to areas that cannot be encompassed easily by the senses or reason.

Literature as a set of procedures and methods for creating a fictional world that should, in Broch's opinion, express something more significant about our real world, offered him the tools for the creation of this corresponding, and yet deeper—as it absorbs irrationality—reality. Uniting the means of the realistic and fantastic narration, he gives rise to a fictional world that is not simply explicable but whose transparency is born of hesitation, which shows that the decision between one or other option at any given time diminishes its semantic potential, its area. Such a fictional world becomes a direct expression of the fragile form of the figuration of meaning—that is, that invoked image of the modern world and its indistinct value system.

> We must read *The Sleepwalkers* carefully, slowly, linger over actions as illogical as they are comprehensible, in order to perceive a hidden, subterranean *order* underlying the decisions of a Pasenow, a Ruzena, an Esch. These characters are not capable of facing reality as a concrete thing. Before their eyes everything turns into a symbol (Elisabeth the symbol of familial serenity, Bertrand the symbol of hell), and it is to symbols they are reacting when they believe they are acting upon reality. (Kundera, *Art of the Novel* 61; original italics)

The symbols the characters use to substitute for reality, and through which they unwittingly detract from this reality, can be seen as an expression of an irrational longing for values which are beyond the reach of their intellectual understanding because they are united with feeling and desire. The symbols thus represent a state of preunderstanding, and at the same time they provide legitimization to understanding—the symbols generalize the unique phenomena. However, the symbols may also have more than one meaning. By interceding between reality and man they cause a blurring of reality. And it is exactly this symbolic reading that causes the separation of man from the world, its misunderstanding.

In 1976, the Gallimard publishing house in Paris published Kundera's third novel, *The Farewell Party*. Kundera wrote it while he was still living in Czechoslovakia, although he was subject to a publishing ban. Kundera completed it in 1971; four years later he left Czechoslovakia and the book was published the following year. It was subsequently translated into most major foreign languages and garnered numerous literary prizes. And it was, of course, extremely widely read. However, most readings go little further than identifying a novel whose plot plays out against the background of the historically factual political situation of a Czechoslovakia occupied by the Soviet army in 1968. But such a reading results in Kundera's novel becoming something that the author himself tried to resist as an essayist pondering the nature of the novel: a mirror of its epoch, of its surface.

The Farewell Party is a novel at whose foundations lie the interconnected issues of freedom, action, murder, and responsibility. These motifs are variously expressed by the characters of the novel; the characters are connected with these motifs and they are their variations. Jazz trumpeter Klíma comes to a small Czech spa town at the end of the season to terminate his relationship with the spa nurse Růžena; the relationship has developed from an occasional affair into an unwanted pregnancy. Klíma wants to persuade Růžena to have an abortion and thereby free himself from the relationship. But for Růžena the unwanted child represents the possibility of escape from the provincial town and a free ticket to the trumpet player's big, wide world. Klíma wants freedom for himself, and this is also what Růžena longs for; but their desires are mutually incompatible. At the same time, another figure arrives at the spa. Before his planned escape from the country (and therefore to freedom), Jakub wants to say goodbye to his friend Škréta, a doctor at the spa, and return a deadly blue pill that Škréta gave him long ago, by means of which Jakub, a victim of Stalinist purges, could have freely decided whether to live or die. Now he is leaving Czechoslovakia and the pill is redundant. Therefore, he wants to symbolically return it to his friend because it represents the last tie with his past, with the country from which he wishes to unbind and free himself.

The whole novel is built around the classical unities of place, time, and action. The plot takes place over the course of five days, and its events are unfolded chronologically and therefore create a compact, transparent fictional world. This external formal transparency is, however, only illusory. The fates of the novel's protagonists are influenced by uncontrolled forces; their deeds abandon them, and from being active doers, they become merely passive witnesses to events that cause a breakup of the system of values upon which they have built their lives. None of the novel's characters escape this destructive movement, and what looks at the beginning of the narrative like a comic instance of unwanted fatherhood consequently turns into an existential drama.

The issue of the transparency and controllability of the world finds expression in the formal means Kundera uses. The principal speaker in the novel is the heterodiegetic (third-person) narrator who maintains a distance from the fictional world and does not thematize his narration or pronounce explicit comments upon the other characters. Nevertheless, this is not to say that the reader is left without evaluation; in fact, everything that happens in the story is constantly judged. Yet rather than this evaluation being provided by the narrator, the novel employs a multiply evaluating perspective as the means by which the fictional world is constructed. From the point of semantic construction, the clear dividing line between "good" and "bad," which runs between the character of Růžena and the other characters, is of considerable importance. The narration judges Růžena constantly by means of the other characters' perspectives. From these multiple perspectives she is shown to be a selfish, moody, calculating, and ruthless person. And the reader has no hesitation in aligning himself with this evaluation. The other characters are thus defined in their interaction with Růžena, which functions as a means of constructing a value-stabilized fictional world.

This situation is confirmed by the idyllic world of the spa, whose choice as the novel's setting can be seen to confirm some sort of pre-negotiated irreverence in the story. The comic situation involving the tricky incident of the unwanted pregnancy, which is announced inter-textually, coupled with the figure of a mysterious doctor who treats sterile female patients by inseminating them himself (so that the women, without apparently suspecting anything, are happy and the whole world is populated by copies of the doctor's elongated nose) can be considered equally "light." Kundera himself calls his novel a "vaude-ville," a theater genre based on superficial entertainment and the comic. The reader is assured at every turn of the uncomplicated nature of what is happening, about the simplicity of this world of high-spirited relations between the characters, about the transparency of this world of realistic fiction.

But such apparent transparency is disrupted by a murder. As a result of an accident, Jakub brings about Růžena's death. Having inadvertently palmed the poisonous pill off onto her, he knowingly lets her swallow it. "But was it really poison?" Jakub asks himself. "Was Škréta perhaps playing some game with me?" "Did I really hold my freedom of choice in my hand?" Jakub does not know the answers to these questions. And he does not know how to get the pill back from Růžena without drawing attention to himself. What if she denounces him? He will be detained and imprisoned, and the martyrdom of persecution will start anew. So he observes Růžena with anxiety; but nothing happens.

He felt an enormous sense of relief: Růžena was still alive. Tablets of the kind the tube contained were generally taken three times a day: she must therefore have taken some last night and this morning, and she must have swallowed his tablet quite some time ago. Suddenly everything became quite clear to him: the pale blue pill which he had been carrying in his pocket as a guarantee of his freedom was a fake. His friend had merely given him an illusion of death. (*Farewell Party* 150)

And Jakub bids farewell to Škréta, to the spa, to his mother country, and heads for exile. He sees himself leave the country where he "had left no traces, no roots, no mark in this land—a land he was now leaving like a puff of wind" (171). And at that very moment Růžena swallows the pale blue poisonous pill.

"Imperceptibly the words with which things are labeled have lapsed into uncertainty: it is as if all words were orphan strays" (*Sleepwalkers* 292). So writes Broch in *The Sleepwalkers*. Guilt and punishment, murder and responsibility, freedom and action—these words are still part of the fictional space, but their meaning becomes unstable in Kundera's novel. Růžena is killed and none of the characters pays any real attention to her murder. Her death is inexplicable, and they simply accept it as such. Jakub leaves for exile, and in a manner echoing Broch's Huguenau, who kills Esch at the end of his story, it does not actually appear to mean anything to him: "He tried to test himself by pretending that the nurse was really dead. No, this idea failed to fill him with any sense of guilt, and Jakub drove calmly and peacefully through the pleasant countryside which was saying its gentle farewell" (*Farewell Party* 171). In *The Sleepwalkers,* Broch says that freedom and murder are as intertwined as conception and death (see *Sleepwalkers* 294). But the murder in Kundera's novel occurs with no apparent significance and is filled with a strange lightness. And the reader is disturbed precisely because he perceives that he has been caught in the novel's trap as he, too, has attributed no significance to this action. It is only at the close of the narration that the reader realizes how unquestioningly he has accepted the perspective offered and thus uncritically adopted the evaluation of another.

However, the primary interest of this essay is focuses on the question of whether these two works can be considered to be connected at the deeper level of fictional world construction. Therefore, it is time now to go back and to concentrate on the semantic construction of the novel and on its formal level of narration.

The key word now will therefore be polyphony, and the focus of our discussion will be on its structures and functions. But is it actually possible to speak of polyphony in the case of Kundera's *The Farewell Party*? The above-mentioned formal characteristics of the novel, which stress transparency and compactness, seem to eliminate such a feature. Still, as we have seen, the result of these processes is not a transparent or compact fictional world, but rather a world of destruction, disintegration, and uncertainty. A polyphony of narrative procedures plays the leading role in the creation of this aesthetic effect of the fictional world.

For Kundera, polyphony is one of the basic means by which a narration can be structured. In his first novel, *The Joke* (1965), it is present in the form of the four narrators who each separately describe their view of the story of the principal character, Ludvík Jahn. In this novel, the reader is unable to arrive at a precise and unambiguous image of either Ludvík or any of the narrators because each storyteller's opinion stands in such contradiction to the others. No simple connection exists between the world of effects and the world of relations, not even in the discourse, because of this polyphonic approach to narration. Three years after the publication of *The Farewell Party*, Gallimard published *The Book of Laughter and Forgetting* (1979). In this work Kundera takes the strategy of variations and polyphony to the very limits of its narrative possibilities. The individual parts of this novel lack connectedness in terms of their story, but they are linked by the topics that they address. The concept of a joined-up plot is abandoned and instead links are formed by means of words, motifs that the characters exchange without knowing one another. Kundera speaks of such words as functioning like musical notes that, in the form of variations, start a novel symphony (see *Art of the Novel* 71–96). The narration of the stories is constantly interrupted by an essay that further studies and plays variations on the key motifs and topics.

However, such an evident, formally marked polyphony is missing from *The Farewell Party*. Nevertheless, polyphony still becomes one of the most important elements of the novel's semantic structure. In one of its forms it is present in what we have already indicated as being the retreat of the heterodiegetic narrator from the narration and the manner in which, by means of the individual characters, the fictional world's value system is constructed. In this form, polyphony is a result of multiperspectival narration. The reader adopts the characters' evaluations whilst presuming that these are shared by the heterodiegetic narrator who thereby somehow gains the status of an omniscient narrator. The polyphony in the novel adopts yet another significant form that can also lead us back to Broch's *The Sleepwalkers*.

If Kundera's world is, at least at first sight, transparent and governed by a rational connection between cause and effect—which characterizes the conduct of the characters of the fictional world, into whose minds we penetrate by means of the narrative competence of the narrator—then there is one character to whom this does not apply: Bartleff. Bartleff is a figure to whose mental space the reader is not admitted. We do not know what he thinks; we only know what he does and says. Bartleff, as a figure of the fictional world, is therefore created only as a point of intersection for the views of other characters. But the way other characters perceive him is rather special.

Bartleff is characterized as a stranger: an elderly man, maybe around sixty-five, Růžena thinks. Klíma calls him a rich American and convivial bon vivant. To Olga, Jakub's protégée, Bartleff seems ridiculously theatrical and complacent. When Bartleff speaks, his speech—syntactically, lexically, and thematically—evokes that of a priest; indeed, this is what Klíma feels during their first meeting in the novel:

> "I understand you and I am not going to try to change your mind. I am too old to take on the job of improving the world. I have given you my opinion, and that's that. I will remain your friend even if you disregard my advice, and I will help you even if I don't agree with you."

The trumpet player looked at Bartleff, who delivered the last words in the ringing tones of a kind and wise prophet. There was something majestic about him. It seemed to Klíma that everything Bartleff said could serve as homily, a parable, an example, a chapter out of some modern version of the Gospel. He felt like bowing down before him. (*Farewell Party* 24)

We come to associate with Bartleff a bluish glare to which we are introduced at the outset of the novel in relation to the picture of Saint Lazarus that Bartleff is painting, as the color of saints' haloes. A moment later, the trumpet player unexpectedly enters Bartleff's hotel room, "then stopped short, startled. The room was quite dark except for the glow of a fluorescent tube or the yellowish light of an electric bulb. It was blue, a strange blue aura" (46). Later he mentions it to Bartleff, and the latter, smiling, challenges him that this was a hallucination. Růžena, who spends an amorous night with Bartleff, wakes up at one point and:

it seemed to her that the whole room was bathed in a peculiar bluish light. She had never seen such a strange glow before. What was it? Had the moon come down to earth wrapped in a bluish gown? Or was she dreaming with her eyes open? (144)

And it is Bartleff who identifies a characteristic in Růžena that is in stark contrast to all her traits identified previously. In his eyes, Růžena is "a radiant being full of love, tenderness and nobility" (175). The relation between the words and what they are describing becomes blurred. And, simultaneously, so do the contours and personalities of the individual characters. Bartleff destabilizes the whole fictional world, and Růžena functions as a catalyst of this destabilization.

Bartleff's character can be considered disturbing in many ways. Not only does he hide behind the words of others, which forever show Bartleff's character in lights that contradict one another; not only does he enter the story as a *deus ex machina* ("god from a machine," whose sudden appearance is in fact commented on by all the characters); not only do all the threads of the narration constantly intersect with him, thereby making him the compositional center of the whole narration and formally confirming his central significance to the narrative; but on top of all this he boasts attributes that are repugnant to the rules of the world with which we are presented in the form of a small spa, a vaudeville, and a story of unwanted paternity. He is visited by beautiful children akin to angels—children that nobody knows: "'I don't know whether she was an angel,'" said Škréta, "'but it is certainly strange that I have never seen that child before, even though I know just about everybody in these parts'" (*Farewell Party* 90). He is accompanied by a blue halo that shines a light bearing a disturbing meaning, not only upon him but also upon the whole narration. Also Bartleff's speeches are in sharp contrast with the speeches of the others: the consequence of both their form and content is that they seem to develop into parables and pull back from the speeches of the others. Bartleff is a mysterious figure. And the reader hesitates as to how to understand him. And this hesitation is an expression of another, maybe the most important form of the polyphony in the novel.

If we look carefully at the individual motifs in the novel, we find a whole range of similarities that unite intertextually Kundera's Bartleff with Broch's Bertrand: Bertrand's wealth is derived from the docks; this is the place Esch comes from, and Bartleff says that he worked at the docks in his youth. There is a similarity between the names Bartleff and Bertrand, as well as between the speech that characterizes Bertrand during the encounter with Esch and the manner in which Bartleff is conceived by the other characters; both of these introduce mythical elements into the narration. Moreover, Bertrand is connected with the motif of a dream. And Bartleff? The dream motif appears early, at the point of his entrance into the novel and his first meeting with Klíma. Besides, Klíma's fascination with Bartleff and his urge to bow before him are similar to the feeling experienced by Esch when he meets Bernard. As readers we do not and should not know what

Bartleff thinks, and Bertrand's character remains equally inaccessible to us. That places them in opposition to the novels' other characters. I hear two significant voices of fiction polyphony behind the character of Bartleff.

Like Broch, in *The Farewell Party* Kundera uses the means of semantic construction of the world of fantastic literature. The reader's hesitation and inability make up his mind about Bartleff and Bertrand shows that the world is not simply translatable into a single meaning, that it is a structure that absorbs both rationality and irrationality, that chance always challenges causality and context deed, and that words do not match either objects or phenomena. The reader's hesitation, resulting from the crossover of genres, is therefore a productive starting point for the creation of a space that is called the modern world. This hesitation is just as disturbing as what tends to be called modern existence, which stands against both the logic of Cartesian reason and theological concepts of the meaning of the world that direct human actions toward an impersonal (divine) order. The world of Broch and Kundera is one of disintegrating values, where in reality the struggle for values still takes place. By its establishment, this world indicates the unclosedness, nontransparency, and dubiousness of this struggle, because its setting has been brought from an external space into the internal world of an individual standing between reason and sensation, or between rationality and desire, as Broch says. Both Broch and Kundera observe this world of disintegrating values, but what their novels thematize is not the disintegration of these values, but the need for them. And it is this basic tone that makes them part of the same type of modern literature.

Beside the generic polyphony, I can hear another voice in the union of these novels. The touches of intertextuality with which *The Sleepwalkers* and *The Farewell Party* handle the topic of the modern world shape them into a component of fiction polyphony that belongs to an aesthetic project that Kundera calls the heritage of the central European novel—a heritage featuring the names of Franz Kafka, Robert

Musil, Hermann Broch, and Witold Gombrowitz. In a manner similar to Broch, Kundera also observes the moment of murder and invites the traditionally united concepts of guilt and punishment, justice and revenge into the narrative. But this basic logic fails. Murder will remain unpunished and seems to be treated with an unusual lack of respect, with an inappropriate "lightness." Still there remains one outstanding contrast, and this can be labeled as the final and unifying voice of the polyphony. In both cases, it is the reader who feels disconcerted by the disintegration of this natural balance of values. It is the reader who is forced to fill in the empty space left in the world when values disappear. This is the inherent nature of this aesthetic project—its ethics, as Broch calls them; or its noetics, to use Kundera's designation. An observation of the process of disintegration of values is in fact a way of acknowledging their significance. At the same time, this is probably the most important feature that distinguishes the fictional worlds of modern novels from their postmodern successors.

Notes

1. A noetic novel is one that becomes a tool for understanding certain aspects of human existence, and in this sense an experimental space. In this respect, Kundera says that a novel that does not involve cognition is immoral. He here alludes to Broch about whom he said he "could make of the novel the supreme intellectual synthesis" (*Art of the Novel* 16).
2. Broch's novel is set in the years 1888–1918, contains three parts ("Pasenow or The Romantic"; "Esch or The Anarchist"; and "Huguenau or The Realist"), and attempts to highlight the decline of values in society. Each part has a self-contained plot that, whilst not directly interwoven, does create an organic unity. The three central characters represent various possibilities.

Works Cited

Adorno, Theodor W. "Standort des Erzählers im zeitgenossischen Roman." *Moderne Erzähltheorie*. Ed. Karl Wagner. Vienna, Aus.: WUV, 2002. 168–77.

Broch, Hermann. *The Sleepwalkers. A Trilogy.* Trans. Willa Muir and Edwin Muir. New York: Vintage, 1996.

_____. *Román—mýtus—kýč* [Novel—myth—kitsch]. *Eseje*. Ed. Milan Kundera, trans. Naděžda Macurová. Prague: Dauphin, 2009.

Kundera, Milan. *The Farewell Party*. Trans. Peter Kussi. New York: Penguin, 1984.

_____. *The Art of the Novel*. Trans. Linda Asher. London: Faber and Faber, 1990.

_____. *Der Vorhang*. Trans. Uli Aumüller. Frankfurt am Main: Fischer Taschenbuch, 2008.

_____. *Encounter*. Trans. Linda Asher. London: Faber and Faber, 2010.

Todorov, Tzvetan. *The Fantastic: A Structural Approach to a Literary Genre*. Trans. Richard Howard. Ithaca, NY: Cornell UP, 1975.

Thomas Pynchon and the Contemporary Forms of the Fantastic

Eugenio Bolongaro

"A screaming comes across the sky. It has never happened before, but there is nothing to compare it to now." (*Gravity's Rainbow*)

The opening lines of Thomas Pynchon's *Gravity's Rainbow* (1973) are among the most memorable in twentieth-century fiction. On a primary level, the impact of these much-discussed two sentences derives undoubtedly from the brilliant evocation of "death from the air": the hissing "s" sounds in the first sentence "speak" and prolong the scream suddenly stilled by the period and then by the ambiguous pronoun "it" (the "[h]it" of contact before the sound of conflagration can be heard). Pynchon is alluding here to the V2 rocket used by Nazi Germany to bomb London. The first ballistic missile developed by humankind is presented as a new and unprecedented menace that encapsulates all that has gone terrifyingly wrong with the modern world and its hubris of technological mastery.[1] In the subsequent pages this allusion gradually turns into a specific reference and contributes to establishing the historical setting for the initial phases of the novel: London, England during the last year of World War II. And yet this realistic stabilization of the narrative (only a momentary one, in any event) should not blind us to the fact that the impact of the opening crucially relies on the ambiguity of the first two sentences. The screaming is unidentified as well as unprecedented. It cannot be recognized; it punctures our cognitive categories, opening up a new horizon in which we cannot orient ourselves with the tools of realism because it lies beyond what we have learned to recognize as real. Is this, then, the horizon of the fantastic? This question is at the heart of this discussion in which I will argue that in Pynchon's landmark work the fantastic emerges as an interrogation of the accepted distinctions between the real and the imaginary. This interrogation is not, however, an end in itself but rather strives to promote a dialectical overcoming of an insufficient understanding of the real and of the conventions of literary realism that are its corollary.

I. The Fantastic Nebula: From Genre to Mode

Before examining Pynchon's work, it is useful to clarify the meaning of the term *fantastic* on which this discussion relies. Contemporary understanding of the fantastic in literature can be traced back to the publication in 1970 of Tzvetan Todorov's watershed work *Introduction à la littérature fantastique*.[2] The essay was very influential because it seemed to settle the thorny question of what defines the fantastic as a literary genre. Todorov's proposal raises a series of difficulties, as the articles in this collection demonstrate, but for the purposes of this discussion it is more useful to focus on one crucial strength. For Todorov, at the heart of the fantastic is the reader's unresolved "wavering" between a natural and a supernatural explanation of the narrative events. In the end, Todorov can be seen as having defined a common "generic horizon," the cornerstone of which is precisely this "wavering" attitude. This is the fundamental contribution of Todorov's articulation, as long as we realize that the reader's "wavering" constitutes a cognitively valuable stance. To waver involves being forced to let go of one's certainties and then to be given the opportunity to open oneself up to new possibilities. This particular type of imaginative challenge is at the heart of the fantastic, and Todorov has given us the key to understanding it in a rather different way from the one he envisaged.

It was in order to do justice to a growing body of novelistic works that did not fit into Todorov's model of the fantastic that critics like Eric S. Rabkin (*The Fantastic in Literature*, 1976), Robert E. Scholes (*Science Fiction: History, Science, Vision*, 1977), and Darko Suvin (*Metamorphoses of Science Fiction*, 1979) began to lay the foundations for a new conceptualization of the fantastic "nebula" in the 1970s and 1980s. The key distinction that these critics developed and that I later adopted and generalized in my own discussion of genre ("From Literariness to Genre," 1992) was between two modalities of narrative discourse: the "as if" modality of realism and the "what if" modality of the fantastic. This move allows us to conceptualize the fantastic no longer as a genre but rather as a mode that can permeate any number of literary genres and texts, some of which will gravitate closer to the center of the nebula where the fantastic modality dominates the narrative, while others toward the periphery, where the fantastic modality is sporadic and negligible. This move liberates the fantastic from the strictures of genre specificity and allows us to develop Todorov's fundamental intuition.

First, the distinction between the "as if" and "what if" modes makes it clear that both realism and the fantastic are imaginative constructs; in other words, they have the same fundamental relationship to the real: not literally true but, potentially, poetically/symbolically/allegorically true. The difference between realism and the fantastic lies in the way each articulates this relationship. In the case of realism the narrative proceeds by analogy ("as if"), which means that the author does not have to tell us much about the way the fictional world s/he is creating operates because s/he can rely on our empirical knowledge of the world to fill in the gaps. The sentence "Jane was walking down the street when she saw Peter for the first time" can be easily read as realistic without the author having to tell us that Jane and Peter are a female and a male *homo sapiens*, living in an urban community where streets are paved with a combination of asphalt, cement, and stone, and where the reproduction of the species is highly valued and assured by heterosexual intercourse. In the case of the fantastic, however, the situation is quite different. The author will normally signal from the start that we cannot make any easy assumptions. The sentence "Jane felt a shudder as her spaceship emerged from the wormhole" immediately catapults the reader into a world where s/he cannot automatically rely on her/his knowledge of ordinary reality and must instead, as Marc Angenot forcefully argues in his essay "The Absent Paradigm" (1979), gradually construct the paradigm (i.e., the rules) that governs the fictional world. In this case the interest of the narrative lies precisely in how such a world diverges from our own. The author's gambit then is a kind of thought experiment: "what if" life took the form of a sentient spider-like creature on a planet that is plunged in darkness and frozen for two hundred and fifteen years out of each two-and-a-half-century cycle (as in Vernor Vinge's *A Deepness in the Sky*)? What challenges would that species face to develop a civilization?

The second main advantage of the "as if" versus "what if" distinction is that it makes an apparent paradox easier to grasp. The fantastic seems by definition antagonistic to realism: after all, in Todorov's terms the reader wavers because s/he is faced with alternative and incompatible positions. However, it has been widely noted that the fantastic emerges insistently and significantly in realist texts (Jackson). The key to unlocking the conundrum is the fact that realism and the fantastic are deeply related though different and potentially autonomous modes of representation. The realist and fantastic modes are fundamental strategies of narrative elaboration that coexist to varying degrees in most narrative texts, though usually one mode will be dominant, have genre-specific thematics (e.g., the focus on science and technological development in science fiction), and set the tone for the individual work. In the case of Pynchon, the interaction of fantastic and realistic elements is one of the hallmarks of the author's unmistakable style.

Third, there are innumerable ways of posing the "what if" question. The science fiction example used above is the most obvious insofar as the difference of the fictional world is directly thematized. A less direct but equally unmistakable strategy is the one deployed in fantasy, a genre encompassing works such as J. R. R. Tolkien's *Lord of the Rings*, J. K. Rowling's *Harry Potter* saga, or the more run-of-the-mill examples of the "sword and sorcery" subgenre. In all these cases, however, the departure from the laws of ordinary experience is immediate and explicit. A different situation arises when such a departure is more gradual, subtle, and the result not only of thematic elements but also of formal devices. This is the area where Pynchon makes his contribution: his use of the fantastic is an ironic puncturing of the real, a sudden irruption of productive chaos that undermines the very assumptions of what constitutes reality and realistic representation.

II. Pynchon and the Fantastic

Pynchon is universally recognized as one of the leading American writers of the twentieth century and among the most original voices in world literature to emerge after the end of World War II. Pynchon's style is unique; all his works, from his early short stories (collected in the 1988 volume *The Slow Learner*) and his first novel *V.* (1963) to his most recent effort *Inherent Vice* (2009), prove difficult to classify in terms of genre. At the thematic level, the overarching characteristic is a steadfast commitment to identifying, exploring, and critiquing the American way of life as it has evolved since the 1950s. At the formal level, Pynchon's prose is typified by an iconoclastic virtuosity in mixing different languages, rhythms, images, and metaphors, and in pushing English syntax to its limits. Pynchon's texts are not easily approached and his major works to date (*Gravity's Rainbow*, 1974; *Mason & Dixon*, 1997; *Against the Day*, 2007) are as massive and challenging as they are rich.

It is the contention of this essay that one of the hallmarks of Pynchon's narratives is the role played by the fantastic mode. The discussion will now proceed in two stages: first, it will isolate and reflect on the key characteristics of Pynchon's use of the fantastic, and second it will focus on the influence of Pynchon's use of the fantastic mode in works of contemporary fiction (literary and cinematic).

i. Fantastic Irony

We have noted at the beginning of this essay that the opening lines of *Gravity's Rainbow* owe much of their ominous power to a fundamental cognitive uncertainty. The reader vacillates in front of something that is happening but cannot yet be put into words, a phenomenon still at the edge of speech. The strain to capture it in language is felt in the lapidary astonishment that the first two sentences voice. The period and the move to a new paragraph signal a stunned silence, the deadly hesitation as the supersonic bomb drops and before we hear the noise of the explosion. But then "It is too late": the opening of the new paragraph underscores the hiatus between perception and knowledge. The unnamed "him" whose perspective the narrative takes up ("Above him lift girders old as an iron queen") can see nothing ("it's night") and only imagine the glass dome collapsing ("coming down in total blackout . . . only great invisible crashing"). Where are we? This question cannot be answered by trying to establish a referent (albeit a fictional one) that, in fact, is clear enough: an underground station, the precise identity of which does not seem to matter. The way the experience is described leads the reader to believe that the place we inhabit is not only a "real" place but also very much a place of the imagination, a place of nightmare, yes, but also a place that challenges us to see a new world. Supersonic weapons outstrip our understanding of what the ordinary world is like (we can be killed by a bomb before we hear it); we have to posit the imaginary in order to attempt a first approximation of the hitherto unthinkable real. And indeed the first page and a half of *Gravity's Rainbow* hovers constantly between realistic details and an infernal atmosphere of Dantesque proportion:

The Evacuation still proceeds, but it's all theatre. . . .

Inside the carriage, . . . all the others pressed in around, feeble ones, second sheep, all out of luck and time: . . . stacked about among the rest of the things to be carried out to salvation. . . .

They have begun to move. They pass in line . . . Is this the way out? Faces turn to the windows but no one dares ask, not out loud. Rain comes down. No, this is not a disentanglement from, but a progressive *knotting into* . . . to try to bring events to Absolute Zero . . . and it is poorer the deeper they go . . . ruinous secret cities of the poor, places whose *names he has never heard* . . . the walls break down, the roofs get fewer and so do the chances for light. . . .

There is no way out. Lie and wait, lie still and be quiet. Screaming holds across the sky. When it comes, will it come in darkness, or will it bring its own light? Will the light come before or after? (3–4; emphasis original)

Even the flow of time is scrambled in this radically uncertain world. It could all be real or it could all be imaginary; better, it is real and it is imaginary. The reader vacillates but in order to understand, both dimensions have to be kept in momentary balance. And then, an additional sudden twist: "*But it is already light.* How long has it been light?" (5; emphasis original). And an equally sudden change in mood: "All these horizontal here, these comrades in arms, look just as rosy as a bunch of Dutch peasants dreaming of their certain resurrection in the next few minutes" (5). A character distinctly emerges: "His name is Capt. Geoffrey ('Pirate') Prentice" (5). But the fantastic mode is not abandoned: "Pirate has become famous for his Banana Breakfasts" (5). Hell turns into a tropical paradise with banana trees!

A realistic justification for Prentice's horticultural endeavor may be possible but is, once again, not pertinent. The point and impact of the passage is to establish a world in which our cognitive coordinates are constantly under attack. The reader never knows in advance what kind of world s/he will encounter in the next page, what leap of imagination it will be necessary to perform in order to make sense of the text. In order to continue reading, the reader must be willing to live with this uncertainty and eventually even come to enjoy it. But why? What are the stakes of this strange and difficult game to which Pynchon is convening the reader? The answer begins to emerge as we keep up with our newly found and very temporary protagonist Pirate Prentice.

In addition to the cultivation of bananas, Pirate's main talent lies in "getting inside the fantasies of others" (13) and as a result of this unusual capacity Pirate is enlisted by the powers that be (the omnipresent "Firm" or simply "They") to deal with the Giant Adenoid, a monster produced by the imagination of Lord Blatherard Osmo, a high official in the Foreign Office. After rampaging through London and defying all weapons deployed against it, the "lymphatic monster" (16) settles in the St. James's area but requires constant monitoring. This is the task entrusted to Pirate so that Lord Blatherard can return to his more important diplomatic duties.

The Giant Adenoid episode is a notable example of Pynchon's use of grotesque imagery (Meindl 201), which, however, is narrativized in the fantastic mode. The richness of Pynchon's strategy deserves exploration, especially since the farcical tone of the story may mislead the reader about the significance of the author's manipulations. The fantastic mode is ushered in by the very premise of the episode: "what if" we could have access to other people's fantasies, and in particular to the fantasies of those in power, military leaders on whom the fate of the world may at times depend? What monsters will we find in those fantasies? More importantly, what catastrophes can these people (the "They" of the novel) occasion as a result of their monstrous fantasies? With each question, the stakes are raised: there is a crescendo in parallel to the growth of the Adenoid; the story gathers a momentum that is paradoxically comic and tragic, satirically carnival and disturbingly serious.

The Giant Adenoid is simultaneously a monster from B movies (e.g., *The Blob* from 1959) and an allegory of the body; its rampage is the struggle of the organic against the inorganic weapons of modern technology—a synecdoche of the human pitted against the inhuman power of manipulative bureaucracy. It is also a figure of hypertrophy, which develops the central theme of the cancerous explosion of modern civilization but also reflects meta-discursively on the character of the text itself: a hypertrophic narrative of the highest order. The hypertrophic figure is therefore ambivalent: both the representation of a deadly illness (the cancer) and of the possible remedy to such illness (the work of art). Finally, Pirate's ability to communicate, albeit with difficulty, with the Adenoid confirms his placement on the side of the organic, a location already signaled by his cultivation of bananas. And Pirate will be a key member of the "counterforce" keeping up the good

fight against domination by the "Firm." In sum, the Adenoid is anything but a facile fantasy (offered by Lord Blatherard to Pirate, and by
the author to the reader). Rather, it is a cognitive tool that Pynchon uses
to begin mapping out a constellation of issues vital to the novel. These,
then, are the stakes of the game: the sudden irruptions of the fantastic
in *Gravity's Rainbow* cajole the reader into contemplating the unthinkable: a world where human technology embodies monstrous fantasies
and reason is driven by the insane desire for orgasmic death. At first
this happens through laughter—as in Pirate's encounter with the Giant
Adenoid (16–18) or Slothrop's voyage down the toilet bowl (75–81).
Later, however, these irruptions of the fantastic involve ominous episodes as we reach the heart of the "They" system.

In the end, the most accomplished product of the fantastic mode in
Pynchon's masterpiece is the "Zone." By far the longest of the four
"books" that compose *Gravity's Rainbow*, "In the Zone" occupies almost four hundred pages in which Pynchon creates an unprecedented narrative space. Part hallucination, part reality, the receptacle of a
seemingly inexhaustible series of disparate allusions and digressions,
the Zone is as much a place of the mind as of the body, an imaginative/
imaginary site as well as a physical location. This begins to be made
clear in the opening passage of "In the Zone":

> We are safely past the days of the Eis-Heiligen—St. Pancratius, St.
> Servatius, St. Bonifacius, die kalte Sophie . . . they hover in clouds above
> the vineyards, holy beings of ice, ready with a breath, an intention, to ruin
> the year with frost and cold. In certain years, especially War years, they
> are short on charity, peevish, smug in their power: not quite saintly or
> even Christian. The prayers of growers, pickers and wine enthusiasts must
> reach them, but there's no telling how the ice-saints feel—coarse laughter,
> pagan annoyance, who understands this rear-guard who preserves winter
> against the revolutionaries in May? (327)

Immediately striking in this passage are the echoes of "Little Gidding," the last poem in T. S. Eliot's collection *Four Quartets* (1936–42). There are similar images of winter (frost, ice, cold), and of a special time both in terms of calendar cycles and of historical events (Eliot's "midwinter's spring" is similar to Pynchon's winter grape harvest; Pynchon's war years remind the reader of Eliot's year of the king's execution). There is the religious atmosphere (All Saints in Pynchon and "Pentecostal fire" in Eliot) that produces a time out of time and a place out of place: the saints are menacing in Pynchon as "they hover in clouds . . . ready with a breath, an intention"; while in Eliot there is an ominous series of negation of the human world "no earth smell / Or smell of living thing" ("Little Gidding" II. 12–13), "not in time's covenant" (14), "Not in the scheme of generation" (18). And Pynchon's paragraph ends on a question: "Who understands the rear-guard who preserves winter against the revolutionaries of May?" (327), just like the ending of the first stanza of "Little Gidding": "Where is the summer, the unimaginable / Zero summer?" (19–20).[3]

For our purposes, this intertextual evidence is important because it sets the tone for the kind of world we encounter in the Zone: a world hovering between reality and fantasy, between this-worldliness and other-worldliness, between realistic representation and the fantastic. The device that triggers this oscillation here, however, is not the grotesque but rather the sublime, which the allusions to Eliot's poetry assist in evoking. The question that this passage and the Zone in general insistently raise is a radical "what if": what if it were true that, as Eliot states in "Burnt Norton" (the first of the *Four Quartets*) "human kind / Cannot bear very much reality" (42–43)? What if, to be more explicit, our understanding of the world, of what counts for us as real is a cognitive limit that we should be struggling to overcome? Slothrop (the evanescent protagonist of *Gravity's Rainbow*) can only experience much of the Zone in the modality of the fantastic, through the glimmer of a hypothesis, because what he faces is on the edge of the imaginable—

and indeed this is the kind of challenge to human understanding that for philosopher Immanuel Kant defines the experience of the sublime.[4]

A fully developed example of this use of the fantastic occurs immediately after the opening passage. As he enters the Zone, Slothrop is obsessed by the memory of Katje, the beautiful and vulnerable woman he met in London and with whom he feels he has a mysterious connection. This obsession is a kind of paranoia that leads Slothrop to (over) interpret everything he sees as a sign of/from Katje: "a red tulip between Slothrop's toes. He has taken it for a sign. A reminder of Katje. Signs will find him here in the Zone . . ." (327). There is much more to these signs, however, than Slothrop realizes: "Signs of Katje, and doubles too. One night he sat in a children's play house on an abandoned estate, feeding a fire from the hair of a blonde doll with lapis lazuli eyes. He kept those eyes. A few days later he traded them for a ride and half a boiled potato" (328). Here, the preoccupation with Katje erupts into a narrative that manifests unconscious processes. The blonde doll with lapis lazuli eyes stands in as Katje's double, clearly, but what is much less obvious is why Slothrop is tearing her apart: burning her hair, tearing out her eyes. For the moment, the story remains within the compass of realism and yet there are elements of the fantastic creeping in. The setting (a playhouse on an abandoned estate) evokes fairy tales and within that mode the cruelty of Slothrop's actions is both emphasized and, for the moment, contained: horrible things can happen in fairy tales and their meaning is not literal but symbolic. This is not the fantastic mode yet; it is just a hint that realism is under pressure from another mode: events can be explained not only realistically but also as determined by the narrative conventions of a nonrealist genre (namely the fairy tale). In the ensuing paragraph, the pressure on realism mounts but at the same time the fairy tale's capacity to contain and defuse horrific content is undermined:

The doll's hair was human. The smell of it burning is horrible. Slothrop hears movement from the other side of the fire. A ratcheting noise—he grasps his blanket, ready to vault away out of the empty window frame, expecting a grenade. Instead, one of these little brightly painted German toys, an orangutan on wheels comes ki-ki-ki-ing into the firelight . . . It rolls nearly into the fire before the clockwork runs down, the wagging head coming to dead center to stare at Slothrop. (328)

Notice how the syntactical structure in the first sentence places a heavy stress on the last word, "human." Even more striking is the shift from the past tense of the first sentence to the present tense of the second: the hair "was human"; its smell, as it burns, "is horrible." The hair both is still and is no longer human: it remains human hair but it is also part of a toy. Time collapses ("One night he sat" but now "Slothrop hears") and the reader tumbles into the world of Slothrop's memory, a world haunted by death: human remains are burning as in a funeral pyre. Then another toy comes ominously "alive": the mechanical orangutan (the most humanlike of the apes) is at first perceived as a threat, an engine liable to explode and kill. When it lies still "staring" at Slothrop, the threat seems contained and yet the uncanny elements in the scene have set the stage for the final conflagration of the fantastic. Slothrop's gesture becomes an incantation:

He feeds the fire another tuft of golden hair. "Evening."
Laughter, somewhere. A child. But old laughter.
"Come on out, I'm harmless." . . .
"Why are you burning my doll's hair?"
"Well, it's not her own hair, you know."
"Father said it belonged to a Russian Jewess."
"Why don't you come in to the fire?"
"Hurts my eyes." . . . "Dance with me."
"I can't see you."
"Here." Out of the fire's pale, a tiny frost-flower. He reaches and just manages to find her hand, to grasp her little waist. . . .
He never saw her face. She felt like voile and organdy. . . .

A faint smell reached him exactly then . . . as he turned back to her to ask if she really was Katje. . . . But the music had run down. She had vaporized from his arms. (328–29)

A memory? A hallucination? A dream? All of these, probably. The point is that Slothrop cannot face, grasp, even cognize what he is facing except through recourse to the fantastic. In this case, the "real" is both so horrifying (the reference to the Holocaust) and so complex (the connections between technology, sexuality, and death exposed by the Holocaust; the connection between this constellation and Katje; and so on) that it can only emerge into consciousness as a bubbling up of fantastic images and narratives. The fantastic irrupts when the resources of realism fail, when realistic representation is not yet possible.

Gravity's Rainbow plays a crucial role in Pynchon's development of the fantastic mode. The section "In the Zone" in particular makes clear that for the author the fantastic serves to explore dimensions of the real that the conventions of realism cannot yet reach. The last adverb, "yet," is critical here. Pynchon uses the fantastic to show the limits of realism but never abandons the project of imagining what is actually the case though we cannot, do not want, or do not "yet" know how to see it, speak of it, even cognize it. The fantastic becomes a kind of safety valve when experience forces us to revise what we consider "real," but at the same time, realism keeps the explorations of the fantastic within the orbit (even a distant one) of the actual.[5] In Pynchon, it is the oscillation and tension between the two modes that produces a brilliantly imaginative and dynamic narration.

Two additional observations need to be made before we discuss the impact of Pynchon's development of the fantastic on contemporary fiction. First, it is important to note that the fantastic mode that achieves its definitive formulation in *Gravity's Rainbow* is the result of an exploration of literary forms which can be traced back to Pynchon's earliest work. Not only do Pynchon's early short stories, such as "Low Lands" (1960), "Entropy" (1960), and "Under The Rose" (1961) display a tendency to break out of realism, but most importantly his first novel *V.* (1963) contains striking examples of the fantastic strategy that would come to full fruition in his mature works. One of the most notable fantastic episodes in *V.* is the death of the "Bad Priest" at the end of the "Confessions of Fausto Maijstral" (286–323). The passage is intricate and only its highlights can be considered here. It starts with an important assertion on the part of the narrator: this is "a horrible encounter with the one we only knew as the Bad Priest. An encounter I am only now attempting to put in English" (286)—once again the reality that needs to be described is at the edge of language. We are in Malta, during WWII; the Italians are bombing the island and the Bad Priest (who used to preach against procreation and had counseled the narrator's mother to have an abortion) is one of the victims:

I heard cries: hostile shouting. Children. . . . The children inside were clustered round a figure in black. The Bad Priest. Wedged under a fallen beam. Face—what could be seen—impassive.

"Is he dead," one asked. Others were picking already at the black rags. . . .

"Funny hat," giggled a little girl. She reached out and tugged off the hat. A long coil of white hair came loose and fell into the plaster-dust. . . .

"It's a lady," said the girl.

. . . "It's not real hair," the boy announced. "See." He removed the long white wig from the priest's head.

"That's Jesus," cried a tall boy. Tattooed on the bare scalp was a two-colour Crucifixion. It was to be only the first of many surprises. (320–21)

What follows is a very disturbing scene of children like ants tearing apart a dying organism. Except that many of the parts are not organic but metallic and mineral: gold teeth, sapphire navel, a glass eye. Then, the narrator interpolates:

I wondered if the disassembly of the Bad Priest might not go on, and on, into the evening. Surely her arms and breasts could be detached; the skin of her legs be peeled away to reveal some intricate understructure of silver openwork. Perhaps the trunk itself contained other wonders: intestines of parti-coloured silk, gay balloon-lungs, a rococo heart. But the sirens started up then. The children dispersed. . . . (322)

This vision and this episode are key moments in the novel, one of the central themes of which is precisely the relation, the tension, and the struggle between the organic and the inorganic. The impact of the passage is due to the cognitive disorientation that the discovery of the Bad Priest's body produces. The first challenge is gender: the Bad Priest is in effect a transvestite. But that is only the beginning, and by the end of the scene we confront a being whose life-form is undecidable: monstrous and wondrous at the same time; as deeply ambivalent and mysterious as all the incarnations of the elusive principle that is V. And Pynchon relies on the fantastic mode to deliver such a vision.

A second comment must be made in order to conclude an initial mapping of Pynchon's fantastic. The examples discussed so far illustrate how the fantastic in Pynchon can be triggered by grotesque exaggeration (the Giant Adenoid), metaphysical high-mindedness (the opening of "In the Zone" and its intertextual evocation of Eliot's "Little Gidding"), and by an admixture of the uncanny, the ominous, and the horrific (the doll with human hair and the Bad Priest episodes). These modulations by no means provide a complete catalogue of the ways in which Pynchon invokes the fantastic. However, they are distinctive of the author's style, and in this context it should be emphasized that the first—that is, grotesque amplification—is overall the most common and most typically associated with Pynchon's oeuvre, especially when accompanied by a broadly comedic tone. One of the most memorable examples of this particular modulation is the hairspray bottle episode in Chapter 2 of Pynchon's novella *The Crying of Lot 49* (1966), when the sexual encounter between Oedipa (the protagonist) and Metzger (one of the many rather insignificant male figures she encounters in the course of her quest) ends with a punctured can jetting wildly about, wreaking havoc in the motel room and spraying a sticky mist over the whole scene. Pynchon's fantastic spans from the sublime to the ridiculous—but in either case it alerts the reader to a critical passage in the narrative: in Oedipa's case the encounter with Metzger definitively commits the protagonist to the vortex of suppositions and mysteries around which the novel revolves.

ii. Pynchon's Legacy

Pynchon's impact on contemporary culture is wide ranging. Through his well-known and well-publicized reclusiveness, Pynchon has even achieved the status of a cult figure in popular culture and ensured that the appearance of one of his novels is automatically an event. For our purposes, however, the key issue is the impact of Pynchon's use of the fantastic mode, and from this angle we should begin by considering the connection between the fantastic mode and certain features of literary postmodernism.

In his influential book *Postmodernist Fiction* (1987), Brian McHale has argued that what distinguishes modernist from postmodernist literature is the fact that while the former's basic concerns are epistemological, the latter's are ontological. For McHale, modernist writers (like Proust and Joyce) are still primarily concerned with how we can know the world. On the other hand, postmodernist writers (like Calvino and Pynchon) have been primarily preoccupied with ontological questions such as: what kind of world do we live in? Pynchon is a key figure in this "change of dominant" (McHale 3) and McHale devotes the entire third chapter of his book to an analysis of *Gravity's Rainbow*'s "Zone," which he describes as a heterotopia:[6] a place that is both real and imaginary, where contradictory states can coexist (43–58). McHale's argument helps us to clarify a couple of important points:

First, there is a connection between the "ontological dominant" in postmodernist fiction and the fantastic. The question "what kind of world do we inhabit?" is akin to the question *"what if* the world we inhabited were like . . . ?": in both cases the objective is to explore a world that cannot be understood according to our conventional notions of how reality functions. However, in the former case the world which turns out to be strange and mysterious is the one around us, while in the latter a world is posited as manifestly different from the one around us though such other worlds can in the final analysis tell us something important about what our world may become (for better or for ill).

Second, in Pynchon, these two questions are constantly at play and the dynamic energy of the narrative derives from the dialectical interaction of these two different narrative strategies. In Pynchon, realism (postmodernly inflected, as per McHale) and the fantastic constantly react upon each other forcing a never-ending evolution of what can be written about in both modes. In the end, neither category predominates, and both remain programmatically open to challenge by the other. It is this oscillation that most clearly distinguishes Pynchon's work from science fiction in spite of a shared preoccupation with scientific knowledge and technology.

These observations help us frame the discussion of Pynchon's legacy. The impact of his work is most evident in two overlapping but not coterminous currents in contemporary culture: postmodernism and science fiction. For the purposes of this discussion, Pynchon's most important contribution to postmodernism is the development of the fantastic as a cognitive tool: our effort to grasp the strangeness of the world around us can exploit the resources of fantasy. The imagination exceeds the real not to escape it but to overcome conventional understanding and widen the horizon of what we might in due course be able to understand and talk about more precisely when we recognize it as belonging to the ever-expanding horizon of our reality. To science fiction, conversely but consistently, Pynchon contributes a key reminder that no matter how strange the posited world might be, no matter how technologically advanced or backward, the link with contemporary reality must always be acknowledged and creatively addressed.

Postmodernist works that show Pynchon's influence are so numerous as to make citation problematic. Yet the case of Salmon Rushdie (*Midnight's Children*, 1980; *The Satanic Verses*, 1988) is especially important insofar as it points to a much-acclaimed trend in postcolonial fiction that is unimaginable without Pynchon's contribution, though other legacies are undoubtedly also involved (such as Gabriel Garcia Márquez's novel *One Hundred Years of Solitude* (1967) and, more generally, South American magical realism). It should also be noted that *Gravity's Rainbow* culminates in an apocalyptic vision that has strongly influenced contemporary catastrophic narratives, such as the 2006 novel *The Road* by Cormac McCarthy.

Just as numerous are the science fiction works clearly indebted to Pynchon. Science fiction writers often explicitly acknowledge his influence, as did William Gibson when he stated:

Pynchon has been a favorite writer and a major influence all along. In many ways I see him as almost the start of a certain mutant pop culture imagery with esoteric historical and scientific information. Pynchon is a kind of mythic hero of mine, and I suspect that if you talk with a lot of recent science fiction writers you'll find they've all read *Gravity's Rainbow* (1973) several times and have been very much influenced by it. (McCaffery 138)

As the founder and the most critically acclaimed practitioner of cyberpunk, Gibson has become an essential point of reference in contemporary science fiction with works such as *The Neuromancer* (1984), *The Difference Engine* (1990), *All Tomorrow's Parties* (1999), and *Zero History* (2010). Gibson's oeuvre has reached a mass audience and exploits precisely Pynchon's ability to oscillate between the highly imaginative and the grittily realistic, though in Gibson's case we remain with the science horizon of posited "other" / future worlds.

An intriguing example of Pynchon's impact on science fiction film is Andrei Tarkovsky's haunting work *Stalker* (1979).[7] At the center of the narratives is "the Zone"—a place that, in addition to sharing a name, is remarkably similar to Pynchon's "Zone" in *Gravity's Rainbow*. Though the film is usually considered to belong to the science fiction genre, *Stalker* is fundamentally an oneiric narrative, and Tarkovsky's "Zone" bears striking similarities to the landscape within which Slothrop eventually vanishes. While no direct filiation has been yet established between Pynchon and Tarkovsky, it seems unlikely that the Russian director would not have been aware of the former's work; the affinity between their imaginative worlds is compelling.

Finally, in popular culture, Pynchon's impact can be detected in the increasing appeal of plots that, set in apparently "ordinary" environments, quickly drift toward the fantastic while never relinquishing what may be called "detail realism." For example, today's massively popular "horror" narratives display a Pynchonesque inflection when they rely on a grotesquely ironic self-referentiality (e.g., the *Scream* movies). Also worth mentioning is Pynchon's participation in *The Simpsons* TV series. It is telling that Pynchon agreed to lend his mark of approval to a program that deploys fantastic means—the condensations and displacements of the cartoon genre—to challenge (albeit rather blandly and ambivalently) the contemporary American way of life.

III. Conclusion: The Fantastic and Contemporary Culture

From today's perspective it is possible to see that Todorov's theory of the fantastic concludes an epoch. The subtitle of the English translation of Todorov's book is telling: *A Structural Approach to a Literary Genre*. The key terms are "structural" and "genre." The former indicates Todorov's indebtedness to structuralism, a critical orientation that dominated literary studies (especially in continental Europe) in the 1960s and sought to disengage the literary text from its context (historical, ideological, etc.), focusing rather on the immanent features of each work. Though undoubtedly valuable, this approach tended to use wide atemporal categories (such as "genre" in Todorov's sense) which as Medusa's gaze froze the text rather than understood it as an instrument in the ongoing struggle for cognition. The need for a more flexible approach began to manifest itself at the end of the 1970s, and over the course of the decade, many critics abandoned structuralism in order to focus on the dialogue between text and context and on the productive reciprocal impact of such a dialogue on literature and society. Post-structuralism emphasized conceptual fluidity, more nuanced theoretical claims and constant self-reflection and criticism. The move from genre to mode responded to this change in approach and led to our contemporary definition of the fantastic as a narrative strategy based on a hypothesis—the "what if" question—which destabilizes the commonsense notion of what the world is in order to reveal what is not yet the case but perhaps could be.

One last question should be asked in conclusion: what is the connection between our contemporary cultural predicaments and the strong revival of the fantastic mode in today's fiction (literature, film, TV programs, etc.)? This is a complex and fascinating question. In this context, we can at least say that Pynchon's use of the fantastic speaks directly to the condition alluded to in the title of Andy Grundberg's important book *Crisis of the Real* (1990). There can be little doubt that one of the most evident features of contemporary (Western?) culture is a growing skepticism about the human ability to identify and understand the foundations of reality. Philosophical relativism, suspicions about science, and, finally, a growing sense of the impossibility of mastering the complexity of the world we inhabit are undermining our ability to distinguish the real from the imaginary. Media saturation has contributed to this predicament by both too much content and too little reflection about the reasons and conditions concomitant to the production of that content. When fiction and reality tend to merge, when a key cultural predicament is the redefinition of what constitutes the real and how to navigate this unprecedented virtual dimension, the power of the fantastic to step outside the conventions of realism and posit new worlds must become very appealing.

Appealing but also dangerous. Pynchon's fantastic explorations remain, as we have seen, firmly within the orbit of actuality. He uses the fantastic as a cognitive tool that can help us come to grips with what we do not yet quite understand and do not yet quite know how to speak about. On the other hand, the fantastic mode can also be merely a veneer, a facile dressing-up in bizarre costume of trite situations, emotions, and relationships, thus providing an escape from, rather than a way into, the complexity of the real. In this too, the fantastic and realism are closely allied: both can be articulated with seriousness of purpose or for shallow entertainment. Pynchon's work reminds us of the rewards of seriousness and provides a model of rigor in using one mode to interrogate the other.

Notes

1. This image has been vividly revived in the Western imaginary by the September 11, 2001, terrorist attack on the World Trade Center in New York City.

2. The English translation appeared in 1973 under the title *The Fantastic: A Structural Approach to a Literary Genre*. For ease of reference, however, all citations are taken from the Cornell UP edition of 1975.

3. It should be noted that the second book of *Gravity's Rainbow* is entitled "Beyond the Zero."

4. For reasons of space, the concept of the "sublime" cannot be explored here. For our purposes, it will suffice to say that the term is used not to mean an "elevated style" but rather in the philosophical sense developed by Kant in his *Critique of Judgment* (*Kritik der Urteilskraft*, 1790). In describing the character of the sublime experience, Kant points to the most awe-inspiring and overwhelming spectacles of nature (e.g., a storm at sea) that challenge our very ability to comprehend them (97–126).

5. This formulation is indebted to Todorov's insight that "the fantastic permits us to cross certain frontiers that are inaccessible so long as we have no recourse to it" (158). But while for the French critic these "frontiers" turn out to be those of repression, leading him to the rather startling conclusion that "psychoanalysis [insofar as it speaks of taboos and seeks to undo repression] has replaced (and thereby has made useless) the literature of the fantastic" (160), my discussion here develops the cognitive dimension of Todorov's insight: the frontiers in questions are those of the knowable and the imaginable.

6. McHale derives this term from Michel Foucault's essay "Of Other Spaces" (1967).

7. The Russian director is best known in the West for his science fiction classic film *Solaris* (1972).

Works Cited

Alighieri, Dante. *Dante's Inferno*. Trans. Mark Musa. Bloomington, IN: Indiana UP, 1971.

Angenot, Marc. "The Absent Paradigm: An Introduction to the Semiotics of Science Fiction." *Science Fiction Studies* 6.1 (Mar. 1979): 9–19.

Arnold, Matthew. *Culture and Anarchy*. 1869. Oxford: Oxford UP, 2006.

Bolongaro, Eugenio. "From Literariness to Genre: Establishing the Foundations for a Theory of Literary Genre." *Genre* 25 (1992): 277–313.

Eliot, T. S. *Four Quartets*. London: Faber & Faber, 1944.

Foucault, Michel. "Of Other Spaces." *Diacritics* 16.1 (1986): 22–27.

Frye, Northrop. *The Anatomy of Criticism: Four Essays*. 1957. Toronto: U of Toronto P, 2006.

Gibson, William. *All Tomorrow's Parties*. New York: Putnam, 1999.

_____. *Burning Chrome*. New York: HarperCollins, 2003.

_____. *The Neuromancer*. New York: Ace, 2004.

_____. *Zero History*. New York: G. P. Putnam's Sons, 2010.

Gibson, William, and Bruce Sterling. *The Difference Engine*. New York: Bantam, 1991.

Grant, Kerry J. *A Companion to* The Crying of Lot 49. 2nd ed. Athens: U of Georgia P, 2008.

Grundberg, Andy. *Crisis of the Real: Essays on Photography since 1974*. New York: Aperture, 1999.

Jackson, Rosemary. *Fantasy: The Literature of Subversion*. London: Methuen, 1981.

Kant, Immanuel. *Critique of Judgment*. Trans. Werner S. Pluhar. Indianapolis, IN: Hackett, 1987.

Márquez, Gabriel Garcia. *One Hundred Years of Solitude*. Trans. Gregory Rabassa. New York: Harper, 1970.

McCaffery, Larry. "An Interview with William Gibson." *Across the Wounded Galaxies: Interviews with Contemporary American Science Fiction Writers*. Ed. Larry McCaffery. Urbana: U of Illinois P, 1990. 130–50.

McHale, Brian. *Postmodernist Fiction*. London: Routledge, 1987.

Meindl, Dieter. *American Fiction and the Metaphysics of the Grotesque*. Columbia: U of Missouri P, 1996.

Pynchon, Thomas. *Against the Day*. New York: Penguin, 2006.

_____. *The Crying of Lot 49*. New York: HarperPerennial, 1999.

_____. *Gravity's Rainbow*. New York: Viking, 1973.

_____. *Inherent Vice*. New York: Penguin, 2009.

_____. *Mason & Dixon*. New York: Holt, 1997.

_____. *V.: A Novel*. Philadelphia: Lippincott, 1963.

Rabkin, Eric S. *The Fantastic in Literature*. Princeton, NJ: Princeton UP, 1976.

The Road. Dir. John Hillcoat. Dimension Films, 2009.

Rowling, J. K. *Harry Potter*. 7 vols. Vancouver, BC: Raincoast, 1997–2007.

Rushdie, Salman. *Midnight's Children*. London: Cape, 1981.

_____. *The Satanic Verses*. London: Viking, 1989.

Scholes, Robert, and Eric S. Rabkin. *Science Fiction: History, Science, Vision*. New York: Oxford UP, 1977.

Suvin, Darko. *Metamorphoses of Science Fiction: On the Poetics and History of a Literary Genre*. New Haven: Yale UP, 1979.

Tarkovsky, Andrei, dir. *Solaris*. Criterion Collection. HVE, 2002. DVD.

_____. *Stalker*. Kino International, 2006. DVD.

Todorov, Tzvetan. *The Fantastic: A Structural Approach to a Literary Genre*. Trans. Richard Howard. Ithaca, NY: Cornell UP, 1975.

Vinge, Vernor. *A Deepness in the Sky*. New York: Tor, 1999.

Calvino, the Fairytale, and Two *Stories for Children*

Daniela De Pau

Introduction

One of the most fruitful ways in which the Italian intellectual, writer, and critic Italo Calvino (1923–85) explored his profound interest in the literature of the fantastic was through his passion for fairy tales, whose rich world had appealed to him from the time of his early works and continued to inform his poetics in more or less overt ways, in his fictional and nonfictional works, until his final writings. This predilection was mainly due to the fact that, for Calvino, the fantastic did not hold an emotive fascination and did not include fantasy. On the contrary, it was deeply rooted in the rational, representing for him an intellectual tool through which he could try to understand the complex relationship between perceptions and reality, or rather, the different and multiple levels through which reality presents itself, a concept on which he believed literature to be founded. In a chapter entitled "Definitions of Territory: The Fantastic"[1] (1970), written on the occasion of the publication of Tzvetan Todorov's book *Introduction à la littérature fantastique*, Calvino explained his approach to the fantastic: "The central point of narration for me is not the explanation of an extraordinary fact; rather the order that this extraordinary fact develops within and around itself, the design, the symmetry, the web of images that are deposited around it as in the formation of a crystal" (*Una Pietra Sopra* 261). The author here is clearly distancing himself from Todorov, for whom the fantastic was constituted by the hesitation experienced before an extraordinary event that cannot be explained by the laws of nature. Calvino's vision of the fantastic instead centered on the architectural and logical aspects that could be derived from this event and for this reason coincided with his conception of the fairy tale. Indeed, as I will explain below, Calvino saw in both the fantastic and the fairy tale the possibility of building a lucid intellectual narrative design.

Roberto Deidier specifies that the fairy-tale components, an underlying leitmotif in all of Calvino's oeuvre, whether fantastic or not, constitute a model that functions both as the "identification of a perspective" (e.g., structure) and as a "modulation of the writing" (e.g., style) (41). Calvino's own belief in the importance of these two aspects in their most essential forms can be deduced from two passages in which he explicitly discusses the genre of the fairy tale. The reference to the first element, the identification of a perspective, is taken from the preface to *Italian Folk Tales* (1956), in which Calvino collected and then rewrote two hundred of the most significant tales of the last one hundred years from different Italian regions. It is important to note that, by undertaking such an onerous task, Calvino created the first national collection of traditional Italian fables since the unification of Italy in 1861. This study acquired historical, philological, and anthropological significance, equaling in importance, for instance, the collection of the Grimm brothers in Germany and of Alexander Nikolayevich Afanasyev in Russia.[2] While studying these Italian fairy tales in depth, at a time when "collating, categorizing, comparing became a fever" (*Italian Folk Tales* xvii), Calvino came to discover and appreciate specific narrative qualities that were characteristic of the genre and that profoundly influenced his poetics from that moment on.[3] He states:

> For two years I have lived in woodlands and enchanted castles . . . where everything that happened was a spell or a metamorphosis, where individuals, plucked away from a chiaroscuro of a state of mind, were carried away by predestined loves, or were bewitched; where sudden disappearances, monstrous transformations occurred, where right had to be discerned from wrong, where paths bristling with obstacles led to a happiness held captive by dragons. Also, in the lives of people and nations, which until now had seemed to be at a standstill, anything seemed possible. . . . I had the impression that the lost rules which govern the world of folklore were

tumbling out of the magic box I had opened. Now that the book is finished I know that this was not a hallucination . . . but the confirmation . . . folktales are real. (xviii)[4]

As mentioned above, the element that Calvino claims to appreciate here is the clear (and almost binary) logic of fairy tales, according to which circumstances are depicted in black or white and decisions and actions are extremely significant, since they possess the power to effect reversals of fortune. At the same time, this logic is governed by pure imagination, through which stories can magically be altered thanks to those same metamorphic attributes that had characterized the writing of the Latin poet Ovid, whom Calvino greatly admired. In other words, in fairy tales the path toward a resolution is found through the fantastic, a pseudo-"geological" or pseudoscientific reasoning that, applied to old rules evocative of the rites of primitive societies, is instrumental in changing fixed situations and helping events to unfold. It is evident here that it is the structure of the genre that appealed to the author, in which he identifies a (scientific) "perspective" to serve as a starting point for the construction of a story that might resemble real life (Lavagetto 38). Calvino specifies:

> Taken all together, they [the fairy tales] offer, in their oft-repeated and constantly varying examinations of human vicissitudes, a general explanation of life preserved in the slow ripening of rustic consciences; the folktales are the catalog of the potential destinies of men and women, especially for the stage in life when destiny is formed. (*Italian Folk Tales* xviii)

The author sees in fairy tales the potential to forge one's own destiny precisely in the effort of the main protagonist, the hero, to recognize, face, and overcome obstacles, thus attaining different phases of development that eventually lead to the character's maturity. Calvino, who was mainly a writer of action and adventure stories, was notoriously fascinated by the concept of trials. Indeed, challenges, and the way they are confronted, provide the opportunity to discover oneself and the world, and therefore also the ability to affirm oneself in it, according to an ancestral and mythical-ritual understanding of life. In *Italian Folk Tales,* Calvino concludes the discourse on his "Journey through Folklore" thus:

> This sketch, although summary, encompasses everything: the arbitrary division of humans, albeit in essence equal, into kings and poor people, the persecution of the innocent and their subsequent vindication, which are terms inherent in every life, love unrecognized when first encountered and then no sooner experienced than lost; the common fate of subjection to spells, or having one's existence predetermined by complex and unknown forces. This complexity pervades one's entire existence and forces one to struggle to free oneself, to determine one's own fate; at the same time we can liberate ourselves only if we liberate other people, for this is a sine qua non of one's own liberation. There must be fidelity to a goal and purity of the heart, a sign of grace that can be masked by the humble, ugly guise of a frog; and above all, there must be the infinite possibilities of mutation, the unifying elements in everything men, beasts, plants, things. (xix)

According to Mario Lavagetto, in essence, the world of the fairy tale represented for Calvino "a vast encyclopedia of the stories to be told, a repertoire of primary functions that, in different guises, can be rediscovered in every story" (38). For Calvino, fairy tales are the archetype of narration, the result of a combination of stories that finally converge, balancing the opposites—good and bad, beauty and ugliness, and so on—and thus portray the ancient struggle for life.

The second aspect of fairy tales that interested him, and on which he based the modulation (the style) of his writing, is expressed in *Six Memos for the Next Millennium*, a posthumous work published in 1988 constituted by a series of six prestigious lectures (the Norton lectures) that he was invited to deliver at Harvard University but never finished or gave. With these beautiful and complex lectures that can also be read as an autobiography and an overview of his entire literary career, he intended to identify and discuss six literary values to be preserved for the next millennium. He completed only five lectures: "Lightness," "Quickness," "Exactitude," "Visibility," and "Multiplicity." The last one would have been on "Consistency," and it is known that he was planning to write two more. In the chapter of *Six Memos for the Next Millennium* entitled "Quickness" he returns to the subject of fairy tales, saying:

> If during a certain period of my career as a writer I was attracted by folk-tales and fairytales, this was not the result of loyalty to an ethnic tradition (seeing that my roots are planted in an entirely modern and cosmopolitan Italy), nor the result of nostalgia for things I read as a child (in my family, a child could read only educational books, particularly those with some scientific basis). It was rather because of my interest in style and structure, in the economy, rhythm, and hard logic with which they are told. (35)

This passage shows that, reflecting back on his career, Calvino wanted to exclude any sentimentality as a determining factor for his predilection for the genre. He also clarified that fairy tales provided him with a model of the way to tell a story, as they contained a lesson in the use of language, which served as a "modulation" for his writing. Fairy tales represented for him an example of "economy of expression" (*Six Memos* 37) due to their ability to present a story by giving a synthesis of the most important facts, without pausing to give explanations or provide analysis. Instead, they focus on the description of the action, with brevity and conciseness, qualities to which Calvino had always aspired in his prose.

Traces of these elements of the fairy tale and their diverse meanings are found throughout his writing and have being accurately noted and studied by several critics, including Cesare Segre, who wrote the preface to Delia Frigessi's important work on the subject, *Inchiesta sulle fate* (*An Inquiry into Fairies,* 1988). The Italian critic drew attention in this preface to the fact that the two complementary interests present in Calvino, that of the collector of fairy tales and of the fairy-tale elements in his writing, merge into a unified vision that allowed Calvino to "intellectually exploit the gap between the real and the rational" and "to expand reality, going much further than our experience" (*Inchiesta sulle fate* 14). This merging can be seen in certain of the short stories he wrote for children, which also illustrate Calvino's conceptualization of the fantastic through his passion for fairy tales. These short stories, although less known and studied than much of his work, contain equally important themes for Calvino. They also carry the advantage of possessing a high level of symbolism and of being written in a particularly fresh and lively style.

This essay examines two of these stories, taking into account the parameters of fairy tales, according to two literary categories discussed in *Six Memos for the Next Millennium*. They are: "The Evil Drawings" (1977), read through Calvino's lens of "Exactitude," and "The Dragon and the Butterflies" (1978) read through his lens of "Quickness." The other two categories of "Lightness" and "Visibility" are appropriate for analysis of two other short stories Calvino wrote for children: "The Three Faraway Islands" (1978) and "The Forest-Root-Labyrinth" (1977). For reasons of space, however, they cannot be discussed here. The last category, "Multiplicity," is briefly cited at the end of this essay in summarizing considerations regarding Calvino's beliefs about the overall function of literature.

"The Evil Drawings"

This story can be considered a nontraditional fairy tale that illustrates the role of the fantastic in Calvino at a conceptual level. "The Evil Drawings" tells the story of two children, Lodolinda and Federico who, one day, are left alone at home by their parents. There are few similarities between the two children: the girl likes to make drawings that represent mimetically her inner world; the boy likes to conduct experiments that interrogate the ideas of common sense. Their interaction is marked, at least initially, by disagreement, but also by unexpected events. To prove the other wrong, the two engage in a ferocious battle that generates several strange adventures, in which they appear to metamorphose into, for instance, a terrified bull and a tiger that acts as a victim, or in which a boa constrictor is carried off by a vulture that is sent down the wrong track by a dead horse. These adventures eventually lead them to imagine a scene from a Western film, in which Lodolinda becomes Hawkeye, an American Indian, and Federico a cowboy, and in which both risk their lives. In the end they must run away together, threatened by their own previous creations, and in order to do so they start collaborating, drawing on the same "sheet." When their parents come home, they are happy to see the children calm, but the tranquility is broken at the children's first scream.

The struggle between two opposing forces and the importance of a balance between them constitute two of the main themes of this story. These forces are rationality on the one side (Lodolinda) and imagination on the other (Federico), which Calvino wants to conflate into what has been frequently referred to as "fantastic realism." For Calvino, rationality alone, if it inhabits the realm of artistic expression, offers only a limited understanding of the world because it is trapped within subjective viewpoints. On the contrary, imagination, if it inhabits the realm of science, represents the possibility of exploring reality in new ways. Mario Barenghi rightly observed, in fact, that Calvino subversively attributed the qualities of a constructive logic to fairy tales and those of imagination and creativity to science (qtd. in Frigessi 35).

The fairy-tale elements in this story do not adhere to the functions elaborated by Vladimir Propp in his seminal *Morphology of the Folktale* (1928), but relate to other elements.[5] For instance, the protagonists are children, or undeveloped human beings who need to learn their true path by means of conflict. Also, there is not a hero who acts in opposition to an antihero. Because the author never seems to prefer one character over the other, victory does not consist in the defeat of the opponent, but in the peaceful coexistence of the two. Furthermore, the story is like a fairy tale because, along the way, the two children acquire different forms, transferring within their drawings their identity from the human world into the animal world and back again into the human, without their discourse losing credibility. Rather, all these transformations accentuate one element that precisely characterizes the story: its tendency toward exactness, visible in the perfect symmetry of the opposition of these two forces. To better understand the meaning of this aspect of Calvino, we can refer to the chapter "Exactitude" in his *Six Memos for the Next Millennium*.

In "Exactitude," often associated with his other fictional works, *Cosmicomics* (1965) and *T zero* (1967), and that is based on his passion for science and combinatorial games,[6] Calvino first clearly defined the three implications that this concept entailed for him: (1) "a well-defined and well-calculated plan for the question"; (2) "an evocation of clear, incisive, memorable visual images"; and (3) a language as precise as possible both in choice of words and in expression of the subtleties of thought and imagination" (*Six Memos* 55–56). However, he also specified that his praise for exactness encompasses a great consideration for its opposite—vagueness—because, as the great Italian poet Giacomo Leopardi (author of the famous ca. 1819 poem *The Infinite*) showed, the beauty of vagueness can only be reached thanks to an exact and meticulous attention to a number of details that eventually and paradoxically lead to vagueness in its desired quantity. Calvino further claimed that his preference for geometrical compositions is based on the opposition of the dyad (or binary) of order and disorder that is so fundamental to the discourse of contemporary science (*Six Memos* 69), and that is condensed in the emblems of the crystal and the flame. The crystal represents the premise that starting from order one can reach order and is based on the existence of general laws from which it is possible to deduce the particular (determinism). The theory symbolized by the flame instead derives order from chaos, by studying all the components in which chaos cannot be brought back to simple and necessary laws (probabilism) (Piacentini 330).

Calvino's wish in "The Evil Drawings" is primarily for these two paradigms (determinism and probabilism) to interact by playing with each other. It is well known that the writer had a deep interest in games in their various forms and meanings, as well as in game theory. What is noteworthy here is that, as Roberto Bertoni observes, Calvino seemed to write as if "images on paper could animate themselves, become alive" so that "the fictitious dimension of the game would impose itself on that of the world" (80). This aspect of adherence to the truth is also crucial to an understanding of how, in Calvino's work, the fantastic element is so intrinsically linked to that of the realistic. Calvino explained his passion for combinatorial games in an article written in 1967 entitled "Cybernetics and Ghosts," featured as a chapter of the book *The Uses of Literature*. Starting his analysis on storytelling by recounting the fixed structures of primitive oral narrative (such as folktales), and referring to the mathematical processes used by both Propp in his study of the Russian folktales and by Claude Lévi-Strauss in his study of the myths of Brazilian Indians, Calvino notes that "the combinatorial play of narrative possibilities soon passes beyond the level of content to touch upon the relationship of the narrator to the material related and to the reader," which brings us "to the toughest set of problems facing contemporary fiction" (*The Uses of Literature* 6–7).

Toward the end of the chapter, Calvino rightly addresses such passion in relation to the role of the unconscious in literature (and in arts in general), stating that "literature is a combinatorial game that pursues the possibilities implicit in its own material, independent of the personality of the poet, but it is a game that at a certain point is invested with an unexpected meaning," that takes place when "the writing machine is surrounded by the hidden ghosts of the individual and of his society" (22). In fact, as Bertoni recalls, the game is by nature ambiguous. Because it is a human activity, it is constituted not only by rules and constraints, as exemplified by the French literary group Oulipo, but also by freedom, as articulated by play theorist Huizinga in *Homo Ludens* (1938), in which he discusses the idea that play may be the primary activity from which human culture derives (Bertoni and Ferraro 11). Therefore, the most evident part of the fantastic element in "The Evil Drawings" lies precisely in the combinatory logic of an imaginary game between two real scientific paradigms. Arguably, though, there is also an important "invisible" part to it. According to Fabio Maria Rosolo, the more Calvino tried to display the visible image of his conception of fantastic, the more he was attempting to conceal the unconscious image of it (qtd. in De Caprio and Olivieri 91), leaving some unresolved issues in the individualization of the fantastic in the author (87). Possibly, some traces of the personal anxiety Calvino refers to in the article "Cybernetics and Ghosts," the "intellectual agoraphobia" toward "that which cannot be counted or classified because it is in a constant state of flux" that he felt reassured reducing "to a system" (17, my translation), appear toward the end of "The Evil Drawings" in the temporary and apparent peace achieved between the two children.

Against this unconscious "ghost" in Calvino's rational world, the aim for these two opposite forces (rationality and imagination) is that they should enter into a dialogue and maybe eventually reconcile, or the implied moral of the fairy tale will fail. The author thus demonstrates a desire for unity that brings him close to an Eastern frame of mind, and in particular, close to the thought of Buddha (Piacentini 346). Another relevant element in the story that highlights this need for unity is the link that Calvino makes between words and drawings, adopted without distinction by the children to express themselves, thus combining the two into one discourse. Regarding this point, at the end of his essay on "Exactitude," Calvino recalled the Renaissance artist Leonardo da Vinci and his attempts to prove his theory of the earth's expansion. In his effort to evoke the apparition of a prehistoric sea monster as proof of his theory—while describing the image of his "furrowing the sea waters"—da Vinci in fact traced the very birth of his imagination, according to Calvino. In a passage in his chapter on "Visibility," in relation to his experience as a writer of fantastic narratives, Calvino specifies that his own "procedure aims at uniting the spontaneous generation of images [unconscious/the prehistoric sea monster] and the intentionality of discursive thought [conscious/da Vinci's theory]" (90).

"The Dragon and the Butterflies"

The second story to be discussed follows a more conventional fairy-tale narration, containing several functions identified by Vladimir Propp,[7] and it provides a good illustration of how the fantastic is achieved through stylistic choices. The story has three main protagonists, around whose adventures Calvino constructs a plot based on the juxtaposition of stillness in the first part and quickness in the second. They are the castaway Valdemaro who, after having been robbed of the treasure map that is hidden in the dragon's cave, can finally, one lucky day, reach the shore of the island and start his hunt for the treasure; the dragon who, on the same day, after having waited 177 years due to a prophecy, can come out of the cave and search for the thing he likes the most, butterflies; and Biancaperla, the daughter of the governor, who has been waiting for the dragon to appear, in the hope of being saved from him by a knight, to break the monotony of her days on the island. Once the dragon leaves the cave and Valdemaro finds its footprints, the sense of stillness is over. The story picks up sudden speed and quickly unfolds toward an ingenious happy ending. By catching the dragon with a stratagem while it is about to attack Biancaperla, Valdemaro succeeds in reclaiming his treasure and winning Biancaperla's love and his right to marry her.

The tale uses time in an intriguing fashion in particular with reference to the concept of quickness, a quality that strongly characterizes Calvino's style, and that he discussed, logically enough, in the chapter of *The Six Memos* entitled "Quickness." This quality is often associated with his fairy tale–like novel *The Path to the Spider's Nests*. In "Quickness," Calvino recalled the importance that the ancient legend of Charlemagne, "taken from a book of magic" and narrated by the French romantic writer Jules Barbey d'Aurevilly, acquired for him. The legend is centered on a magic ring that has the power to make the emperor fall desperately in love with whomever or whatever possesses it, to the point of making him forget about his kingdom. Calvino remarked that in the story of Charlemagne the word "love" establishes a verbal link that guarantees continuity between the different types of attraction, and that the ring serves as a narrative link between the episodes, which are held in place by the logic of cause and effect, giving to the imaginary story the necessary resemblance to truth in order to appear plausible or realistic. Moreover, like every object in a narration, the ring acquires a symbolic value and becomes magical.

Clear parallels exist between this legend and Calvino's story. In "The Dragon and the Butterflies," there is also a magical object, the treasure that directs the story in a truthful manner and makes Valdemaro, the protagonist, experience danger in order to possess it. But here the magical object functions in the opposite way. The ring contained a curse for Charlemagne, making him fall in love first with a young woman, then with a corpse, then with the archbishop Turpino, and finally with Lake Constanza, into which it was thrown (it is a historical fact that the ailing king died there). In Calvino, the treasure instead has the positive power to break a negative prophecy, otherwise understood as a curse. The (underlying) verbal link is desire, which leads everybody to look for his/her "treasure": the dragon wants to be a butterfly, Biancaperla wants to meet her prince, and the governor wants normality to reign on the island. Only the hero, however, once he physically holds the treasure in his hands, can satisfy (or not) each desire and he decides that the dragon is to remain a dragon.

Calvino further specified that his preference for Barbey d'Aurevilly's spare and concise version of the story over all others transmitted throughout the centuries is because "everything is left to the imagination and the speed with which events follow one another conveys a feeling of the ineluctable" (*Six Memos* 33). The secret of its beauty lies for him in the fact that in this version "the events, however long they last, become punctiform, connected by rectilinear segments, in a zigzag pattern that suggests incessant motion" (35). These stylistic choices clearly also characterize Calvino's story. Nevertheless Calvino does not want to negate the value of its opposite, slowness, or "the pleasure of delay" (46) in a story, as he recognized that "quickness of style and thought means above all agility, mobility, and ease," but that all these qualities "go with writing where it is natural to digress, to jump from one subject to another, to lose the thread a hundred times and find it again after a hundred more twists and turns" (46). The author in fact specified that a story, especially one belonging to oral narrative (from which fairy tales derive), "is an operation carried out for the length of time involved, an enchantment that acts on the passing of time, either contracting or dilating it" (35). "The Dragon and the Butterflies" adheres to this rule as well: the enchantment first dilates time when characters long for their treasures, and then the increasing pace signals the approach to the solution of the spell. This enchantment that magically dilates and contracts time is also the precise "visible" element that stylistically characterizes the fantastic in the story. In addition, the strategy, toward the end, succeeds in instantaneously bringing all the pieces of the narrative together, therefore ultimately encompassing and enclosing the whole web of fantastic images suggested up to this point by the plot. Particularly regarding his predilection for adventures and fairy tales, the author spoke (in this essay on Quickness) of his search for "some inner energy, some motion of the mind" (48) that arises from an image and its motion, and that then must patiently find its equivalent in words. He thus waited for a "quick flash of inspiration," the *mot juste*, just like a writer of poetry: in this case, Valdemaro's improvised pretence of being a superintendent of the metamorphoses of the Lepidoptera,[8] a clever "fantastic" trick to simulate a false identity in order to catch the dragon who hopes to become a butterfly.

In concluding his essay on Quickness, Calvino talked about his predilection for two gods: Mercury, the god of "communication and mediation" and inventor of writing; and Vulcan-Hephaestus, the god of "constructive concentration" (53). One who "roams the heavens" with his winged feet; the other who "lurks at the bottom of the craters," tirelessly forging objects. These two gods represented for him "two inseparable and complementary functions in life" (53) and two necessary times to the act of writing: that of immediacy (the former), which is achieved through patient and meticulous adjustments (the latter). It is easy to trace in these two gods the emblem representing a crab and a butterfly together, which illustrated *Festina Lente* (his favorite Latin motto since his youth, meaning "Hurry Slowly") in the sixteenth-century collection of emblems by Paolo Giovio (Calvino, *Six Memos* 48). Calvino expressed his appreciation for enigmatic emblems, and this one in particular, because the butterfly and the crab are "both bizarre, both symmetrical in shape and between them establish an unexpected kind of harmony" (ibid.).[9] If we substitute the crab with the dragon/monster (basing such an association on the fact that the semblance of the mask of the cephalothorax of the crab is often intended as the head of Medusa, herself a monster in Greek mythology), and since its claws were often associated with Vulcan, the blacksmith of Roman mythology who tirelessly forged objects with his tools (Piacentini 169), it may be possible to find the "invisible" component of Calvino's fantastic style, that of the "emblematic" link between these two times of writing (immediacy and slowness). Calvino's story about the dragon and the butterfly is also reminiscent of his search for wholeness. This desire for unity explains why the dragon remains a dragon after he is captured and is not transformed into a caterpillar (and then a butterfly). The two animals need each other and their complementary natures, just as Calvino's fantastic needs its opposite, reality, to exist.

Conclusion

The two short stories written for children discussed in this essay, despite their brevity, succeed in conveying Calvino's conception of the fantastic in its dual forms, visible and invisible, both thematically and stylistically and in exploring, as previously mentioned, that "gap between the real and the rational" noted by Segre. They also convey one of the most characteristic traits of the whole of Calvino's poetics: duality. As the Italian critic Alberto Asor Rosa says in this regard, Calvino is:

A twofold writer "constantly oscillating" (using his own expression) between reason and imagination, intellect and myth, human history and nature, the individual and the cosmos, deterministic biology and a stubbornly conscious choice; and consequently, on the level of existential and stylistic tonalities between irony and pessimism, cosmic and tragic, positive and negative, shadow and sun. (XI)

Because of this trait, Calvino remains averse to definitions, and while he constantly searched for balance and continuity among different elements, (a trait linking him with Eastern philosophy), he was excited by new discoveries. By experimenting with children's literature so late in his career thanks to his passion for fairy tales, Calvino also demonstrated that writing for children does not diminish a writer's reputation. An author who writes children's literature can be as equally engaged as one that does not and therefore can be taken just as "seriously." Indeed, children fascinated Calvino for a long time because in them he rightly saw a reflection of the open-mindedness he advocated. He believed that the world might even be "saved" by children, in the sense that the real and the literary universe is explored with its instruments, as in Morgenstern's theory of games (which Calvino knew). The imaginary is in fact often rationalized by Calvino, similarly to children's games (Bertoni and Ferraro 14). Fairy tales, with their "blend of real and unreal" (*Italian Folktales*, xviii), their "infinite variety and infinite repetition" (xviii), and their mix of conventions and free imagination mirroring reality, constituted for Calvino an ideal platform for the exploration of new possibilities which naturally contained a projection into the future, with an implicit ethical message; a future that Calvino would envision through the fantastic.

Furthermore, as he stated in his last chapter of *Six Memos*, the one on "Multiplicity," the great challenge for literature in the future was "to be capable of weaving together the various branches of knowledge, the various codes, into a manifold and multifaceted vision of the world" (112). Combining the imagination, seen as a repertoire of the potential and the hypothetical, (91) with the multiplicity of knowledge, Calvino envisioned a type of literature that, with exactitude, would aim to portray "immeasurable goals, far beyond all hope of achievement" (112). Calvino, at the end of the essay, even hoped for a work "outside of the *self*," "to give speech to that which has no language" (124). With this last postulate, Calvino seems to ludically and fantastically want to subject himself to a new trial, just like one of the characters of his fairy tales.

Notes

1. All translations are mine, unless otherwise stated.

2. The Grimm brothers published the book *Children's and Household Tales* in 1812, which, together with the second volume in 1814, was composed of two hundred fairy tales and ten children's legends. The book is now known by the title *Grimm's Fairy Tales*. Afanasyev collected the impressive number of eight volumes of Russian folk tales between 1855 and 1867.

3. Qualities that had already existed in his writings and of which he was, at that time, only partially aware. The writer Cesare Pavese identified these narrative components in a review of *The Path to the Spiders' Nests* (1947), in which he observed that Calvino narrated the story of the partisans in that book in a ludic manner, as a "fable of the wood," and coined for him the famous nickname "squirrel of the pen" (*L'Unità* 26 Sept. 1947).

4. Calvino used the word *fiabe*, which in English can be translated as folktales as well as fairy tales. The translator George Martin here opted for the word *folktales*. I would prefer to use that of *fairy tale*, especially when referring to the *Stories for Children*, to better refer to their imaginative and magical components rather than their legendary ones.

5. Vladimir Propp (1895–1970) was a Russian formalist scholar (linguist and anthropologist) who studied the structure of Russian fairy tales. He wrote a seminal book on the subject entitled *The Morphology of the Folktale* (1928), in which he identified thirty-one functions (or narrative elements) and eight main characters as constituents of their plot.

6. Calvino's passion for combinatorial games was modeled after the conception of literature as "potential laboratory" developed by Oulipo, a French group founded in 1960 by Raymond Queneau and François Le Lionnais, of which Calvino

was a member. The movement sought constrained techniques and various structures, often based on mathematical equations and games theories (such as that of chess for instance) to formulate a literature conceived in opposition to that proposed by the surrealists, which was based on the concept of automatic writing. Calvino's work *If on a Winter's Night a Traveler* is the most representative of Oulipo's school of thought, as the structure of the novel is primarily based on a combinatorial game.

7. Among the thirty-one possible functions, this story contains the main following ones: as an introduction, the hero, Valdemaro, presented as a everyday fellow, is being removed from his ship, thrown into the water, and deprived of the map of the treasure by three pirates (abstention) and lands on an island, where he is told by another castaway (warning) that he needs to face a hard test, due to the fact that the dragon (the impending threat or danger) will soon appear. He courageously decides to remain on the island and waits for a confrontation (nonadherence of the warning). Then, the dragon appears, and Valdemaro consequently finds on the beach the bodies of the three pirates killed and also the map that has now become unintelligible (villainy). Valdemaro demonstrates his heroic valor and decides to follow the footprints of the dragon (counteraction and departure), finally confronts and defeats his rival (struggle and victory), and is then recognized as a hero, obtains the treasure, and can finally marry the woman he has saved (recognition, solution, and wedding).

8. *Lepidoptera* is an order of insects that includes butterflies.

9. Collections of emblems were a popular genre between the years 1500 and 1600 that prefigured the combination of text and image with strong moral implications. Emblems, by nature, have a high correlation between visible and invisible elements, leaving space to the imagination to link those two spheres, one sensorial and the other mental, which, not surprisingly, suited Calvino's conception of the fantastic well.

Works cited

Asor Rosa, Alberto. *Stile Calvino*. Turin, It.: Einaudi, 2001.

Barenghi, Mario, and Falcetto Bruno. *Italo Calvino. Romanzi e Racconti*. Milan, It.: Mondadori, 1994.

Bertoni, Roberto, and Bruno Ferraro. *Calvino ludico. Riflessioni sul gioco in Italo Calvino*. Lucca, It.: Baroni, 2003.

Calvino, Italo. *Italian Folk Tales. Selected and Retold by Italo Calvino*. Trans. George Martin. New York: Pantheon, 1980.

_____. *Six Memos for the Next Millennium*. New York: Vintage International, 1993.

_____. *The Uses of Literature*. Trans. William Waiver. New York: Harcourt, 1986.

_____. *Una pietra sopra. Discorsi di letteratura e società*. Milan, It.: Mondadori, 1995.

De Caprio, Caterina, and Ugo Maria Olivieri, eds. *Il fantastico e il visibile*. Naples, It.: Libreria Dante & Descartes, 2000.

Deidier, Roberto. *Le forme del tempo. Miti, fiabe, immagini in Calvino.* Palermo, It.: Sellerio, 2004.

Frigessi, Delia, ed. *Inchiesta sulle fate. Italo Calvino e la fiaba.* Bergamo, It.: Pierluigi Lubrina, 1988.

Lavagetto, Mario. *Dovuto a Calvino*. Turin, It.: Bollati Bolinghieri, 2001.

Piacentini, Adriano. *Tra il cristallo e la fiamma: le Lezioni Americane di Italo Calvino*. Florence, It.: Firenze Atheneum, 2002.

Propp, Vladimir, *Morphology of the Folk Tale*. 2nd ed. Trans. Laurence Scott. Austin: U of Texas P, 1968.

Marie NDiaye's Uncanny Realism _____

Daisy Connon

I.

For a number of literary theorists, including the frequently cited structuralist thinker Tzvetan Todorov, the fantastic in a work of literature refers to an apparently supernatural event that the reader has difficulty assimilating to the otherwise highly realist world that the author has generated (25). Many authors of contemporary French fiction have recourse to imagery and strategies that, according to the above definition, could be characterized as fantastic or relating to fantasy. This trend is visible in a variety of forms and techniques that range from classic gothic themes, such as ghosts in the novels of Marie Darrieussecq and Linda Lê, to contemporary twists on traditional figures of the uncanny, such as the double, or doppelganger, in works by French novelist Marie NDiaye. For author and director Emmanuel Carrère, a sense of the fantastic is expressed through Kafkaesque scenarios in which a protagonist finds herself inhabiting a version of our ordinary world that has undergone a number of strange distortions. Writers Marie Redonnet, Eugène Savitzkaya, and Sylvie Germain have produced works that are at first glance less conventionally fantastic, in the sense that they create a more dream-like fictional realm in which the reader is encouraged to abandon her expectations of collective reality. While these various occurrences of fantasy found in current French writing may at times appear disconcerting to the reader or protagonist, they often take the form of harmless or even welcome apparitions resembling those found in Latin American magic realism or traditional tales of the marvelous.

Among these contemporary writers of the fantastic, NDiaye, perhaps more than any other, has exploited the uncanny (discussed below) as an essential part of her global approach to fiction. Her writing is distinguished by a tendency to reappropriate classic fantastic imagery within a familiar, present-day context. NDiaye's novels frequently feature contemporary incarnations of supernatural themes such as ghosts, doubles, metamorphosis, or sorcery. However, rather than conveying a quest for the otherworldly, these images are often brought into proximity with an exploration of the most familiar spaces and phenomena: the home, the self, and everyday relationships and environments in today's society.

The fictional realm generated by NDiaye is at first strikingly familiar, resembling a realist world that is very similar to our own. The reader identifies a re-creation of her own everyday environment and recognizes the commonplace landscape of contemporary suburban and urban France (or other countries, in certain cases). The action unfolds in familiar locations such as family homes, shopping malls, fast-food restaurants, administrative offices, or public transport. The reader sympathizes to a large degree with the protagonists, who are generally unheroic individuals, simply carrying on their day-to-day lives and facing the minor challenges that confront many people: sustaining marriages and negotiating family dynamics, keeping up with finances or fulfilling career-related responsibilities, maintaining the home. In fact, literary critics tend to view NDiaye's approach as participating in a contemporary "return to realism" (Rabaté, *Le Roman* 116; Garnier 79–89), given her tendency to foreground banal settings in suburban France and her choice of very ordinary characters and occurrences.

However, the term "realism" might be viewed as problematic given the unsettling, dream-like quality of NDiaye's writing and her frequent reliance on fantasy. Despite the sense of ordinariness her works evoke, she also presents the reader with a world where teenage girls can metamorphose into crows, where sorcery and clairvoyance exist as regular elements of day-to-day life, where familiar people shapeshift into complete strangers, where individuals must regularly confront their own doubles, and where annoying relatives may simply be transformed into slugs.

Due to this constant tension between the familiar and the strange found in NDiaye's writing, her readers often emphasize the uncanny nature of her work describing it as "inquiétante, presque fantastique" (Rabaté, "L'Éternelle" 49) [disconcerting, almost fantastic], "entre le désir et le réel" (Tulinius 69) [between desire and reality], or generating "une sensation de malaise" (Bonomo 218) [a feeling of uneasiness]. Within psychoanalytic and literary theory, the word "uncanny" suggests an unusual moment in which the boundaries between the familiar and the strange collapse, creating a strange sense of uprootedness within our familiar world. As a literary term, it can refer to a selection of disconcerting imagery, such as ghosts or doubles, or to an atmosphere of strangeness generated by a particular work of literature. Freud explained the uncanny as the experience of something strange that harks back to something familiar or inseparable from the self, perhaps something repressed (Freud 224). However, the uncanny is not an easy concept to define, but is rather something simply felt in response to certain destabilizing phenomena or experiences.

With a focus on the themes of metamorphosis and the double in a selection of novels by NDiaye, this chapter will explore the unique ways in which the author borrows from a repertoire of fantastic imagery and techniques so as to revive and estrange the reader's perception of everyday life and draw her attention to the "extra-ordinary" nature of commonplace phenomena, subjective experience, and family relations within the home. NDiaye creates a fictional realm that we might describe with the Freudian term "*unheimlich*" (uncanny). It is one in which the contending codes of strange and familiar remain unresolved; one that is banal and domestic, yet in which the protagonist—and reader—cannot quite feel at home.

II.

The fantastic did not play a central role in NDiaye's writing from the outset. Her first novel, *Quant au riche avenir* (*As for the Promising Future*), was published in 1985 when the author was just eighteen. Her second work, *Comédie classique* (*Classic Comedy*, 1987), was narrated in a single sentence, taking the form of a linguistic exercise. Both of these novels sought to express a certain form of strangeness within human relationships and everyday life, yet both were essentially anchored in collective reality as we know it. Her next novel, however, *La Femme changée en bûche* (*The Woman Who Turned into a Log*, 1989), veered into fantasy to tell the story of a woman who enlists the aid of the devil in punishing her husband for his infidelity. It was perhaps this story that marked the emergence of the distinctive style we associate with NDiaye's writing today, which is characterized by a distortion of the codes of realism to expose unusual dimensions of contemporary life. NDiaye then went on to write numerous works of fiction and drama—including seven more novels, four plays, three children's texts, and a collection of short stories—many of which contain a fantastic element and are centered on the family.

A prime example of the author's tendency to reveal the strangeness of familiar locations is her representation of home. One of NDiaye's most uniquely reinterpreted fantastic images is that of the haunted house. Her version, however, has little in common with the classic gothic mansion. It is more often simply a somewhat frightening depiction of the run-of-the-mill lower-middle-class family home in suburban France. NDiaye depicts the home in such a way as to emphasize its discomfort and foreignness, rather than its familiarity and reassuring qualities. *La Sorcière* (*The Witch*, 1996), *En famille* (*Among Family*, 1991), and *Rosie Carpe* (2001) are all set in dismal suburban flats or malodorous family homes, in which we find many unloving or monstrous parents, dispersed families, siblings with fluctuating identities, and protagonists who, for different reasons, cannot feel at home. All of the families in *Rosie Carpe*, for example, display some transgression of family norms. Marriages are often cross-generational, defying conventional family hierarchies, or bordering on incestuous. Rosie's mother and father divorce during the story and begin relationships with a father and daughter, respectively. Near the end of the novel, the daughter, Lisbeth, leaves Rosie's father to marry Titi, his grandchild. The ongoing breakdown and reconstruction of the various ties between

---

members of the "family unit" cause it to appear as an impossible ideal rather than a norm. In addition to being unattainable, the reader has the sense that home and family are disturbing and unsettling phenomena, rather than sources of comfort.

A theme that resurfaces in nearly all of NDiaye's texts is that of the impossibility or fear of "going home." The protagonists of her stories share a desire to retrieve their family origins, yet this identity quest is often met with hostility, resulting in a feeling of dislocation. For example, in *En famille*, Fanny arrives at her grandmother's home, where all her relatives have gathered to celebrate a birthday, only to discover that none of these familiar people recognize her or believe her to be part of their family. For the author, the home always contains a disconcerting or monstrous element, and there is a sense that individuals are haunted by the strange and familiar forms that are their mothers, fathers, brothers, and sisters. Yet at the same time, they constantly turn to their kin to constitute their identities or to find themselves. This dual quest for home and self evokes the double meaning of the French *chez soi*, a term referring to both "home" and "self." As we will see further on, many of NDiaye's characters are plagued by a feeling of not being "masters in their own houses," to use Freud's famous description of the role of the ego in the human psyche.

III.

Despite the sense of the absurd that infiltrates NDiaye's writing, French criticism has, as mentioned above, tended to associate this author with a renewal of realism and of the novelistic in general, since she displays a taste for certain more traditional elements of the novel, such as unified point of view, linear plots, and in-depth character development (Thomas 81). The dual classification of NDiaye's work as both fantastic and realist is not necessarily paradoxical, since as the majority of recent criticism on the fantastic tells us, realism and fantasy are not mutually exclusive forms, but rather, intertwined and often codependent. Nearly all fantastic texts depend on realist strategies to produce their aesthetic effects, since the reader must identify the narrative world as her own before she can be surprised by any deviation from it. For Gilbert Millet and Denis Labbé:

> Le fantastique ne peut fonctionner qu'avec l'assentiment du lecteur qui doit accepter de se laisser entraîner dans ce train fantôme, autorisant ainsi le narrateur à lui faire peur ou à le déstabiliser. Pour cela, il faut qu'il puisse y croire, qu'il y ait au moins l'impression de se retrouver face à un univers familier ou d'apparence familière. (11)

> [The fantastic can only function with the consent of the reader, who must allow herself to become swept up in the chilling course of events, thereby enabling the narrator to frighten or disconcert her. For this to work, she must be able to believe; she must at least have the impression of being in a familiar world, or one that appears familiar.]¹

As Claire Whitehead puts it, "Before a reader can be prompted to hesitate, she must be encouraged to believe" (13).

In NDiaye's novels, this interplay of the codes of strangeness and familiarity is rather uniquely configured that renders the tension more vivid. In her novel *La Sorcière,* for example, decidedly supernatural imagery appears to coexist with an almost ethnographic portrait of contemporary French life. Themes such as sorcery and metamorphosis are intertwined with an evocation of the main character's dysfunctional family relations and monotonous existence in the contemporary Parisian suburbs. *La Sorcière* is narrated from the point of view of Lucie, a housewife and mother of twin daughters. Early in the narrative, Lucie is abandoned by her husband, a vacation-package salesman who is miserable with his life. The novel tells the story of Lucie's family life—now as a single parent—and her trip to the city of Poitiers with her daughters in an attempt to retrieve her absent husband and to reunite her own separated parents. Like many of today's parents in suburban France, Lucie's day-to-day life is full of trivial activities such as banking, dish washing, defrosting dinners, mopping floors, coffee making, and mothering her twelve-year-old daughters. However, despite this run-of-the-mill lifestyle, she is also a witch with prophetic visionary powers, inherited from her own mother. This gift manifests itself in tears of blood that trickle down her cheeks during her visions. The paradox of Lucie's clairvoyant gift is its banality, both because of the uninspiring content of the visions it brings her, and because of the way this power is seamlessly integrated into everyday life within the fictional world. Clairvoyance is in fact nothing out of the ordinary, since it only enables Lucie to foresee extremely dull occurrences, such as foggy, incomplete images of her husband's whereabouts, or minor details surrounding the person she seeks to perceive: "la couleur d'un habit, l'aspect du ciel, une tasse de café fumant délicatement tenue par la personne . . ." [the color of an article of clothing, the way the sky looks, a cup of steaming coffee being held daintily by the person . . .] (14).

As well as sorcery, the theme of metamorphosis plays a significant role in this novel. During the course of the story there are several allusions to the generational distance that Lucie experiences between herself and her daughters, and to her difficulty in understanding and communicating with them: "Il me semblait toujours que Maud et Lise vivaient en permanence dans un monde hypothétique et lointain, celui de leur gloire future, où les incidents du présent n'avaient pas leur place . . ." [It has always seemed to me that Maud and Lise dwell permanently in a hypothetical and distant world, the world of their future glory, in which present occurrences are of no relevance . . .] (60). Later, the girls' grandmother comments on their aloofness: "Qu'est-il arrivé à tes filles? Pardonne-moi, elles me semblent glacées, lointaines, mauvaises. «Qu'est-ce qu'il leur est donc arrivé?»" [What's happened to your daughters? I'm sorry, but they seem icy, distant, evil. Just what has come over them?] (116). We later learn that, to Lucie's surprise, her daughters have inherited magical abilities that in fact surpass her own. They transform into crows and fly away, leaving behind their lace-up boots, which then growl and twist in front of the abandoned seats: "Soudain, des manches de leur blouson, des cheveux de Maud et Lise, voletèrent quelques plumes légères d'un brun-noir, qui délicatement se posèrent sur le parquet poli. Mes filles riaient, enfantines, glorieuses" [Suddenly, a few light feathers of a blackish-brown shade fluttered out from the sleeves of Maud's and Lise's jackets and from their hair, landing delicately on the polished flooring. My daughters were laughing, childlike and glorious] (101–2). This event is reminiscent of Alfred Hitchcock's film *The Birds* (1963), which exploits the sinister connotation of birds to generate an uncanny atmosphere. Yet this image also bears a metaphoric meaning. The adolescent daughters' transformation, foreshadowed by their mother's sense of their remoteness and distance, appears to be a fantastic incarnation of Lucie's fear of her girls one day "leaving the nest."

More broadly, the very prevalent theme of metamorphosis seems to serve the expression of NDiaye's vision of contemporary subjectivity and identity as anchorless and lacking in substance or meaning. For example, a similar transformation undergone by Lucie's neighbor, Isabelle, is foreshadowed by a subtler version of this same theme. After encountering this woman early in the novel in her dull sports clothes living out a gloomy lower-middle-class existence with her odious son Steve, we later find that she has "mutated" into a very different person. When Isabelle resurfaces near the end of the novel, she informs Lucie that she has launched a new business: the Université Féminine de la Santé Spirituelle d'Isabelle O [Isabelle O's Feminine University for Spiritual Health], where she provides abused women with self-help courses for 80,000 francs per month. Her cunning business scheme has emancipated her from her monotonous existence yet metamorphosed her into a frightening emblem of *nouveau riche* prosperity and urbanism. Just barely recognizable to Lucie, she reappears with a fancy new hairstyle in an elegant silk suit, having acquired a look of "assurance bourgeoise" [bourgeois confidence] (151), the scent of hairspray floating around her "tête parée, frisée, gonflée" [adorned, crinkled, inflated head] (152). The strangeness of this transformation is highlighted when, uncannily, in a more striking incarnation of this theme of metamorphosis, Isabelle reappears as a bird. The first allusion to this event occurs when Lucie is on her way to the train station with her daughters and spots a large crow, which she realizes is Isabelle. Later at her mother's apartment she sees "Isabelle" again, this time as a large brown raven. In each case where a character transforms into a bird, it is always an extremely commonplace, yet sinister bird. This is a world where magic exists, but its incarnations are not particularly remarkable, and therefore not entirely out of the ordinary.

In many of NDiaye's more recent novels, such as *Rosie Carpe*, *Mon cœur à l'étroit* (*Squeezing My Heart*, 2007), and *Trois femmes puissantes* (*Three Strong Women*, 2009), distortions of the codes of realism are relatively subtle, inducing a gentle estrangement of the reader's habitual expectations of the codes of collective reality. A sense of the uncanny is not so much event-related as written into the narrative language itself. Ordinary environments seem imbued with eeriness; characters' identities appear to morph into others; social and natural laws are subtly transgressed. *Trois femmes puissantes*, for instance, contains three long "chapters," but the lack of obvious continuity among them gives the impression that they are three separate stories. In the first of these narratives, NDiaye repeats the technique of employing bird imagery to emblematize or evoke certain human characters who are very close or familiar to her protagonists. The main character in this text experiences her estranged father as a bird, perched in a flame tree. However, while in *La Sorcière* characters in fact transform into crows, Nora's evocation of her father in this more recent work hovers between metaphor and fantasy.

In *Rosie Carpe*, rather than appealing to forms that are explicitly supernatural to express something strange or awry within family dynamics, NDiaye employs a different strategy: while deviating only slightly from the codes of realism, she seeks to bring out a certain monstrous or grotesque element that resides within the most familiar individuals and locations, depicting the elusiveness of the phenomena that should be the most anchoring or well known. This novel recounts the life story and identity quest of a young woman, banished from her home following her scholarly failures in Paris. The protagonist, Rosie, endures a series of traumatic experiences, miserable jobs in the suburbs, unwanted pregnancies, and periods of alcoholism and depression before deciding to travel to Guadeloupe with her son, Titi, in an attempt to retrieve and reunite her lost family. The action unfolds primarily in Guadeloupe, although the character's youth and young adult life in France are later reconstituted for the reader in a lengthy flashback. A disconcerting, surreal atmosphere prevails in the text and renders the narrative events opaque and dream-like. As in *La Sorcière*, this subtly fantastic mood is often the result of the author's tendency to accentuate the nightmarish elements of ordinary reality. The island of Guadeloupe is depicted as a debased tropical inferno, full of consumer-driven, leathery-skinned holidaymakers in panther print bikinis (178). The sun and the heat are suffocating, rather than welcoming, as they only intensify odors of "decay" and "rotting" (180) and provoke nausea and anxiety.

The theme of metamorphosis, so pronounced in *La Sorcière*, makes a less explicit appearance in *Rosie Carpe*, while retaining the sense of strangeness suggested by the sudden dissipation of the familiar world. Characters in the story, and especially relatives of the protagonist, often appear to shape-shift into elusive forms or to turn into strangers. For example, when Rosie is waiting at the airport in Guadeloupe for her brother Lazare to collect her and her son, she sees a black man and assumes that Lazare's skin color has changed since their last encounter. This very familiar person appears to the protagonist in an entirely foreign body. This uncertainty is ultimately resolved in the narrative when it turns out that Lazare has sent his friend Lagrand to collect his sister and nephew. However, Rosie exhibits a nearly fantastic capacity to believe that a person's skin color can simply change with time.

This subtly fantastic logic is also present in many scenes featuring the protagonist's mother. Without being manifestly demonic or ghostly, Madame Carpe subtly defies natural law by appearing never to age and by becoming pregnant with her third child at retirement age. She often surfaces in the midst of an unusual yellow hue with her "horrible yellow stomach" (181), surrounded by an unpleasant vegetal odor. She also has a fluctuating identity, changing her name from Danielle to Diane when she moves to Guadeloupe, to correspond to her new lifestyle as the owner of an apartment complex in a holiday resort. The strangeness of this familiar person is felt by the reader in a scene evoking the confusion of certain dreams. One day prior to her departure for Guadeloupe, Rosie takes a morning stroll in her Parisian suburb of Antony and discovers that her parents (whom she had assumed to be living in Guadeloupe) in fact own a house in the very same neighborhood as Rosie and her little boy. She suddenly perceives her mother in the garden of this house after years of separation:

> It was Mrs. Carpe but so different from what she had been that she could have not been Mrs. Carpe, and Rosie could have then just given a little nod accompanied by a smile of apology for being nosy, then turned and gone on her way. But the small, severe, brashly confident eyes were her mother's, eyes with the brilliance and expressionless glitter of blue-tinted glass that belonged to the Carpe woman whose offspring she was, she, Rosie, who had just now been one with Rosie Carpe enjoying her walk. (111)

The competing codes of strangeness and familiarity make this encounter with the mother unsettling rather than anchoring. Madame Carpe fluctuates between signifying origin, as "the Carpe Rosie herself had come from," and foreignness, since she has transformed to the point that Rosie hesitates to identify her as her mother. The author compares her to the fish of the same name, perhaps drawing on the connotations of the French expression *"muet comme une carpe,"* (literally "quiet as a carp"), meaning silent or taciturn. Rosie's mother has nothing to offer her daughter, other than a blank stare. This oscillation problematizes Rosie's sense of self, as is suggested by her sense of dislocation between Rosie and Rosie Carpe. This elusiveness confers on this very ordinary person an almost ghostly aura, since the reader is unsure if she is being confronted with a "real" encounter or if the mother is a figment of Rosie's imagination, her past coming back to haunt her.

The motif of haunting assumes a more explicit form in NDiaye's semiautobiographical novel, *Autoportrait en vert* (*Self-portrait in Green*, 2005). This work was published as part of a series of books entitled "Traits et portraits." According to Colette Fellous, its initiator, the aim of this ongoing project is to produce a collection of self-portraits that include a visual supplement (NDiaye's text includes photographs by the French artist Julie Ganzin). The participating writers are asked to create a textual space in which to reveal the hidden side of the self. In *Autoportrait en vert*, NDiaye undertakes her self-portrait through fantastic imagery of the double and of haunting. Against a backdrop of familiar landscapes and autobiographical details, she presents us with the uncanny experience of a narrator struggling with the uncertainties that surface during her attempt at self-representation.

Once again, this narrative first appears to foreground a realistic depiction of everyday life. NDiaye figures in the story as character, narrator, and author, and the book contains some factual content, being set, for example, in contemporary southwestern France, where the author at one point resided. We recognize the narrator as a mother of five, a writer, who engages in conventional tasks of motherhood such as driving her children to and fro or mingling with other parents in the schoolyard. She alludes to details we know to be true of NDiaye's life, such as the name of her husband. She cites the dates and locations of literary conferences she in fact attended, and she shares what appear to be genuine memories from her youth.

Gradually, however, this realist depiction is subordinated to a more fantastic agenda as the author reveals a very different world. At first, for example, we notice that the evocative descriptions of the landscape and vegetation surrounding Bordeaux reach a point of exaggeration with allusions to copious tropical fruit trees. This is a strategy frequently employed by NDiaye. She often endows familiar urban environments with strange climatic or natural characteristics in order to stretch the boundaries of a purely realist description. In her 2007 novel *Mon cœur à l'étroit*, for instance, the city of Bordeaux is depicted in an accurate manner, including verifiable street names and realistic descriptions of the city's tram system. However, the city is consumed by an unusual impenetrable fog, which envelops the characters in a dream-like haze and blurs the reader's perception of the novel's familiar setting. This technique can also be observed in works by other contemporary French writers, such as Darrieussecq. In her novel *Naissance des fantômes* (1998), translated into English in 1999 as *My Phantom Husband*, the suburbs of Paris acquire a nearly fantastic quality by being represented as surrounded by water.

However, more prominent in *Autoportrait en vert* is a more classic fantastic literary device. Throughout the story the narrator is pursued by a series of ethereal presences, women dressed in green, surrounded by a "lueur d'irréalité" [unreal glow] (26), who resurface throughout the story, eluding the gaze of other characters. This image is first introduced in the opening scene of the book when the narrator alludes to a green-clad figure standing next to a banana tree in front of a particular house in her neighbourhood. We learn that she routinely observes this woman on the way to the school, but that her children in the backseat of the car do not perceive her. Although she appears in a ghostly form, she is also capable of assuming the concreteness of an ordinary character, conversing with the narrator "dans une voix phlegmatique" [in a phlegmatic voice], using "phrases monotones" [monotonous sentences], and rambling on about her trivial domestic problems and alcoholic husband (27). What is even more strange, the woman in green's identity is shared among numerous female characters. The author's mother, the first wife of a friend's husband, and the mistress remembered from her primary school days are all at one point or another associated with this woman in green, or designated as such.

Given the title of the text, *Autoportrait en vert*, and the strange ontological status of the woman in green who reveals herself only to the narrator, it seems the reader is urged to view this figure as maintaining a connection to the self. She is an ethereal embodiment through which the author has chosen to depict herself. Although she bears no physical resemblance to the narrator, she might be viewed as a multiplied form of double. The recognition of one's double is, for Freud, an exemplary uncanny experience, which he linked to a regression to a more primitive phase in the development of the psyche. In the fantastic literature of romanticism, the double often takes the form of a malicious counterpart who represents one's sinister side and foreshadows death. According to John Herdman, the romantic writer E. T. A. Hoffmann was influenced by the psychological works of G. H. Schubert, who developed the idea of a "shadow-self," a "dark and hidden counterpart of, or supplement to, the daytime consciousness" (153).

The double is a theme that makes an appearance in other works by NDiaye. The protagonist of her short story "Une journée de Brulard" ("A Day in the Life of Brulard," 2004), for example, receives regular visits from her double, a younger version of herself who watches over her while emitting squawks, yelps, and teasing noises. However, unlike Ève Brulard, who appears mildly annoyed by the existence of this figure, and seems to casually cast it aside, the narrator in *Autoportrait en vert* actively listens to it. She expresses her willingness to enter into dialogue with this hidden side of the self, taking it upon herself to visit the house where she routinely perceives her and accepting her invitation to come in for coffee.

A vision of the self as an unknowable, multiple, or even ghostly phenomenon is very apparent in a branch of French writing originating in the 1980s called *autofiction* (or self-fiction), which combines fiction and autobiography. This term, now generic, was originally coined by the writer Serge Doubrovsky, who used it to describe his novel *Fils* (*Son*) (1977). The main idea behind *autofiction* is that fiction and nonfiction cannot be fully distinguished from one another, since there is no perfectly realistic "or true" representation of something as changeable as the self; we simply cannot know ourselves well enough accurately to portray ourselves in writing. The practitioners of *autofiction* thus seek to obscure the boundaries between reality and fiction in the representation of their life stories. This is performed in the interest of portraying subjectivity not in a straightforward way as coherent and knowable, and therefore inscribable in the codes of nonfiction, but as a product of fantasy and desire and a victim of the ambiguity of memory. In her novel *Enfance* (1983) (translated into English in 1984 as *Childhood*), for example, the writer Nathalie Sarraute presents a dialogue between two voices, those of a narrator and an interlocutor, which are parts of the "same" self. In other works of *autofiction,* by writers such as Alain Robbe-Grillet, Doubrovsky, or Marguerite Duras, distortions of temporality and the use of fantastic atmospheres express the inability of the self to be seized in a cohesive narrative or a purely nonfictional text.

NDiaye's use of the fantastic to portray the unthematizable nature of selfhood and its resistance to autobiographical representation echoes some of these ideas, but further insists upon the positive value of the self's foreignness and its inability to be captured through the codes of realism. While the double is usually an image that expresses a threat to the self, in NDiaye this shape-shifting companion is a welcome form of haunting. In a passage near the end of her self-portrait, the narrator affirms the productive value of the ghostly presences that enrich her life and her writing:

> I am afraid I would feel like a madwoman, should all the women in green disappear one by one, making it impossible for me to prove their existence, my own originality. I then wonder, sitting in my sisters' tidy kitchen, how I would find life bearable without the elusive figures of the women in green hovering in the background. In order to survive with calm these moments of stupor and profound boredom, of crippling lassitude, I must remind myself that they adorn my thoughts, my secret life, that they are there, both real beings and literary figures without whom the bitterness of existence grates my skin and flesh down to the bone. (77)

It seems that for NDiaye, the uncanny double is not so much a dark foreshadowing of death as it is the essential condition for life and indeed the foundation of her originality as a writer. Her openness to the strangeness of the everyday is the basis of her literary inspiration and, in fact, what keeps her alive.

IV.

It is interesting to note that, as well as being a welcome presence, the figure of the woman in green in *Autoportrait en vert* is also one whose existence is not particularly surprising to the main character. Indeed, many of NDiaye's protagonists have a strange tendency passively to accept the outlandish nature of their environments and the uncanny forms that haunt them. In *La Sorcière*, *Rosie Carpe*, or *Autoportrait en vert*, fantastic events such as ghostly apparitions or the transformation of characters into birds or slugs are everyday images, appearing no more or less strange than ordinary phenomena in today's world. The fantastic never becomes an element of surprise in itself, but is in fact often either cast aside or seamlessly blended into the commonplace interactions of characters. In *La Sorcière*, for instance, when Maud and Lise suddenly begin to sprout feathers in their grandfather's kitchen, no one is distressed, and the conversation moves directly on to trivial familial exchanges between characters concerning Lucie's mother's new partner. Lucie's father hardly notices his grandchildren's transformation and appears more interested in discussing the reimbursement of money Lucie has borrowed.

This is a deviation from the majority of traditional fantastic texts, in which the strangeness of a character's situation is the object of incessant reflection; its interrogation by various characters determines the trajectory of the narrative. Fantastic tales by romantic writers such as Hoffmann are peppered with adjectives of horror such as "ghastly," "wretched," "monstrous," or "uncanny," which qualify the characters' emotional responses to events that depart from the ordinary. In her study of the nineteenth-century French and Russian fantastic, Claire

Whitehead points out that one of the generic conventions of the fantastic is that the characters generally display surprise or fear in reaction to irrational or supernatural occurrences (125). In his study on the Fantastic, Todorov also stresses the implicit function of the reader and the likelihood of her identification with the bewilderment of the character: "the fantastic is based essentially on a hesitation of the reader—a reader who identifies with the chief character—as to the nature of an uncanny event" (157). Without this affective solidarity between the reader and the character, a novel may be more accurately classified in the genre of the marvelous or in that of allegory or poetry, where a more conventionally realist representation of the world is not expected (157).

Although Todorov's structural analysis imposes a sense of rigidity on the fantastic, which might appear contrived, he does point out certain tendencies within traditional fantastic writing that do not apply to NDiaye's work. In fact, much contemporary French "fantastic" writing eludes characterization by any of Todorov's categories. In the texts of women writers such as Darrieussecq or Lê, for example, metamorphosis or imagery of the grotesque are integrated into the everyday lives of the characters, often appearing to reflect or at least to be intertwined with a revelation of disconcerting, even monstrous elements of contemporary society. The theme of metamorphosis, for instance, which is present to varying degrees in many of NDiaye's works, forms the basis of Darrieussecq's first novel, *Truismes* (1996) (translated into English in 1997 as *Pig Tales*). This text tells the story of a young masseuse who discovers—and accepts as normal—the fact that she is gradually transforming into a pig. *Truismes* has been interpreted as a commentary on the experience of feminine bodily experience in a phallocentric (male-dominated) world (Caine 45–47).

In some ways NDiaye's approach thus resembles the mechanisms at work in Latin American and postcolonial Anglophone magical realism. In her book on this genre, Wendy B. Faris states that its principal objective is to represent an irreducible element that "defamiliarizes, underlines, or critiques ordinary aspects of the real" in order to highlight the extraordinary nature of reality (13). Critics of this genre often stress the fact that the supernatural events evoked by magical realists such as Gabriel Garcia Márquez are stated in a matter-of-fact manner and never appear shocking to any of the characters (Chanady 24). The reader easily suspends her disbelief and accepts fantasy as reality. However, another quality of magical realism is that it does not usually disconcert the reader (Chanady 24). It seems that fantasy for NDiaye is neither a mode of escapism nor an expression of the enchantment of the everyday but rather serves to generate an uncanny reflection of our own ordinary world and to explore an array of strange images to add depth or texture to everyday experience.

In discussions of the uncanny, our attention is often drawn to the German word *das Unheimliche*, which contains the root *heim*, meaning "home." The term denotes a feeling of being uprooted within the ordinary. As Lucie Armitt suggests, it is an experience in which we are not entirely removed from reality, even in a world of fantasy. Instead we maintain a close connection with the familiar world and solicit its codes to explain the strangeness we encounter: "In order for us to feel something to be uncanny, it must derive from a situation, object or incident that ought to feel (and usually has felt) familiar and reassuring, but which has undergone some form of slight shift that results in . . . a form of *dis-ease*" (Armitt 49). In his landmark 1919 essay "Das Unheimliche" ("The Uncanny"), Freud links the uncanny to castration anxiety and to the return of the repressed. He explains the concept as a side effect of infantile psychosexual development or unsurmounted archaic human beliefs. However, it seems that for NDiaye, the uncanny is much more than just a "symptom" or a "dis-ease." Rather, it is a way of renewing our gaze on familiar spaces or phenomena. In amplifying and reconfiguring the fantastic tension between strangeness and familiarity, NDiaye's novels seem to lean toward a form of "uncanny realism" whereby fantasy expresses, often with humor, forms of absurdity and a sense of strangeness that are extremely "close to home."

Notes

1. All translations of citations from French works are my own. Citations from the novel *Rosie Carpe* are taken from the English translation by Tamsin Black (2004).

Works Cited

Argand, Catherine. "Entretien avec Marie NDiaye." *Lire* 1 Apr. 2001: 32–37.

Armitt, Lucie. *Theorising the Fantastic.* London: Arnold, 1996.

Bonnet, Véronique. "Où situer Marie NDiaye ?" *Portrait.* Africultures, 1 Feb. 2002. Web. 7 Mar. 2012.

Bonomo, Sara. «La Mise en œuvre de la peur dans le roman d'aujourd'hui: *Rosie Carpe* de Marie NDiaye.» *Travaux de littérature* 17: 218-225.

Caine, Philippa. «Redefining the boundaries of corpo-reality for *la femme* in Marie Darrieussecq's *Naissance des fantômes.*" *Redefining the Real: The Fantastic in Contemporary French and Francophone Women's Writing.* Ed. Margaret-Anne Hutton. Bern: Lang, 2009. 45–64.

Carrère, Emmanuel. *The Mustache.* Trans. Lanie Goodman. New York: Scribner, 1988.

Chanady, Amaryll Beatrice. *Magical Realism and the Fantastic: Resolved Versus Unresolved Antinomy.* New York: Garland, 1985.

Cixous, Hélène. "Fiction and its Phantoms: A Reading of Freud's Das Unheimliche." *New Literary History* 7.3. (Spring 1976): 525–48, 619–45.

Darrieussecq, Marie. *Truismes.* Paris: P.O.L., 1996.

_____. *My Phantom Husband.* Trans. Helen Stevenson. London: Faber, 1999.

Faris, Wendy B. *Ordinary Enchantments: Magical Realism and the Remystification of Narrative.* Nashville: Vanderbilt UP, 2004.

Freud, Sigmund. "The Uncanny." *The Complete Psychological Works of Sigmund Freud.* Trans. and ed. James Strachey. Vol. 17. London: Hogarth, 1955. 219–56.

Garnier, Xavier. "Métamorphoses réalistes dans les romans de Marie NDiaye." *Itinéraires et contacts de cultures.* Paris: L'Harmattan, 1982. 79–89.

Germain, Sylvie. *Magnus.* Trans. Christine Donougher. Sawtry, Eng.: Dedalus, 2008.

Herdman, John. *The Double in Nineteenth-Century Fiction.* London: MacMillan, 1990.

Kristeva, Julia. *Strangers to Ourselves.* Trans. Leon S. Roudiez. New York: Columbia UP, 1988.

Lê, Linda. *The Three Fates.* Trans. Mark Polizzotti. New York: New Directions, 2010.

Millet, Gilbert, and Labbé, Denis. *Le Fantastique.* Paris: Belin, 2005.

NDiaye, Marie. *Among Family.* Trans. Heather Doyal. Tunbridge Wells, Kent: Angela Royal, 1997.

_____. *Autoportrait en vert.* Paris: Mercure de France, 2005.

_____. *Comédie classique.* Paris: P.O.L., 1987.

_____. *La Femme changée en bûche.* Paris: Minuit, 1989.

_____. *La Sorcière*. Paris: Minuit, 1996.

_____. *Les Serpents*. Paris: Minuit, 2004.

_____. *Mon cœur à l'étroit*. Paris: Gallimard, 2007.

_____. *Quant au riche avenir*. Paris: Minuit, 1985.

_____. *Rosie Carpe*. Trans. Tamsin Black. Lincoln: U of Nebraska P, 2004.

_____. *Three Strong Women*. Trans. John Fletcher. London: Quercus, 2012.

Rabaté, Dominique. *Le Roman français depuis 1900*. Paris: PUF, 1998.

_____. «L'Éternelle Tentation de l'hébétude, le nom de Rosie Carpe.» *L'Atelier du roman* 35 (Sept. 2003): 48–55.

_____. *Marie NDiaye*. Paris: Textuel, 2008.

Rank, Otto. *The Double: A Psychoanalytic Study.* London: Karnac, 1971.

Royle, Nicholas. *The Uncanny*. Manchester, Eng.: Manchester UP, 2003.

Sarraute, Nathalie. *Childhood*. Trans. Barbara Wright. New York: Braziller, 1984.

Sarrey-Strack, Colette. *Fictions contemporaines au féminin: Marie Darrieussecq, Marie NDiaye, Marie Nimier, Marie Redonnet.* Paris: L'Harmattan, 2002.

Thomas, A. «Marie NDiaye. Renaissance de la littérature française.» *Amina* 253 (May 1991): 81.

Todorov, Tzvetan. *The Fantastic: A Structural Approach to a Literary Genre.* Trans. Richard Howard. Cleveland: P of Case Western Reserve U, 1973.

Tulinius, Torfi H. "Relations proches." *L'Atelier du roman* 35 (Sept. 2003): 68–75.

Vercier, Bruno, and Dominique Viart, *La Littérature française au présent: Héritage, modernité, mutations*. Paris: Bordas, 2005.

Whitehead, Claire. *The Fantastic in France and Russia in the Nineteenth Century. In Pursuit of Hesitation*. London: Legenda, 2006.

Zamora, Lois Parkinson, and Faris, Wendy B. *Magical Realism: Theory, History, Community*. Durham: Duke UP, 1995.

Monsters of the Fantastic: Fusions of the Mythical and the Real _____

Joseph Andriano

What Monsters Signify

Whether they appear in myth, folklore, literature, film, or video, monsters continue to proliferate in the human imagination. They embody what we fear, what we dread, although the fear often becomes fascination and the dread becomes desire. Monsters are protean: they shift their shape just when we think we have grasped them. Some of the fears they embody appear to be primordial and universal, like fear of the dark; but what comes out of the dark keeps changing, evolving. And some fears are less warranted than they used to be, like the fear of being eaten. Most of us do not need to worry about that as much as our ancient ancestors did. And yet, man-eating ogres are as abundant in our films and fictions as ever.

Since monstrous beasts were once a very real threat, it should come as no surprise that our fear of them may be a result of natural selection, hardwired in our brains, encoded perhaps in our DNA and bundled in our amygdala (Asma 4; Gilmore 187). The fear of being eaten is so primordial, so ingrained that common-sense attention to low probability does not curtail our anxiety and dread. Monstrous man-eating beasts like crocodiles and sharks should not bother us at all in our everyday lives, unless we seek them out or happen to invade their space. And yet they are magnified in our films and fictions into fantastic beasts we love to watch on the rampage, purging our fear as we thrill to them on page and screen, all the while secure in the knowledge they are not and can never be real. Sociopathic human cannibals, in contrast, are very real monsters, and it is perfectly understandable why we find them so disturbing. Still, although it is possible, we are not likely to be victims of serial killers such as Jeffrey Dahmer, on whose life Joyce Carol Oates based her novel *Zombie* (1995). The sheer number of monsters, both bestial and human, that appear in our cultural productions is completely out of proportion to their actual threat, suggesting that we need the catharsis they provide.

What exactly is a monster? Some scholars assert that it is indefinable: Stephen Asma, for example, claims that no single defining criterion can be said to capture all monsters (282), although for him "an action or a person or a thing is monstrous when it can't be processed by our rationality" (10); "monstrosity is that which exists outside rational coherence" (251). Many scholars rely on etymology to define the term, which derives from the Latin *monstrum*, a warning or portent (Gilmore 9): sometimes "*demonstrating* what to avoid, and *remonstrating*" with transgressors who break established boundaries (Beal 195; italics original), but other times warning that occasionally it may be necessary to buck the establishment and cross the boundaries. Monsters are often two-faced; they "swing us both ways, soliciting both conservative and radical impulses" (Beal 196). As Jeffrey Cohen suggests, they offer possibilities of liberation from the very norms they warn us not to transgress; they "serve as secondary bodies through which the possibilities of other genders, other sexual practices . . . can be explored" (18).[1] We let our monsters do the transgressing for us, but then we identify with them.

Most monsterologists agree on this much: the monster is a malevolent creature we wish to believe is totally Other, alien, but that we know, deep down, is not (Beal 196; Gilmore 16). It is often gigantic (think of its usage as an adjective in, for example, "monster truck"), but it may be as little as a gremlin. It is often ugly, but may even be, at least in appearance, beautiful. Monstrous beauty approaches the sublime (e.g., Peter Jackson's King Kong), but more often the monster is grotesque—through hybridity, distortion, or repulsive behavior.[2] It is a predator, living either to devour or destroy human beings, but sometimes doing so because human beings have been monstrous to it or its kind. The monster's depredation in medieval times was thought to be motiveless, simply evil. In the ancient Anglo-Saxon epic *Beowulf*,

Grendel, as a descendant of the biblical figure Cain and the son of a monster, is evil by nature. Later versions of Grendel, especially in the movies, suggest that the monster is bad because he has been cast out, rejected by callous human beings (Asma 100–1). That the homicidal behavior of the monster is provoked not by its own nature but by the inhumane treatment it has received from humans was first powerfully dramatized by the writer Mary Shelley in her novel *Frankenstein; Or, The Modern Prometheus* (1818).

Regardless of its cause, malevolence is a defining factor of the monstrous. Once the fantastic creature becomes benevolent, s/he ceases to be a monster. Often, as we will see, what appears to be a monster turns out to be the opposite because the creature's behavior was mistaken for malevolence. It is not the physical grotesque alone that makes a monster; it is malicious behavior—the less rationally motivated, the more twisted the motive, the more monstrous the creature.

Monsters demonstrate that boundaries between human and animal are elusive if not downright illusory. Grendel inhabits "the murky borderland where human nature and animal nature merge" (Foust 451), and yet "Beowulf is disturbingly like Grendel" (Gilmore 191); twentieth-century writer John Gardner even has Beowulf call Grendel his brother (170) in his reworking of the Beowulf epic in his novel *Grendel* (1971). The monster is a liminal creature, often hovering "between categories" (Asma 40), whether it is a mish-mash of two or more animals (like the griffin, the chimera, the dragon) or a hybrid of human and animal (the Minotaur, the gorgon, the werewolf), or (most recently) of human and machine (the cyborg). One of Jeffrey Cohen's "Seven Theses" about the monster's cultural significance is that it is "the harbinger of category crisis," "a form suspended between forms that threatens to smash distinctions" (6). The monster often represents the enemy of the society or culture imagining it, like the dragon of the apocalypse embodying the political and religious enemies of Christianity (Beal 30), or the aliens likened to terrorists in recent movies such as *Independence*

Day (1996) and *War of the Worlds* (2005). But more often than not, the monster gets out of control, refusing to remain the Other.

This deconstruction of boundaries between Self and Other is usually accomplished in monster tales through the process of doubling. At least since *Frankenstein,* the fantastic monster has been a doppelganger, either of its creator or of its pursuers. The double is often the dark side of the self, whether id or shadow (like Mr. Hyde), but it can also be the conscience (individual or societal), appearing as a monstrous embodiment of guilt. Such monsters often become scapegoats or victims (e.g., King Kong). Just as Shelley's novel was the first to posit the monster as victim, it was also the first to suggest that science could create monsters. The gothic novel had already shown, somewhat obsessively, that the Sleep of Reason could breed demonic monsters, but Shelley now suggested that Reason, awake, might create new monsters, those of science and technology. As Brian Aldiss first pointed out, Shelley's novel was a favorable mutation of the gothic that gave rise to a new species, science fiction (16–17).

Perhaps Daniel Cohen is right that the monsters of science fiction are more unsettling and disturbing than those of horror fantasy because they are possible, sometimes even plausible (10), whereas impossible monsters tend to validate and reinforce some readers' need to believe in the supernatural—if demons exist, then so do angels. Even completely skeptical readers, however, can derive pleasure from impossible monsters that allow us to suspend our disbelief, exercise our imaginations, and purge our fear of the unknown. Possible monsters are also cathartic; they encourage us to act out our anxieties and purge our fears of the dangers of science run amok, of scientists playing God, of technology out of our control.

Is there really any significant difference, then, between the monsters of fantasy and those of science fiction? Does the issue of plausibility really matter when we consider the monsters as signs and symbols, as cultural icons, and as indexes of our own identity? A figure like the dragon inhabits both the realms of fable/fantasy and of science fiction; in fact, the creature often fuses the two genres. Anne McCaffrey's *Dragonriders of Pern* series, first appearing in 1967 in *Analog*, a magazine that eschewed fantasy, was perhaps the first to redefine the dragon as a naturally evolved creature, with some genetic modifications. Fire breathing, flying, and even the telepathic bond between rider and dragon were all given (pseudo)scientific explanations. In both science fiction and fantasy, the dragon remains a powerful symbol, more complex than a mere allegory of evil. It ultimately does not matter to us if the dragon is a product of nature or of magic; in both cases it fills a need, creating a sense of either the sublime or the grotesque, depending of course on the behavior of the dragon.

And yet, surely in many cases, especially in cautionary tales of technology or science run amok, it must matter that the monster is not supernatural. Richard Matheson's novel *I Am Legend* (1954) has been very influential in this regard, instituting "the germ theory of vampirism" (Clasen 314). Matheson's natural explanation turned demons into zombies through disease. In many other tales, vampires are actually aliens, possible creatures. And in Gardner's novel, Grendel is not a demon; he is a Neanderthal or an ape-man, the last of his kind. Still, even in such texts, the science fiction monster (as shown below) always seems to retain some very ancient components from myth and fantasy.

Since monsters feel free to inhabit literature, film, television, to haunt highbrow as well as pop culture, serious films as well as B movies, I make no distinctions between media, or between "serious" and "junk" fiction. *Jaws* is no *Moby-Dick*, and Gardner's *Grendel* is certainly a more sophisticated treatment of the monster than, say, *Star Trek Voyager*'s "photonic" version (in the episode "Heroes and Demons"). But no matter the medium, the monster's cultural dismantling of boundaries, its fusion of science and fantasy, can stimulate our intellects as well as our imaginations.

Revelations of Leviathan

Perhaps the most ancient example of monstrous fusion is the biblical sea-monster/dragon Leviathan, still very much alive in our fantastic fictions. In Hebrew mythology, Leviathan is on the one hand the greatest of the sea-monsters God created (Ps. 104), and on the other a demonic chaos-monster, adversary to God (Ps. 74; Beal 25–27). Leviathan is the archetype of ambiguous monstrosity. The Bible does not consistently envision him as evil. Sometimes he is even a metaphor for God himself, as when he answers Job out of the whirlwind: "Canst thou draw out Leviathan with a fishhook?" (*King James Version*, Job 40:25). Can you, in other words, grasp the deity with your puny human mind? God deliberately draws parallels between himself and Leviathan: "None is so fierce that dare stir him up; / Who then is able to stand before Me?" (Job 41:2–3).

Explicitly and emphatically described as a fire-breathing dragon (Job 41:11–13), Leviathan is a sublime creature in both Job and Psalm 104:26, where he is seen sporting in the waters. Psalm 74, in contrast, was written in a time of political and theological crisis—the invasion of Jerusalem by Babylonians in 587 BCE (Beal 26). The psalmist begs God to destroy Babylon as he destroyed Leviathan the chaos-monster (Beal 27–30). Biblical texts often use monsters to symbolize enemy nations, but in Job, arguably, the monster symbolizes God himself. The result is what Noel Carroll calls "category jamming" (194): so many contradictory elements comprise the monster that we cannot get a complete picture of it; it is ultimately unrepresentable (Beal 52). As Herman Melville also pointed out in his novel *Moby-Dick* (1851), "The great Leviathan is that one creature in the world that must remain unpainted to the last" (228). He is both satanic and deific (like Ahab, Moby Dick's doppelganger, both godlike and ungodly). As monster, Leviathan creates and revels in chaos; as god, he creates order and grandeur. Which role dominates depends on the perceiver's view of the great beast and what it symbolizes. In *Moby-Dick*, the White Whale can evoke horror, terror, worship, or wonder.

It was Melville who recast Leviathan for modern fantastic fiction, paving the way for the naturalization of the once-supernatural dragon as a product of evolution (Andriano 9–13). *Moby-Dick* was the inspiration for many fantastic texts and films that recreate Leviathan, though not always retaining its ambiguity. The great white shark in Peter Benchley's 1974 novel *Jaws* is a notorious example of demonizing Leviathan—along with Spielberg's film adaptation that became responsible for what Arthur C. Clarke called a "pogrom" against sharks (qtd. in Ellis 160). I have written extensively elsewhere about Leviathan in *Jaws* and similar fantastic texts, which often start with a creature of Nature, such as a shark or a giant squid (Benchley's *Beast*), and invest it with enough fantastic elements that it becomes a leviathanic dragon. The dragon is then deployed as a symbol to convey ecological themes (in *Beast*) or to suggest that humans are as predatory as sharks (*Jaws*). In both texts Benchley asserts a continuum between human and animal (Andriano 17–44), but the natural killing machine that is the shark is not as monstrous as human killing machines—a point he drives home yet again in his novel *White Shark* (1994).

In this novel, the creature is an artificial monster created by a Nazi scientist. Its teeth and claws are stainless steel; it is essentially a mechanism, impelled only by the instinct to kill, as opposed even to a pregnant great white shark that at least also has a procreative instinct, and to the humpback whale, whose eye clearly reflects a vast intelligence (Benchley 223). Although the monster's human component does not make it any less monstrous, it is defeated by humanity at its best, a group of sympathetic (though rather stereotyped) animal-lovers.

"We need dragons to keep our imaginations alive," says the protagonist Chase during a discussion of the mysterious songs of the humpback whale (Benchley 212). For Benchley, as for Melville, there are two kinds of dragon, embodying the essential ambiguity of the Leviathan archetype: the Dragon of Eden (astronomer and writer Carl Sagan's term) and the Dragon of the Apocalypse. The former takes the creature out of the realm of the monstrous and acknowledges our kinship with other animals (think of the telepathic bond between human and dragon in *The Dragonriders of Pern* or even the 2010 animated film *How to Train Your Dragon*), our common ancestry with reptiles and raptors, and our recognition that all human races are one; while the latter asserts the monstrosity of the dragon, embodying Otherness, discontinuity between races, nations, religions, erecting a hierarchic ladder onto the Tree of Life. Even though *White Shark* is not great literature, not even as good a novel as *Jaws*, it provides a kind of corrective to that novel, as it makes peace with the shark and asserts that true monstrosity resides in humanity when it is inhumane.

Although the "stainless steel" machine grafted onto human and animal makes the creature even more monstrous, it does not have to be that way. As Donna Haraway pointed out in "The Cyborg Manifesto," a "cyborg world might be about lived social and bodily realities in which people are not afraid of their joint kinship with animals and machines, not afraid of permanently partial identities and contradictory standpoints" (154). The Leviathan archetype is especially useful for triangulating what is human, animal, and machine. At the end of chapter 57 of *Moby-Dick*, Melville has Ishmael imagine the white whale as a sort of spaceship (233), which Ray Bradbury would later transform into the rocket, gliding through space "like a pale sea leviathan" (*Planet Stories*). Of course, large ships were often called Leviathans in the nineteenth century; well before Bradbury, nineteenth-century author Jules Verne effectively suggested that Leviathan could be artificial. Technology, he knew, was becoming leviathanic: the *Nautilus* in the novel *Twenty Thousand Leagues under the Sea* (1870), first assumed by observers to be a sea monster, is revealed to be a machine, as sublime as the giant squid it battles (Csicsery-Ronay, "Grotesque" 72). Indeed, the mechanical Leviathan is often viewed as sublime, like the mysterious cetacean space probe in the film *Star Trek IV: The Voyage Home* (1986; see Andriano 161–64), which certainly influenced Osamu Desaki's Japanese anime series *Hakugei: Legend of the Moby Dick* (1997–99). In both cases, the mechanical space whale is capable of global annihilation, which is averted only when human beings come to their senses and exhibit some ecological awareness. In *Star Trek IV*, Leviathan has evolved into an interstellar cybernetic probe of unknown origin: inscrutable, impenetrable, apparently dismissing humankind as inferior to the whale, which it recognizes as kin. The probe's lack of respect for humans is meant to remind us of our own callous disregard for creatures we have considered our inferiors. The icon of the cetacean galactic probe suggests that the future path of evolution will be through artificial selection toward the cyborganic, an idea more fully explored by Desaki.

Viewers of *Hakugei* gradually learn about a "white demon" that will later be identified as Moby Dick, the Federation of Planets' most powerful weapon, a whale-shaped warship capable of destroying a whole planet, which is exactly what it may do to the protagonist's homeworld Moäd if she cannot get Ahab's help. Desaki makes clear that it is not "the Moby Dick" itself that is evil but the power-hungry, energy-wasting Federation. In an interview for the DVD collection (2006), he emphasized the ambiguous nature of the monster: "I thought I'd try to focus . . . more on what exactly this White Whale was. . . . Maybe it's a cyborg. But each viewer will have a different interpretation" (Interview, Disk 1). This viewer sees it as a vehicle for exploring human identity, which is becoming more and more entangled in the machine. The planet Moäd has been strip-mined, polluted, and virtually drained of its oil and resources by the Federation, which declares the moribund world a total loss and orders a mandatory evacuation. Moäd has been selected for the first planetary demolition in human history. Toward the end of the series, after quashing the resistance, the Federation announces to all planets the upcoming "Great Space Show of 4701, the Big Bang to usher in the new century: the first time humans are able to blow up a whole planet . . . broadcast live on your home monitors" (episode 25). This dubious milestone in human achievement will also be a demonstration of the Federation's superior technology.

The Federation's big show is of course spoiled by the noble Captain Ahab and his frenetic crew. Ahab's first encounter with the "white demon" has left him one-eyed as well as one-legged. Now a quasi-cyborg with a prosthetic leg and a mechanical crutch, he is one of many characters in the series who are part machine. In suggesting that human identity is now inevitably linked with the machine, Desaki presents a wide range of human-machine hybrids, dissolving any clear boundaries between the two. Several characters begin as human but are transformed into androids or cyborgs. The whole series may be taken as a kind of cyborg manifesto for adolescents; rather than asserting a violent dichotomy between human and machine (as in *The Matrix* film series), Desaki asserts a continuity. The android singer Sara is not only capable of love, she is also capable of religious sensibility: seeing Moby Dick in orbit above her, she thinks it is God and prays to it to save Moäd. As always, Leviathan makes us ask, is it God or monster? The cyborg whale-ship orbiting Moäd is programmed by the Federation to be detonated, but the human consciousness within it resists and actually helps bring about its own self-destruction to save the world. Altruism and self-sacrifice defeat the forces of oppression and exploitation. But only a battle has been won; the Federation is still in power.

Hakugei is a fascinating free adaptation of *Moby-Dick* that conveys many of Melville's themes, from the ambiguous whiteness of the whale to the dissolution of traditional boundaries to the encouragement of ecological awareness. And Leviathan is revealed not to be a monster, except when it becomes an oppressive political state. The real monster is the Federation.

A more recent example of the sublime space Leviathan on television is a 2010 episode of *Doctor Who* entitled "The Beast Below," written by Steven Moffat. Like *The X-Files* in the 1990s, *Doctor Who* is an especially rich source of monsters, although in this particular episode the apparent monster turns out to be quite otherwise.[3] The space/time–traveling Doctor and his companion Amy arrive in their TARDIS on Starship *UK* in the twenty-ninth century. Much of the British population has escaped the earth before its incineration by solar flares; the opening montage reveals that London is now a metropolis moving through space. The society inhabiting the giant nation-starship, we quickly learn, is a grotesque dystopian police-state, replete with "Smilers," mechanical robot watch-fiends installed in booths; and "Winders," cowled monk-like figures that take offenders away and feed them to the Beast below. This hidden creature is fed "protestors and citizens of limited value."

After several adventures, including a repulsively hilarious sequence in which Amy and the Doctor fall down a chute into the mouth of the Beast, they finally learn the truth: Starship *UK* is supported by a giant "star whale," which propels it through space. Like the Doctor, the creature is the last of its kind, which at one time guided space travelers through the asteroid belt. With the onslaught of the solar flares, it was captured and the ship was constructed around it. In order to control it, the pain center of its brain was exposed to receive frequent jolts of electricity, which originate from a device reminiscent of many a *Frankenstein* film. A beast of burden like a horse under the whip, the creature is tortured "just to keep it moving." When Amy realizes that the star whale, who refuses to eat children, is just like the benevolent Doctor, she finds a way to relieve the Beast of its pain while still driving the starship.

Shortly after the Doctor and Amy return to the TARDIS, they get a call from historic politician Winston Churchill (in the twentieth century, on Earth). The camera cuts to the prime minister sitting in his office. He tells the Doctor he needs him because a situation has developed. The camera then pans to the wall, on which appears a gigantic shadow of a Dalek, the ultimate monster in *Doctor Who*, a cyborg dedicated to the destruction of all sentient creatures that are not Daleks. From this grotesque we cut to the final shot, the sublime star whale, seen for the first time in all its titanic glory, Leviathan as Atlas rather than Satan, supporting a world.

"The Beast Below" is a satirical fable demonstrating that genuine monstrosity lies not in the beast but in humanity when it is devoid of empathy. Without it, men become mechanical manikins (the Smilers are often visually doubled with the cowled Winders). Starship *UK* is a microcosm of any prosperous society that chooses to forget that its prosperity often comes at a terrible price paid by those who do not share in it but whose pain actually makes it possible. The toothy grimace of the Smiler is a reminder that such a society has become a monster, malevolent though appearing benevolent. As in *Hakugei*, the real monster is the oppressive state, turned monstrous when hegemonic thinking infects the rulers, who consider some citizens "of limited value."

As these texts and videos reveal, the ancient sea-dragon Leviathan is still very much alive in science fiction, which has transformed the mythical beast into an icon of our hopes and fears for the future.

The Extraterrestrial Monster

Perhaps the most expected monster of science fiction is the alien. Not all aliens are monsters, of course; well before the motion picture *ET* (1982), science fiction fans delighted in friendly if enigmatic aliens like the famous Tweel in Stanley Weinbaum's short story "A Martian Odyssey" (1934). But the very word "alien" now conjures up H. R. Giger's grotesque invader of bodies and ships, first seen in Ridley Scott's film *Alien* (1979).[4] Our collective anxiety over HIV and other viruses, our fear of the incursion of the Other, whether human, insect, or beast, gets repeatedly played out and purged through invading aliens depicted ad nauseam in every medium.

Products of evolution, monstrous aliens are the demons of the post-Darwinian age (cf. Csicsery-Ronay, "Aliens" 6). We use them as symbols not only of cultural dread but of "what we oppress and repress" (3): "Sf's [science fiction's] aliens have been modeled on . . . categories of otherness that fascinate [and repel] the regulators of culture: . . . women, marginalized peoples, animals, and 'anomalous genders'"— with animals being "by far the most frequent models for alien forms and behavior" ("Aliens" 12). Even after Darwin taught us otherwise, we like to think we are different in kind from other animals, and when we try to imagine beings that evolved on other worlds, we often picture them as insects, cephalopods, and reptiles.

It was H. G. Wells who paved the way for the plausible depiction of the alien by adapting the gothic monstrous to the new scientific romance (Stableford 818). Unlike Verne, who preferred the heroic sublime, Wells was a master of the grotesque in his early fictions—with his Morlocks, Selenites, Beast-folk, and of course Martians (Csicsery-Ronay, "Grotesque" 72). In *The War of the Worlds* (1898), he infuses his text with gothic imagery; the Martians are vampires, although their method of feeding is through injection. They are brains with tentacles, and while a clear pattern of imagery invests them with mythical monstrosity, they are relentlessly natural: their invasion, likened variously to volcanic eruption (Wells 127), earthquake (185), and cyclone (266), is a natural disaster. And yet they are Medusan, equipped with a "Gorgon group of tentacles" (139); their machines hiss like serpents (131, 143), and they emerge like serpents of evil from a hellish pit.

While the horror that readers feel imagining the monsters is partly a result of the gothic atmosphere Wells provides, the Martians are clearly a new kind of creature—the first cyborgs in literature. Once they inhabit the giant tripods they create, they become the machines' brains, and the tripods are repeatedly called Martians. Wells makes no distinction between the Martian and its machine. The tripods, first seen on a dark and stormy night, are hooded giants, "huge black shapes, grotesque and strange" (167), but their strangeness comes not from the ghostly but from the mechanical. They seem in fact to flicker between the two, as the lightning creates a horrific strobe effect (164). This is a perfect example of Asma's view of the monstrous as something Reason cannot process, and of Csicsery-Ronay's definition of the grotesque as an object "that consciousness cannot accommodate" because it "disturbs the sense of rational, natural categorization" ("Grotesque" 71). Invested with gothic attributes, the tripods are actually something totally new, products of science and engineering rather than superstition, "glittering Titans" of myth, yet possible products of advanced science.

The octopus-like Martians are "ugly brutes" that seem at first (before they construct their machines) to be helpless and easily defeated. But Wells is giving his complacent audience that has reaped the benefits of imperialism and colonization a lesson in humility and relativism. To the Martians we are the brutes, the dodos to be exterminated, the inferior race to be extirpated. What makes the Martians monsters is what makes humans monsters: "they took no more notice . . . of the people . . . than a man would of the confusion of ants in a nest against which his foot has kicked" (Wells 181). "What are these Martians?" the curate asks. "What are we?" responds the narrator (188).

The Martian invasion was meant in part as a cautionary scenario of what kinds of very human war (from poison gas to heat rays) might lie ahead, but the novel also cautions against hierarchic, hegemonic thinking. The Martians are not the Other; they are what we might evolve into (246–47). The narrator learns to feel empathy both for indigenous peoples colonized by empire, and for animals displaced by human encroachment. Thinking of a rabbit "returning to his burrow" to find men "digging the foundations of a house" (264), he feels "a sense of dethronement" as the Martians have devastated his homeland. Now "an animal among the animals," he fears "the empire of man [has] passed away." Now he feels like "a rat leaving its hiding place . . . an inferior animal" (268). Ironically, creatures even more "inferior" defeat the Martians—bacteria. While they were perpetrating an invasion, they were being invaded, not by sentient monsters but by the microbes Nature uses both to create and destroy.

The War of the Worlds was of course much imitated (and has been repeatedly adapted), but Wells's evolutionary speculations and satirical relativistic themes were usually omitted from the alien monster-tales of the 1920s, 1930s, and 1940s, when "bug-eyed monsters" (BEMs) threatening thinly clad damsels dominated the covers of American pulp science fiction (where, by the way, Wells was reprinted). Some aliens from the pulps remain intriguing, however, especially those of writer H. P. Lovecraft, whose infamous Cthulhu is a fusion of Leviathan, gothic monster, and unearthly alien. Another much-imitated monster is John W. Campbell's shape-shifting Thing in his novella *Who Goes There?* (1938). The thawed alien has much of the mythical Gorgon in its original form, but its monstrosity lies as much in its "unearthly hatred" (Campbell 51) as in "the writhing, loathsome nest of worms" (44) ringing its face. The Thing's ability to imitate what it digests is what makes it especially horrific, but it does not turn humans into monsters; it merely simulates them. It does not symbolize human monstrosity, at least not explicitly as Wells's Martians do.

Campbell, unlike Wells, insists on a dichotomy between human and monster (later deconstructed in John Carpenter's postmodern film *The Thing*, an adaptation of Campbell's *Who Goes There?*). As the crew at the Antarctic research station becomes infiltrated with a shape-shifter, they have to worry, "Is the man next to me an inhuman monster?" (Campbell 79). If he is, it is no longer a man, the original man having been consumed. It is a simulacrum. "The basic quality of the monster" (79) is essentially nonhuman; in the test McReady develops the monster's blood actually "crawls away from a hot needle" (80). The Thing is clearly much more alien than Wells's Martians. As such, it may be terrifying, but it is ultimately less disturbing because it asserts the essential Otherness of the creature, even though it can simulate human beings (and dogs). We are much more horrified to see the monster reflected in the mirror.

Perhaps this explains why the grotesque gorgon in Catherine Moore's short story "Shambleau" (1933) is so unsettling. The alien is identified as "the" Medusa; the myth is "explained" by the supposed "fact" that ancient Greeks actually encountered this extraterrestrial (Moore 525). But the literal identity of the alien makes her no less symbolic. As object of both fear and desire, the mythical Medusa is the archetypal "projection of fascinated repulsion/attraction" (Csiscery-Ronay, "Grotesque" 71) for the Other—in this case both gender and race. Shambleau's skin is brown; with her turban she appears as a pretty "brown girl" (Moore 528), and she is pursued by a lynch mob as the story opens on the planet Mars. We could just as easily be in a Western as in a pulp science fiction tale, with the title character a prostitute dressed in scarlet. When the protagonist, Northwest Smith, saves her and claims her as his own, her pursuers are disgusted and leave her in his "care" (527).

He takes her in, and what follows in his apartment is an extraordinary encounter with the alien, anticipating in its complexity the aliens of later writers such as James Tiptree Jr. and Octavia Butler. Like most writers of science fiction, Moore relies heavily on animal imagery to convey Shambleau's alien nature. When Smith gets a good look at her, "though the brown, sweet body was shaped like a woman's," she has the "look of the beast," namely a kitten (528). A few pages later she's a full-fledged cat-woman, alluring, "stirring excitement within him" (531). Her being half-animal at first arouses him, but then a deeper instinct kicks in, and "the very touch of her was suddenly loathsome" (531).

She is as much a gothic *femme fatale* as she is a mythical gorgon, like Samuel Taylor Coleridge's Geraldine or Sheridan Le Fanu's Carmilla, and like them she is a symbol of men's fear of women's power, agency, and sexuality. But since Shambleau is also a woman of color, the white man's desire becomes doubly conflicted, as Smith is enchanted and befuddled "in a rapture of revulsion, hateful, horrible—but still most foully sweet" (532). When she does not eat, he thinks she may be a vampire (534). But this fear makes her no less desirable to him. Even though she has claws, as long as her hair remains hidden in her turban, Shambleau appears to Smith "so like a woman . . . — sweet and submissive and demure, and softer than soft fur" (535). But her flat animal gaze finally turns him off, and he goes to his own bed.

Coming out of a deep sleep he sees her remove her turban and reveal her "worms, hair, what?—that writhed over her head." When she comes to him, casting a witchlike spell, she engulfs him like a succubus, but then turns him to stone: he is rigid, as in sleep paralysis, but also aroused (537). She is only interested in devouring him, however. Smith's friend Yarol comes just in time to rescue him from this Medusa, again likened to a vampire—indeed the alien is now offered as an explanation for that legend (541).[5] Remembering Perseus, a figure from Greek mythology who battled Medusa, Yarol defeats the gorgon by sighting her in a mirror and shooting her with his gun behind his back. He warns Smith to be certain, if he should ever encounter another Shambleau, to draw his gun and "burn it to hell" (543). But Smith's response is hardly resolute: "I'll—try," he says, his voice actually imitating Shambleau's manner of speech.

Noted feminist critics Sandra Gilbert and Susan Gubar dismissed the story because of Moore's apparent complicity in "the male imperative to murder the alien female"; for them, Shambleau in the mirror reflected "the female author's culturally conditioned self-loathing" (qtd. in Bredehoft 370). But Bredehoft convincingly demonstrates that Smith has been changed for the better by his experience. He is unwilling to join the mob (383). Yarol's view of Shambleau as completely nonhuman, as a simulacrum akin to Campbell's Thing, is actually rejected in the tale, which instead suggests that the alien is more like Wells's Martians, an embodiment of guilt over colonization, exploitation, and racism. Once again, whether ultimate Other or thinly disguised Self, the alien is a symbol of all that we dread and desire.

The more one thinks about "our monsters, ourselves" (as both Gilmore and Beal titled a chapter of their books), the more one is forced to conclude that, semiotically at least, there is no significant distinction between the impossible monsters of myth or fantasy and the possible ones of science fiction. Mythical and gothic monsters emerge from the past, while the monsters of science fiction loom in an imagined future. But that future carries baggage from the past, as the first science fiction novel revealed: Dr. Frankenstein is as much an alchemist and necromancer as he is a scientist; his monster is therefore as much a demonic fiend as he is a constructed human. And the futuristic star whale is still the ancient Leviathan, transformed to serve new purposes. The cultural heritage of myth helps to shape the monster's body. Perhaps this is why the symbolically richest creatures of science fiction, like Shambleau, are often just barely plausible, teetering on "the borders of the possible" (J. Cohen 12). So Grendel alternates between supernatural ogre and natural hominid, and then morphs into a photonic being. As an immaterial alien life-form aboard starship *Voyager*, he may seem futuristic, but he has become a spirit again, an ancient sprite. There will always be fantastic monsters trampling on our murky borderlines.

Notes

1. The monstrosity of "the other gender" is a common element of fairy tales and heroic fantasies. For an informative discussion of male writers' female monsters and female writers' male monsters, see Veglahn's article (esp. 112–16). Regardless of gender, the monster's threat, danger, aggression, is often sexual—and often desired as well as dreaded.

2. Istvan Csicsery-Ronay contrasts the sublime with the grotesque in his article "On the Grotesque in Science Fiction." Jules Verne used the sublime "to present the reader with a wider and wider extension of the imperial domain of received science, the imperial status quo." Following H. G. Wells instead, Csicsery-Ronay argues that modern science fiction "favors grotesque ordeals of consciousness" (80).

3. Both programs have continuing story arcs often interrupted by "monster of the week" episodes, parading a menagerie of creatures: *The X-Files* included (among many others) a golem ("Kaddish"), a were-reptile ("Alone"), and a lake-monster Leviathan ("Quagmire"); *Doctor Who* has cybermen, weeping demonic alien "angels" (in several episodes), fishlike aliens disguised as vampires ("The Vampires of Venice"), and synthetic human doppelgangers ("The Almost People").

4. More has been written about this creature than almost any other. Istvan Csicsery-Ronay, in both essays cited here, gives an excellent overview of "the trajectory of the *Alien* series, as the first film's classic monster-gothic evolved into a more complex cyborg fable," with the creature itself evolving "from a quasi-mechanical package of irresistible instincts into a conscious being" ("Grotesque" 5); the xenomorph also evolves from something totally Other (in *Alien*) to a creature contaminated by "humanity's own self-disgust" (in *Alien Resurrection*) ("Aliens" 14).

5. See Veronica Hollinger's "The Vampire and the Alien." Focusing on Colin Wilson's *The Space Vampires* (1976) and Jody Scott's *I, Vampire* (1984), she concludes that Wilson's "conflation of vampire with alien maintains the role of the

former as a threat from outside, the quintessential Other" (155), whereas Scott makes the vampire a metaphor for the Self (154). Like Veglahn, she sees these authorial differences as gender specific.

Works Cited

Aldiss, Brian W. *Trillion Year Spree: The History of Science Fiction*. New York: Avon, 1988.

Andriano, Joseph. *Immortal Monster: Mythological Evolution of the Fantastic Beast in Modern Fiction and Film*. Westport, CT: Greenwood, 1999.

Asma, Stephen T. *On Monsters: An Unnatural History of Our Worst Fears*. New York: Oxford UP, 2009.

Beal, Timothy K. *Religion and Its Monsters*. New York: Routledge, 2002.

"The Beast Below." *Doctor Who: The Complete Fifth Series*. Writ. Steven Moffat. Dir. Andrew Gunn. BBC Warner, 2010.

Benchley, Peter. *White Shark*. New York, St. Martin's, 1994.

Bradbury, Ray. "Mars Is Heaven!" *Planet Stories* 3.12 (Fall 1948).

Bredehoft, Thomas A. "Origin Stories: Feminist Science Fiction and C. L. Moore's 'Shambleau.'" *Science Fiction Studies* 24.3 (Nov. 1997): 369–86.

Campbell, John W., Jr. "*Who Goes There?*" 1938. *The Science Fiction Hall of Fame*. Vol. 2 A. Ed. Ben Bova. New York: Tor, 2004. 34–87.

Carroll, Noël. *The Philosophy of Horror; or, Paradoxes of the Heart*. New York: Routledge, 1990.

Clasen, Matthias. "Vampire Apocalypse: A Biocultural Critique of Richard Matheson's *I Am Legend*." *Philosophy and Literature* 34.2 (2010): 313–28.

Cohen, Daniel. *Science Fiction's Greatest Monsters*. New York: Pocket, 1980.

Cohen, Jeffrey Jerome. "Monster Culture (Seven Theses)." *Monster Theory*. Ed. Jeffrey J. Cohen. Minneapolis: U of Minnesota P, 1996. 3–25.

Csicsery-Ronay, Istvan. "On the Grotesque in Science Fiction." *Science Fiction Studies* 29.1 (2002): 71–99.

_____. "Some Things We Know about Aliens." *Yearbook of English Studies* 37.2 (2007): 1–23.

Ellis, Richard. *Monsters of the Sea*. New York: Doubleday, 1994.

Foote, Timothy. "Fish Story." *Arts*. The New York Times Company, 5 June 1994. Web. 13 Mar. 2012.

Foust, R. E. "Monstrous Image: Theory of Fantasy Antagonists." *Genre* 13 (1980): 441–53.

Gardner, John. *Grendel*. 1971. New York: Random House, 1989.

Gilmore, David D. *Monsters: Evil Beings, Mythical Beasts, and All Manner of Imaginary Terrors*. Philadelphia: U of Pennsylvania P, 2003.

Hakugei: The Legend of the Moby Dick. Dir. Osamu Desaki. ADV Films, 2005–6.

Haraway, Donna. "A Cyborg Manifesto: Science, Technology, and Socialist Feminism in the Late Twentieth Century." *Simians, Cyborgs, and Women: The Reinvention of Nature*. New York: Routledge, 1991. 149–81.

"Heroes and Demons." *Star Trek Voyager*. Dir. Les Landau. UPN. 24 Apr. 1995.

Hollinger, Veronica. "The Vampire and the Alien: Variations on the Outsider." *Science Fiction Studies* 16.2 (1989): 145–60.

Melville, Herman. *Moby-Dick*. 1851. New York: Norton, 1967.

Moore, Catherine L. "Shambleau." 1933. *The Prentice Hall Anthology of Science Fiction and Fantasy*. Ed. Garyn G. Roberts. Upper Saddle River, NJ: Prentice Hall, 2001. 525–43.

Sagan, Carl. *The Dragons of Eden*. New York, Random House, 1977.

Stableford, Brian. "Monsters." *The Encyclopedia of Science Fiction*. Eds. John Clute and Peter Nicholls. New York: St. Martin's, 1993. 818–19.

Star Trek IV: The Voyage Home. Dir. Leonard Nimoy. Paramount, 1986.

Veglahn, Nancy. "Images of Evil: Male and Female Monsters in Heroic Fantasy." *Children's Literature* 15.1 (1987): 106–19.

Wells, Herbert George. *The War of the Worlds*. 1898. The Time Machine *and* The War of the Worlds. *A Critical Edition*. Ed. Frank D. McConnell. New York: Oxford UP, 1977. 119–300.

Zondervan Bible Publishers. *Holy Bible*: King James Version. Grand Rapids, MI: Zondervan, 2002.

RESOURCES

Additional Works on the Fantastic ─────

Long Fiction

The Castle of Otranto by Horace Walpole, 1764

The Mysteries of Udolpho: A Romance by Ann Radcliffe, 1794

Frankenstein; Or, The Modern Prometheus by Mary Shelley, 1818

Moby-Dick; or The Whale by Herman Melville, 1851

Alice in Wonderland by Lewis Carroll, 1865

The Picture of Dorian Gray by Oscar Wilde, 1890

The Invisible Man by H. G. Wells, 1897

The Turn of the Screw by Henry James, 1898

The Wonderful Wizard of Oz by L. Frank Baum, 1900

Peter Pan by J. M. Barrie, 1911

Metamorphosis by Franz Kafka, 1915

The Chronicles of Narnia by C. S. Lewis, 1950–55

One Hundred Years of Solitude by Gabriel García Márquez, 1967

The Earthsea Novels by Ursula Le Guin, 1968–2003

Breakfast of Champions by Kurt Vonnegut, 1973

Danse Macabre by Stephen King, 1981

The House of Spirits by Isabel Allende, 1982

The Colour of Magic by Terry Pratchett, 1983

Nights at the Circus by Angela Carter, 1984

The Handmaid's Tale by Margaret Atwood, 1985

His Dark Materials Trilogy by Philip Pullman, 1995–2000

The Eyre Affair (Thursday Next) by Jasper Fforde, 2001

American Gods by Neil Gaiman, 2005

Short Fiction

"Love Charm" by Ludwig Tieck, 1811

"The Devil and Tom Walker" by Washington Irving, 1824

"The Queen of Spades" by Alexander Pushkin, 1834

"The Diary of a Madman" by Nikolai Gogol, 1835

"The Sylph" by Vladimir Odoevsky, 1837

"The Venus of Ille" by Prosper Mérimée, 1837

"The Fall of the House of Usher" by Edgar Allan Poe, 1839

"The Black Cat" by Edgar Allan Poe, 1843

"The Double" by Fyodor Dostoevsky, 1846/1866

"Carmilla" by J. Sheridan Le Fanu, 1872

"The Horla" by Guy de Maupassant, 1887

"The Black Monk" by Anton Chekhov, 1894
"The Ripper of Yesteryear" by Emilia Pardo Bazán, 1900
"The Jolly Corner" by Henry James, 1908
"The Call of Cthulhu" by H. P. Lovecraft, 1928
"Midnight Express" by Alfred Noyes, 1935
"The Bird Spider" by Juan José Arreola, 1949
"Continuity of Parks" by Julio Cortázar, 1956
Cosmicomics by Italo Calvino, 1965
Invisible Cities by Italo Calvino, 1972

Bibliography

Abrams, M. H. *Natural Supernaturalism: Tradition and Revolution in Romantic Literature*. New York: Norton, 1971.

Apter, T. E. *Fantasy Literature: An Approach to Reality*. London: Macmillan, 1982.

Armitt, Lucie. *Theorising the Fantastic*. London: Edward Arnold, 1996.

_____. *Contemporary Women's Fiction and the Fantastic*. London: Macmillan, 2000.

_____. *The Twentieth Century Gothic*. Cardiff: U of Wales P, 2011.

Attebery, Brian. *The Fantasy Tradition in American Literature: From Irving to Le Guin*. Bloomington: Indiana UP, 1980.

_____. *Strategies of Fantasy*. Bloomington: Indiana UP, 1992.

Auerbach, Erich. *Mimesis: The Representation of Reality in Western Literature*. Trans. W. R. Trask. Princeton: Princeton UP, 1953.

Baldick, Chris. *In Frankenstein's Shadow: Myth, Monstrosity, and Nineteenth-Century Writing*. Oxford: Clarendon, 1987.

Bettelheim, Bruno. *The Uses of Enchantment: The Meaning and Importance of Fairy Tales*. New York: Knopf, 1976.

Botting, Fred. *Gothic*. London: Routledge, 1996.

Bronfen, Elisabeth. *Over Her Dead Body: Death, Femininity and the Aesthetic*. Manchester, Eng.: Manchester UP, 1992.

Brooke-Rose, Christine. *A Rhetoric of the Unreal: Studies in Narrative and Structure, Especially of the Fantastic*. Cambridge, Eng.: Cambridge UP, 1981.

Chanady, Amaryll. *Magical Realism and the Fantastic: Resolved versus Unresolved Antinomy*. New York: Garland, 1985.

Chen, Fanfan. *Fantasticism: Poetics of Fantastic Literature: The Imaginary and Rhetoric*. Frankfurt am Main: Lang, 2007.

Clareson, Thomas D. *SF: The Other Side of Realism: Essays on Modern Fantasy and Science Fiction*. Bowling Green U Popular P, 1971.

Cornwell, Neil. *The Literary Fantastic: From Gothic to Postmodernism*. London: Harvester Wheatsheaf, 1990.

Faris, Wendy. *Ordinary Enchantments: Magical Realism and the Remystification of Narrative*. Nashville: Vanderbilt UP, 2004.

Germana, Monica. *Scottish Women's Gothic and Fantastic Writing: Fiction Since 1978*. Edinburgh: Edinburgh UP, 2010.

Hall, Daniel. *French and German Gothic Fiction in the Late Eighteenth Century*. Bern: Lang, 2005.

Harter, Deborah. *Bodies in Pieces: Fantastic Narrative and the Poetics of the Fragment*. Stanford: Stanford UP, 1996.

Hume, Kathryn. *Fantasy and Mimesis: Representations of Reality in Western Literature*. New York: Methuen, 1984.

Irwin, W. R. *The Game of the Impossible: A Rhetoric of Fantasy*. Urbana: U of Illinois P, 1976.

Jackson, Rosemary. *Fantasy: The Literature of Subversion*. New York: Methuen, 1981.

Kennard, Jean E. *Number and Nightmare: Forms of Fantasy in Contemporary Fiction*. Hamden, CT: Archon, 1975.

Landy, Joshua, and Michael Saler, eds. *The Re-Enchantment of the World: Secular Magic in a Rational Age*. Stanford: Stanford UP, 2009.

Lewis, C. S. *Of Other Worlds: Essays and Stories*. Ed. Walter Hooper. New York: Harcourt, 1966.

Little, T. E. *The Fantasts: Studies in J. R. R. Tolkien, Lewis Carroll, Mervyn Peake, Nikolay Gogol, and Kenneth Grahame*. Amersham, Eng.: Avebury, 1982.

Lovecraft, H. P. *Supernatural Horror in Literature*. First published 1938.

Manlove, C. N. *Modern Fantasy: Five Studies*. Cambridge, Eng.: Cambridge UP, 1975.

_____, ed. *The Impulse of Fantasy Literature*. London: Macmillan, 1983.

Masschelein, Anneleen. *The Unconcept: The Freudian Uncanny in Late Twentieth-Century Theory*. Albany: State U of New York P, 2011.

Massey, Irving. *The Gaping Pig: Literature and Metamorphosis*. London: U of California P, 1976.

Monleón, José. *A Specter Is Haunting Europe: A Sociohistorical Approach to the Fantastic*. Princeton: Princeton UP, 1990.

Mücke, Dorothea von. *The Seduction of the Occult and the Rise of the Fantastic Tale*. Stanford: Stanford UP, 2003.

Pearson, Wendy Gay, ed. *Queer Universes: Sexualities in Science Fiction*. Liverpool, Eng.: Liverpool UP, 2008.

Penzoldt, Peter. *The Supernatural in Fiction*. London: Nevill, 1952.

Punter, David. *The Literature of Terror: A History of Gothic Fictions from 1765 to the Present Day*. London: Longman, 1980.

_____, ed. *A Companion to the Gothic*. Oxford, Eng.: Blackwell, 2000.

Rabkin, Eric. *The Fantastic in Literature*. Princeton: Princeton UP, 1976.

Rank, Otto. *The Double: A Psychoanalytic Study*. Chapel Hill: U of North Carolina P, 1971.

Royle, Nicholas. *The Uncanny: An Introduction*. Manchester, Eng.: Manchester UP, 2003.

Scholes, Robert. *Structural Fabulation: An Essay on Fiction of the Future*. Notre Dame: U of Notre Dame P, 1975.

Siebers, Tobin. *The Romantic Fantastic*. Ithaca: Cornell UP, 1984.

Suvin, Darko. *Metamorphoses of Science Fiction: On the Poetics and History of a Literary Genre*. New Haven: Yale UP, 1979.

Swinfen, Ann. *In Defence of Fantasy: A Study of the Genre in English and American Literature since 1945*. London: Routledge & Kegan Paul, 1984.

Todorov, Tzvetan. *The Fantastic. A Structural Approach to a Literary Genre*. Ithaca, NY: Cornell UP, 1975.

Tolkien, J. R. R. "On Fairy-Stories." *The Tolkien Reader*. New York: Ballantine, 1966. 54–5.

Traill, Nancy. *Possible Worlds of the Fantastic: The Rise of the Paranormal in Fiction*. Toronto: Toronto UP, 1996.

Vidler, Anthony. *The Architectural Uncanny*. Cambridge, MA: MIT P, 1992.

Warner, Marina. *Fantastic Metamorphoses, Other Worlds: Ways of Telling the Self*. Oxford, Eng.: Oxford UP, 2002.

Webber, Andrew. *The Doppelgänger: Double Visions in German Literature*. Oxford, Eng.: Clarendon, 1996.

Whitehead, Claire. *The Fantastic in France and Russia in the Nineteenth-Century: In Pursuit of Hesitation*. Oxford, Eng.: Legenda, 2006.

Zamora, Lois Parkinson, and Wendy Faris, eds. *Magical Realism: Theory, History, Community*. Durham, NC: Duke UP, 1995.

Zipes, Jack. *Fairy Tales and the Art of Subversion: The Classical Genre for Children and the Process of Civilization*. New York: Wildman, 1983.

CRITICAL
INSIGHTS

About the Editor

Claire Whitehead is senior lecturer in the Russian Department at the University of St. Andrews in the United Kingdom, where she has worked since 2003. Her research focuses primarily on prose fiction from the nineteenth century up to the present day in both Russia and France. She completed her undergraduate and postgraduate degrees in French and Russian at the University of Bristol, having spent two years working as an English-language teacher at the Université de Bordeaux III in France. Her PhD thesis, offering a comparative analysis of devices of hesitation in the fantastic, was published by Legenda in 2006 under the title *The Fantastic in France and Russia in the Nineteenth Century: In Pursuit of Hesitation.* It offers close readings of works by authors including Alexander Pushkin, Nikolai Gogol, Fyodor Dostoevsky, Théophile Gautier, Prosper Mérimée, and Guy de Maupassant. She is also the author of several other academic articles that examine the fantastic in the writing of Vladimir Odoevsky, Ivan Turgenev, and Anton Chekhov. In 2008 she edited a special issue of the journal *Forum for Modern Language Studies*, which considered the enduring popularity of the fantastic and brought together eight essays studying its presence in a variety of national traditions and a range of historical periods. Alongside her ongoing interest in the fantastic, Whitehead is also researching the development of crime fiction in Russia beginning in the 1860s. She has published articles on the work of Semen Panov, Fyodor Dostoevsky, Alexander Shklyarevsky, and Anton Chekhov.

Contributors

Claire Whitehead is senior lecturer in Russian at the University of St. Andrews in the United Kingdom. She completed both her undergraduate and postgraduate degrees in French and Russian at the University of Bristol. Her PhD thesis, offering a comparative analysis of devices of hesitation in the fantastic, was published by Legenda in 2006 under the title *The Fantastic in France and Russia in the Nineteenth-Century: In Pursuit of Hesitation*. In 2008 she edited a special issue of the journal *Forum for Modern Language Studies*. She is also the author of several other academic articles on the fantastic in the writings of Vladimir Odoevsky, Ivan Turgenev, and Anton Chekhov.

David Sandner is an associate professor of English at California State University, Fullerton, with an interest in the history of fantastic literature and its criticism. His new book on the emerging field is *Critical Discourses of the Fantastic, 1712–1831* (2011). He also wrote *The Fantastic Sublime: Romanticism and Transcendence in Nineteenth-Century Children's Fantasy Literature* (1996), edited *Fantastic Literature: A Critical Reader* (2004), and coedited *The Treasury of the Fantastic: Romanticism to the Early Twentieth Century* (2001).

Dimitra Fimi is a lecturer in English at Cardiff Metropolitan University. She is the author of *Tolkien, Race and Cultural History: From Fairies to Hobbits* (2008), which won the Mythopoeic Scholarship Award in Inklings Studies. She has also published articles and essays in journals (including *Folklore* and *Tolkien Studies*) and in edited collections (including *Old Norse Made New*, 2007, and *Picturing Tolkien*, 2011). She lectures on Tolkien and fantasy literature at undergraduate and postgraduate levels.

Amaryll Chanady is a professor of comparative literature at the Université de Montréal, Canada. Her areas of specialization are inter-American studies, the construction of space, collective identity, hybridity, transculture, the fantastic, magical realism, and postcolonialism. Among her publications are the books *Entre inclusion et exclusion: La Symbolisation de l'autre dans les Amériques* (1999), *Latin American Identity and Constructions of Difference* (ed., 1994), and *America's Worlds and the World's Americas* (coed., 2006). She has also published articles in journals including *Comparative Literature*, *Quebec Studies*, *Universitas humanística*, and *Revista de estudios hispánicos*, among many others.

Bernice M. Murphy is assistant professor in popular literature at the School of English, Trinity College Dublin, Ireland. She is also the director of the School's MPhil in popular literature. She has edited the collection *Shirley Jackson: Essays on the Literary Legacy* (2005), coedited *It Came From the 1950s: Popular Culture, Popular Anxieties* (2011), and is the author of the monograph *The Suburban Gothic in American Popular Culture* (2009). She is the cofounder and editor of the online *Irish Journal of*

Horror and Gothic Studies (2006–) and has also published essays on Stephen King, Shirley Jackson, Jonathan Carroll, the film *Back to the Future*, and the decline of the American horror movie. Her recent work includes a book on the relationship between horror and the landscape in American popular culture.

Lucie Armitt is a professor of literary and cultural studies at the University of Salford, UK, where she is also the director of the Research Centre for English Literature and Language. Her primary publications include *Twentieth-Century Gothic* (2011), *Fantasy Fiction* (2005), *Contemporary Women's Fiction and the Fantastic* (2000), *George Eliot: Readers' Guide to Essential Criticism* (2000), *Theorising the Fantastic* (1996), and *Where No Man Has Gone Before: Women and Science Fiction* (1991).

Birgit Röder was educated at the Heinrich-Heine Universität in Düsseldorf and the University of Reading. She has taught at the Universities of Reading and Nottingham, and is currently a teaching fellow at the University of Warwick. She is the author of *A Study of the Major Novellas of E. T. A. Hoffmann* (2003) and has published articles on Hoffmann's treatment of Orientalism, as well as on literary reworkings of Hoffmann's biography in the work of Peter Härtling.

Peter Cogman read modern and medieval languages at Pembroke College, Cambridge, where he subsequently gained a PhD for research on the work of the poet and novelist P.-J. Toulet. He was a lecturer and senior lecturer in French at the University of Southampton, before retiring in 2004, and is the author of guides to the works of Victor Hugo and Prosper Mérimée. Along with his book *Narration in Nineteenth-Century French Short Fiction: Prosper Mérimée to Marcel Schwob* (2002), Cogman has published a number of articles in academic journals on nineteenth-century French literature and is currently editing some works on English topics by Mérimée for the Champion complete edition of his works.

Slobodan Sucur teaches English and global literature at the University of Alberta in Edmonton, Canada. His publications include articles on comparative literature in *CLCWeb: Comparative Literature and Culture: A WWWeb Journal*, as well as essays on gothic literature and such writers as Edgar Allan Poe, V. F. Odoevsky, and Nathaniel Hawthorne in *The Literary Encyclopedia*. Sucur has also written the book-length study *Poe, Odoyevsky, and Purloined Letters: Questions of Theory and Period Style Analysis* (2001), a work that draws on his broad literary interests, ranging from such topics as romanticism and the "long" eighteenth century to literary history and period style analysis.

Donald Shaw is Brown Forman Professor of Spanish American Literature at the University of Virginia. His areas of research include peninsular literature of the nineteenth and early twentieth centuries and, more especially, modern Spanish American literature, particularly fiction. He has published 16 books and editions and more than 170 articles in academic journals and contributions to books, in English, Spanish, and Italian. These include *A Companion to Spanish American Fiction* (2001); *Borges' Narrative Strategy* (1992); and *A Literary History of Spain: The Nineteenth Century* (1972).

Tomáš Kubíček is a literary historian and theorist and is currently head of the Department of Bohemian Studies at Palacký University in Olomouc in the Czech Republic. His interests include narratology, Czech structuralism, literary theory, and Czech literature after 1930. In addition to numerous other studies, he is the author of several monographs, including *Felix Vodička—Theory and Method: On the History of Czech Structuralism* (2010); *The Narrator: Categories of Narrative Analysis* (2007); *Intersubjectivity in Literary Narrative* (2007); and *Narrate the Story: Narratological Chapters on the Novels by Milan Kundera* (2001). Between 2004 and 2007, he was chief editor of the series *Theoretica*, published by the Institute of Czech Literature at the Academy of Sciences of the Czech Republic. Since 2008, he has been one of the heads of the editorial board of the *Library of Possible Worlds*.

Eugenio Bolongaro is an associate professor of Italian studies at McGill University in Montreal. A native of Italy, he immigrated to Canada in 1976 and studied English and law at the University of British Columbia, receiving a PhD in comparative literature at McGill University. His book *Italo Calvino and the Compass of Literature* (2003) established him as one of the leading North American scholars on a central figure in twentieth-century Italian literature. His other publications focus on contemporary Italian, British, and American literature, as well as on post–World War II Italian cinema. His most recent research interests include ethics and literature; the interaction between realism and the fantastic in fiction; and the representation of homosexual desire in modern Italian culture. He is also preparing a book on the reception of the American writer Thomas Pynchon in Italy.

Daniela De Pau is a native of Sassari, Italy. She obtained her PhD in Italian at the University of Illinois at Urbana-Champaign. She is an associate teaching professor at Drexel University. Her research interests include Italian cinema and literature, the tradition of the Comic and the Fantastic, travel literature, and the documentary. She has published in many international journals and has coedited two books: *Watching Pages, Readings Pictures, Cinema and Modern Literature in Italy* (2008) and *Zoom "d'oltreoceano": Istantanee sui registi italiani e sull'Italia* (2010). She also coauthored *Il Divo* (2011).

Daisy Connon is a freelance translator and independent researcher in Aix-en-Provence, France. She holds a PhD in French literature from Trinity College Dublin. Her research focuses on the contemporary French novel, with an emphasis on the fantastic and the uncanny. She has published articles on French and Anglophone fiction and is the author of *Subjects Not-at-Home: Forms of the Uncanny in the Contemporary French Novel* (2010) and is coauthor of *Aesthetics of Dislocation in French and Francophone Literature and Art* (2009). She has taught French and literature at various universities in Ireland and France and is currently exploring the topic of the uncanny in contemporary French and Francophone cinema and the visual arts.

Joseph Andriano is a professor of English at the University of Louisiana at Lafayette. He has published two books on the fantastic: *Our Ladies of Darkness: Feminine Daemonology in Male Gothic Fiction* (1991) and *Immortal Monster: Mythological Evolution of the Fantastic Beast in Modern Fiction and Film* (1999), as well as several articles on American literature. He also writes short stories, which have appeared in *Argonaut, Louisiana Literature, The Chattahoochee Review,* and other literary journals and anthologies.

Index

Don Ottavio ("Il Viccolo"), 141
Double, The (Dostoevsky), 13
doubles and doppelgängers, 13, 122,
    167, 187–88, 255–66, 276
"Dragon and the Butterflies, The"
    (Calvino), 245–48
dreams and dreaming, 111, 197–99, 208

Earnshaw, Catherine (*Wuthering
    Heights*), 101
Earthsea trilogy (Le Guin), 54
ecocriticism, 56
Eliot, T. S., 221
Elsa (*The Salamander*), 166–70
escapism, nostalgia, and utopianism, 34,
    46–56, 99. *See also* fantastic, the:
    purpose
Esch, August (*The Sleepwalkers*),
    191–200
eucatastrophe and dyscatastrophe
    (Tolkien), 30, 47
"Evil Drawings, The" (Calvino), 240–45

fairy tales and folktales, 27, 129–32,
    235–50. *See also* Kunstmärchen
    (literary fairy tale); myths and
    mythology
"Fall of the House of Usher, The" (Poe),
    82
fantastic, the
    definition, 7, 8, 23–36, 40, 63–76,
        108, 213–15, 253
    fantasy, relation to, 21, 40–41, 63
    language, relation to, 11–15
    pedagogical fantastic, 161–63
    purpose, xiii, 4, 129, 132, 175, 228
    reason, relation to, 4–9
*Fantastic: A Structural Approach to a
    Literary Genre, The* (Todorov), 34
"Fantastic Imagination, The"
    (MacDonald), 27, 52

fantasy literature
    definition, 28, 40, 63
    high (or immersive) fantasy, 42–43
    low (or intrusion) fantasy, 42–43
    Victorian, 27, 51
Farewell Party, The (Kundera), 201–9
fear, 28, 70, 139, 273
Federico ("The Evil Drawings"), 240
fictional world, construction of, 45–52,
    200–209
Fischer, Benjamin Franklin (*Hell
    House*), 88
folktales. *See* fairy tales and folktales
Foucault, Michel, 61, 66
Freud, Sigmund, 4, 99
"fuzzy set theory" (Attebery), 35, 49–50

"Garden of Forking Paths, The"
    (Borges), 185–86
ghosts and spirits, 40, 70, 83–84,
    99–115. *See also* haunted houses;
    paranormal activity, investigations
    of; psychic sensitivity
Goethe, Johann Wolfgang von, 117
Golden Pot, The (Hoffmann), 129–32
Gothic architecture, 81. *See also*
    haunted houses
gothic literature, 3, 25, 99–116, 162,
    171–72, 276. *See also* American vs.
    European gothic
Gravity's Rainbow (Pynchon), 212–27
Grendel (*Beowulf*), 275

Hakugei: Legend of the Moby Dick
    (television series), 281–82
Halloran, Dick (*The Shining*), 92
Harry Potter series (Rowling), 33
haunted houses, 78–95, 99–114, 256
Haunting of Hill House, The (Jackson),
    84–94
Hawthorne, Nathaniel, 82

sorcery and witchcraft, 258. *See also* alchemy; occult, the; paranormal activity, investigations of

"South, The" (Borges), 186

spatial theory, 61–77

spirits. *See* ghosts and spirits

spirituality. *See* religion and spirituality

structuralists and structuralism, 6, 230

sub-creation (Tolkien), 30, 43–46. *See also* fictional world, construction of

sublime, the, 23, 221

suicide, 90, 124, 197. *See also* murder

suspension of disbelief, 26, 52, 176

Talboys, George (*Lady Audley's Secret*), 105

Talboys, Helen (*Lady Audley's Secret*), 105

Todorov, Tzvetan, 6–8, 40, 137–38, 213–14

Tolkien, J. R. R., 43–58

Torrance, Danny (*The Shining*), 91

Torrance, Jack (*The Shining*), 91

Turn of the Screw, The (James), 14, 40, 82–83

uncanny, the

Freud, 4, 28, 99–103, 123, 255, 270

Todorov, 34, 63, 137

Valdemaro ("Dragon and the Butterflies"), 245

Vance, Eleanor (*Haunting of Hill House*), 84

violence, 89–90

"Vision of Charles XI, The" (Mérimée), 138–41

Von Bertrand, Eduard (*The Sleepwalkers*), 191–99

Walpole, Horace, 3

War of the Worlds, The (Wells), 285–86

Water Babies, The (Kingsley), 56

Waters, Sarah, 112

Weetzie Bat (Bloch), 33

Well at the World's End, The (Morris), 53

Wells, H. G., 28, 285

White Shark (Benchley), 279

Who Goes There? (Campbell), 287

Wieland (Brown), 81

witchcraft. *See* sorcery and witchcraft

Wizard of Earthsea, A (Le Guin), 33

women and the home, 99–116. *See also* haunted houses

Wood beyond the World, The (Morris), 53

Wuthering Heights (Brontë), 100–102

Yakko the Finn (*The Salamander*), 166–70

young adult literature, 33. *See also* crossover novels

Yu Tsun ("Garden of Forking Paths"), 186